Marxist Criticism
of the Bible

Marxist Criticism of the Bible

Roland Boer

T & T CLARK INTERNATIONAL
A Continuum imprint
LONDON • NEW YORK

Copyright © 2003 Sheffield Academic Press
A Continuum imprint

Published by Sheffield Academic Press Ltd
The Tower Building, 11 York Road, London SE1 7NX
370 Lexington Avenue, New York NY 10017-6550

www.continuumbooks.com

British Library Cataloguing-in-Publication Data
A catalogue record for this book is available from the British Library

Typeset by Sheffield Academic Press
Printed on acid-free paper in Great Britain by MPG Books, Bodmin, Cornwall

ISBN 0-8264-6327-4 (hb)
     0-8264-6328-2 (pb)

Aan de mijnen,
Samuel, Thomas, Stephanie and Amanda

Thus the criticism of heaven turns into the criticism of earth,
The criticism of religion into the criticism of law
And the criticism of theology into the criticism of politics.

Karl Marx 1843: 244-45

CONTENTS

List of Tables and Figures   ix
Preface   xi
Abbreviations   xiii

INTRODUCTION: WHY MARXIST THEORY?   1

Chapter 1
LOUIS ALTHUSSER: THE DIFFICULT BIRTH
OF ISRAEL IN GENESIS   14

Chapter 2
ANTONIO GRAMSCI: THE EMERGENCE
OF THE 'PRINCE' IN EXODUS   42

Chapter 3
TERRY EAGLETON: THE CLASS STRUGGLES OF RUTH   65

Chapter 4
HENRI LEFEBVRE: THE PRODUCTION OF SPACE IN 1 SAMUEL   87

Chapter 5
GEORG LUKÁCS: THE CONTRADICTORY WORLD OF KINGS   110

Chapter 6
ERNST BLOCH: ANTI-YAHWISM IN EZEKIEL   133

Chapter 7
THEODOR ADORNO: THE LOGIC OF DIVINE JUSTICE IN ISAIAH   158

Chapter 8
FREDRIC JAMESON: THE CONTRADICTIONS
OF FORM IN THE PSALMS   180

Chapter 9
  WALTER BENJAMIN: THE IMPOSSIBLE
  APOCALYPTIC OF DANIEL   204

CONCLUSION: ON THE QUESTION OF MODE OF PRODUCTION   229

Bibliography   247
Index of References   259
Index of Authors   264

LIST OF FIGURES AND TABLES

Table 1.   *Mode of Production and Space*   96

Figure 1.   *Greimas's Semiotic Square*   187

Figure 2.   *Semiotic Square of P.K. Dick's Dr Bloodmoney*   189

Figure 3.   *Semiotic Square of Psalm Superscriptions*   193

Figure 4.   *Primary Contradiction of the Psalms*   196

Figure 5.   *Semiotic Square of the Psalms*   196

Figure 6.   *Semiotic Square of Psalms Criticism*   203

On Sunday, 11 July 1999 I visited the grave of Karl Marx. I arrived in London for the first time via Sheffield, with a strong desire to avoid the city's usual attractions. After depositing my bags at the hotel near St Pancras Station, I joined the crowds at the tube, negotiating my way into the underground headed for Highgate. With some local assistance I finally found Sinian's Lane in Highgate Village and the overgrown entrance to the East Cemetery. An old lady sequestered three pounds from me—one for entry, two for the camera (much more than it was worth)—and warned me that the cemetery was on the verge of closing. I strode down the path, followed the left fork past the graves of George Eliott and Herbert Spencer to be met by the three metre grave, replete with a bust of Karl Marx himself atop a vast headstone. At least this grave wasn't buried in the riot of vegetation found elsewhere in the cemetery. 'Workers of the world unite!' and 'The philosophers have sought to understand the world, the point is to change it' were inscribed above and below the names of those buried—Karl, Jenny von Westfalen, Eleanor and the grandson. I had time to reel off some shots, think for a moment about Marx in London, and slip away to avoid being locked in. Now I needed a toilet and a beer on this humid London day.

Over a second beer, by the window of the Rose and Crown pub on Highgate Road, I reflected on Marx in London, where he found the most advanced workings of capitalism in England (if only he could see it now!) and sought to analyze its trends and workings. I supposed that some of the buildings in Highgate were here when the Marx family moved in, with a little more money, from the grinding poverty of Soho and a chance for some quieter, less cramped living. There is an anecdote about Jenny and Karl: on a Sunday like the one I was cooling with a few beers, Jenny set off for church with the children in tow. Karl, who probably should have gone along with her, if only so that she was not left with their brood on her own, grumbled as she walked out the gate, 'You would do better to read the Hebrew prophets than go to church.'

I read more than the Hebrew prophets in this book, seeking to show how Marxist literary theory—a great tradition in itself—has a distinct contribution to make to the study of the Hebrew Bible. In order to do so, I draw various key motifs from the work of Louis Althusser, Antonio Gramsci, Terry Eagleton, Henri Lefebvre, Georg Lukács, Ernst Bloch, Theodor Adorno, Fredric Jameson and Walter Benjamin—and engage with a range of biblical texts from Genesis to Daniel. The book is one of the first fruits of a Logan Research Fellowship at Monash University, one of those rare and glorious opportunities to read, reflect, discuss and write at my own pace and temperament. Constant Mews, Graeme Davison, Andrew Milner and Gary Bouma have been wonderful supporters of my work at Monash, where the notion of a Marxist intellectual still has some life in the world of commodified knowledge. The writing itself was done at various stages, usually in transit between Melbourne, Sydney and Brisbane, but nearly all of it I discussed and debated with Ed Conrad and Julie Kelso over the occasional wine and cigarette. Anything worthwhile in the pages that follow is the result of those discussions.

Roland Boer
Olinda, Victoria
August 2002

ABBREVIATIONS

AB	Anchor Bible
ICC	International Critical Commentary
Int	*Interpretation*
JBL	*Journal of Biblical Literature*
JSOT	*Journal for the Study of the Old Testament*
JSOTSup	*Journal for the Study of the Old Testament*, Supplement Series
LXX	Septuagint
MT	Masoretic Text
NCB	New Century Bible
VT	*Vetus Testamentum*

INTRODUCTION:
WHY MARXIST THEORY?

My concern is with the contribution of Marxist literary theory to biblical studies. It seems to me that this is one of the most neglected areas of biblical studies. However, before asking the question, why Marxist theory? there is a prior question I must address: why theory at all? Too often in biblical studies, especially in light of the influx of various literary and philosophical theories—deconstruction, feminism, new historicism, post-colonialism, queer studies, the social sciences and so on—I hear the comment that theory is unnecessary, or that it is really not that important for a discipline like biblical studies. This may be accounted for in a number of ways, such as baulking at the immense amount of reading and work that needs to be done to be aware of the various currents of theory, or the notion that biblical studies has an established series of methods that have been tried over time, or the sense that the concerns of theory are foreign.

The obvious point to make is that such responses ignore or refuse to acknowledge the theoretical underpinnings of the so-called agreed methods and questions. Why is it is still important to search for the dates and social settings of the various pieces of biblical literature, whether late or early? Why does the search for the history and development of the biblical literature continue? And why do the historical hypotheses about the background to that literature continue to multiply? Why is it that theological concerns remain important for so many biblical critics? Why do others attempt to wrest biblical criticism away from the dominance of theology? All of these questions, and the methods used to answer them, have their own complex history and theoretical justification that were once hotly debated but are now forgotten: the importance of the search for origins, the use of methods from outside biblical studies (such as the literary and historical theories common in Europe in the nineteenth and twentieth centuries), the theological drive to locate the mythical stories of the Bible in some historical continuum, and so on. Even what appear to be the most radical works in biblical studies at the moment—those of Thomas

Thompson, Niels Lemche, Philip Davies or Keith Whitelam—still operate
with these concerns in mind. All they have done in many respects is return
to the scepticism of some of the early German biblical critics of the late
nineteenth and early twentieth centuries. And the radical edge is that of
the earlier Germans: the questions posed to theology, or to understandings
of the Hebrew Bible in light of the continuing conflict between the
Palestinians and the Israelis.

However, what has happened in biblical studies since the 1970s and
1980s is a consistent questioning of the theoretical assumptions of these
approaches, so much so that any work that wants to ask new questions
must be theoretically aware of what is going on. Hence, in article after
article, in monograph after monograph, the pattern has developed whereby
the analysis of a biblical text must be preceded by some form of theoretical discussion, whether longer or shorter, in order to outline the theory
being used, to delineate the questions being posed and to justify the
theoretical path being taken. Usually this involves the consideration of a
major theorist or literary critic, such as Mikhael Bakhtin, Homi Bhabha,
Julia Kristeva, Jacques Derrida, Michel Foucault, Luce Irigaray or Stephen
Greenblatt. Only then may the interpretation of the text take place. In this
book I have followed this pattern as well, for it seems to me a necessary
approach in the current climate of biblical criticism, which is still in a state
of theoretical flux. Thus, I begin with discussions of the pertinent work
of various Marxist theorists—Louis Althusser, Antonio Gramsci, Terry
Eagelton, Henri Lefebvre, Georg Lukács, Ernst Bloch, Theodor Adorno,
Fredric Jameson and Walter Benjamin—before discussing a particular
biblical text in light of their theories.

One of the implications of the need to consider theory in biblical
studies, and I suspect that this is one of the half-acknowledged challenges,
is that it makes it increasingly clear that biblical studies is in fact a subset
of literary criticism, that the interpretation of the Bible is but part of
a much larger discipline that is concerned with the interpretation of
texts. One of the arguments I have made at various times is that this is a
necessary and valuable move for biblical studies to make, not least because of the continuing interest in the Bible in literary criticism outside
biblical studies. It enables one to engage with these critics in much wider
debates than biblical studies alone. In fact, I have often found a far greater
interest among circles of literary and other critics in the questions I ask of
the biblical text than in biblical studies. For instance, at the Marxism 2000
conference, held in Amherst, Massachusetts, I organized a panel simply

titled 'Marxism and the Bible'. Erin Runions, Gale Yee, Norman Gott-wald, Richard Horsley and I outlined some of the work we were doing in biblical studies at a session that had one of the highest attendances of the whole conference. It included Marxist philosophers, literary critics, historians, economists, geographers and so on. Norman Gottwald commented to me after the session that this sort of thing is sorely needed in biblical studies as well.

However, there is a curious logic to this, for it is not merely a case of reconstituting biblical studies as part of the larger disciplines of literary and cultural studies, or even history and economics. Biblical studies itself, especially with the long heritage of interpretation through the Middle Ages, was one of the traditions from which a whole host of secular disciplines arose, carrying through the questions one might ask of a text without the theological assumptions that went with it. Thus, the various disciplines of English literature, German literature, French literature, or even the study of linguistics and literary criticism per se, may from this perspective be seen as the various secularized developments of biblical studies. The questions asked of texts still remain determined by such issues as meaning, context, the uses of language, politics, and so on. This means that it is not so much the placing of biblical studies within a larger context that is foreign to it, but rather the recognition of this earlier background, the return of biblical studies to a place it has given up. Except that now biblical studies is not the determining discipline, but one that must take its place in a wider panoply of various literary disciplines and the debates that go on within them. To use an image I have used before, it is time that various cheques issued by biblical criticism need to be cashed.

Thus, if biblical criticism can be seen as part of literary criticism, then the issue of theory, which is so important within literary criticism itself, especially under the influence of philosophy, is also one that becomes important within biblical studies. However, I have kept one final problem many biblical critics have with theory until now, and that is the sense of a weariness with theory in literary criticism itself (an implicit recognition that biblical studies cannot remain isolated from this context). For theory has gained a life of its own, generating a host of studies that remain within the realm of theory without considering the literary texts that first generated the need for theoretical reflection. My own position is that this is a valid criticism, but that the way to avoid the tendency to work with theory for theory's sake is to maintain contact with the practice of interpreting texts. Nothing is more satisfying, it seems to me, than the detailed work with a text, that patient attention to a text that often throws up questions for the theoretical material itself. For this reason, along with the theoretical discussions that begin each chapter in this book, I give a great deal of attention to the biblical texts themselves, which are selected from various parts of the Hebrew Bible in order to provide samples of how Marxist criticism works in biblical interpretation.

Yet my theoretical and political passion is Marxism, and the theory with which I engage is Marxist literary criticism. And so I need to ask, why Marxist theory in particular? Apart from the point that Marxist criticism has a distinct place in literary criticism because of the work of critics like the ones with which I deal in this book, the most obvious reason is the sparseness of Marxist literary criticism in biblical studies. Despite the influx of new methods into biblical criticism in the last two decades, as witnessed for instance by the landmark volume *The Postmodern Bible* (Bible and Culture Collective 1995), Marxism is conspicuous by its absence. Although sporadic studies in selected areas of the Bible have dealt with Marxist issues, there has been no sustained consideration in biblical criticism of Marxism compared to the coverage that such areas as postmodernism, poststructuralism, feminism, postcolonialism and queer studies have received. This is all the more surprising given the influence of the major figures of Marxist literary criticism in precisely these and other areas of contemporary criticism, especially the figures I consider in this book. In this respect, this book is a critical introduction to Marxist literary criticism for biblical studies so that biblical critics will be able to use, or at least be aware of, various elements of Marxist criticism in their critical task.

Where Marxist criticism has had an effect is in social-scientific studies of the Bible, especially through the work of Norman Gottwald in Hebrew Bible and Richard Horsley in New Testament studies. Norman Gottwald's monumental work *The Tribes of Yahweh* (1999), as well as his widely used introduction to the Hebrew Bible (Gottwald 1985), work with an explicitly Marxist approach. The reception of his work, however, has tended to neglect the Marxist theory and focus on his arguments concerning the Hebrew Bible itself (see the effort to correct this tendency in Boer 2002). Richard Horsley's work has brought to bear Marxist criticism in both the reception of the New Testament and in an effort to interpret the socio-economic context of the New Testament (see most recently his work in editing *Semeia* 83/84 [Callahan, Horsley and Smith 1998]). Further social-scientific work includes that of the volume on class edited by Mark

Sneed (1999) and the work on mode of production by Simkins (1999). And Gale Yee has brought Marxist feminist approaches to interpreting the Hebrew Bible, most recently in an interpretation of Gen. 2–3 (Yee 1999). However, the issue of *Semeia* in which Yee's and Simkin's articles appear, *The Social World of the Hebrew Bible: Twenty-Five Years of the Social Sciences in the Academy*, is notable also for the fact that it does not include the contribution of literary approaches, let alone Marxist ones, to social-scientific studies, a feature noted by Norman Gottwald in this volume (Gottwald 1999: 256). And yet it is precisely Marxist approaches that enable such a cross-over between literary criticism and social-scientific criticism of the Bible. My hope is that this book will enable more of such interactions between these two areas.

The question of interaction raises another contribution of Marxist literary criticism to biblical studies. Such an approach is often criticized for being reductionist, for bringing everything down to the 'ultimately determining instance' of economics, explaining all that goes on in a text in terms of a certain political and economic theory. This is but another sign of the ignorance of Marxist literary theory in biblical studies, for Marxist approaches enable the opposite, namely, the inclusion of a host of questions normally excluded or compartmentalized in biblical studies. What I mean is that Marxism includes questions of literary form and content, detailed analysis of texts, in conjunction with wider issues of thought and belief, especially of a religious kind in regard to the Bible, of society and social interaction and conflict, of history, politics and economics, to name but a few. It is anything but reductionist, as the following chapters will make clear. It is one of the paradoxes of the continuing ban on master narratives that it is precisely a master narrative like Marxism that enables the inclusion rather than exclusion of a whole range of issues and questions.

There is a further dimension to Marxist criticism that aligns it with various feminist approaches, gay and lesbian studies, and even post-colonialism to some extent: it is also an approach with a distinct politics. In an era when any sign of political passion withers under the cynicism that refuses to see any change to what may now be called *Götterdämmerung* capitalism, it seems to me even more important to hold to a political passion, especially Marxism. For it holds out the utopian—understood in all the best senses of the term—possibility that capitalism will finally collapse, that it is not the end run of political economic systems.

The issues or problems that interest me from Marxist criticism may be understood in two ways, as a list of major issues, and as the methods for reading texts that each writer produces. The issues might be listed as follows: the nature and function of dialectics; ideology and its construction; the understanding of culture, literature and aesthetics in the light of ideology; the nature and role of commodification; economic value; reification; the superstructure (that is, the arena of culture in all its forms, the judiciary, philosophy and reflection, religion and ideology); social class and class conflict; the concept of mode of production, particularly as that has a bearing on interpretation of ancient documents and on the dynamics of history, with one aim being the relativizing of the mode under which they all have done and do their work, capitalism. Each of the writers I have mentioned—Adorno, Althusser, Benjamin, Bloch, Eagleton, Gramsci, Jameson and Lukács—debates some or all of these problems with specific reference to questions of literature and culture. Indeed, in most cases there is a distinct method, or at least cluster of questions, that arises from their own particular positions. I will be interested in such methods, not only because they are important items in themselves and need to be subjected to critical reflection, but also because they offer possibilities for the reading of the Bible.

What I have done in this book is focus on key questions from the critics I have chosen in order to interpret a selection of biblical texts. Thus, in regard to Althusser I discuss his theory of ideology and ideological state apparatuses in order to interpret Gen. 25. From Gramsci I am interested in his treatment of Machiavelli and the notion of hegemony in order to read Exod. 32. Eagleton's work on class, gender and ethnicity enables an interpretation of Ruth, whereas Lefebvre's study of the production of space provides me with a distinct angle on 1 Sam. 1–2. Lukács's discussions of genre I bring to bear on the structure of the books of Kings. Bloch's argument for the protest atheism of some biblical texts becomes the starting point for my interpretation of Ezek. 20, whereas Adorno's immanent dialectical criticism is the basis for reading Isa. 5. Jameson's treatment of the ideology of form gives me an angle on the study of the Psalms and Benjamin's reflections on allegory and language enable an interpretation of Dan. 7–12.

Let me summarize the main arguments of each chapter below, in order to provide a foretaste of what is to come, and also to allow those who do not wish to read everything at once a chance to pick and choose. In Chapter 1 I focus on Louis Althusser's most famous essay—'Ideology and Ideological State Apparatuses (Notes towards an Investigation)' (1971: 121-73)—where he argues for the central role of institutions in the production and reproduction of socio-economic relations. Later, in his 'autobiography', *The Future Lasts a Long Time* (Althusser 1994), he states that the family is the most powerful ideological state apparatus. The term itself designates the role of such institutions, especially religion and the family, in ensuring the perpetuation of ideologies that secure the perpetuation of the socio-economic system. However, such state apparatuses are also the sites of profound ideological conflict and tension, where opposing ideologies continually work against each other. These tensions may show up at various points, often displaced. Since written texts and other cultural products are prime sites of ideology, as well as being the products of the institutions to which Althusser refers, the application of his methods has become very common in literary and cultural theory. The reason for focusing on Genesis is that, apart from being a text itself, its major concerns are 'family' (in a broad sense), religion and the state. However, the collective entity of 'Israel' only appears at the division of the books between Genesis and Exodus. At this level, I want to ask why it is that the narratives of Genesis focus on family narratives, running through from Adam and Eve to Jacob and Joseph. However, Althusser's approach also stresses that ideological state apparatuses are sites of ideological tensions, and the tension in this text concerns the perpetual delay of the birth of a people. While other nations arise, often through names themselves, the repeated promise of a people is held off until the next book. If family and religion are crucial aspects of the 'state', why is Israel's emergence as a 'state' held back? Given the importance of the family in Genesis, I analyze Gen. 25, arguing that the tensions may be found in the birth narratives of women. The maternal body of Rebekah becomes a site of the most profound tensions in Genesis, for here all of the ideological state apparatuses comes together in a contradictory effort to bring about the 'birth' of Israel.

In Chapter 2 I turn to Antonio Gramsci, whose work has become very influential in such areas as postcolonial criticism, cultural criticism, feminism and so on, particularly through the widespread use of the term 'hegemony'. Apart from his deepening of the Marxist categories of ideology and class consciousness in terms of hegemony—the revolutionary struggle over the ruling ideas of an age—Gramsci also contributed to understanding the role of intellectuals, ideology, the state, politics, civil society, the philosophy of praxis, reformation and revolution. These ideas were generated in the tension between the Marxist tradition, Italian fascism and the overwhelming presence of the Roman Catholic Church. In this case, it is Gramsci's reflections on the state and ideology that provide a continuation of some of the concerns of my reading of Genesis with the help of Althusser. In particular, it is his reflections on Machiavelli's *The Prince* (1988) that I will develop for an understanding of the figure of Moses in Exodus. In *The Prince* we find the literary construction of a 'state' and a focus on Moses as leader, one of Machiavelli's own major examples of the ideal Prince. Given that hegemony is always a contested zone, attempting to deal with opposition, the stories of revolt or opposition become crucial, for they indicate not merely a textual nervousness about the uniformity of an ideological position, but also a more complex strategy of incorporating opposition within such an ideology. For this reason the key text will be the story of the golden calf in Gen. 32. I close this discussion by reflecting on Gramsci's argument that *The Prince* is a utopian text.

Terry Eagleton, the concern of Chapter 3, has been a major figure in transmitting continental Marxism to the English-speaking world. Some of the key terms of Eagleton's work include the engaged intellectual and the consequent interaction of theory and practice, the reassertion of traditional categories of Marxist analysis, such as class, revolutionary transformation, ideology, mode of production and politics. Eagleton's encyclopaedic critical work has engaged with Althusser, Benjamin, postcolonialism, feminism, novels, plays and major critical works. In this chapter I will pick up a particular insistence of Eagleton on the various strategies found in literature in order to efface the presence of class, class struggle and gender. The texts I consider are *The Rape of Clarissa* (Eagleton 1982), an effort to bring together Marxism, feminism and psychoanalysis in the interpretation of Samuel Richardson's novels, and 'Heathcliff and the Great Hunger' (Eagleton 1995: 1-26), a study of class and ethnicity in *Wuthering Heights*. Even though Eagleton falls short of a full integration of Marxism, feminism and ethnicity, I argue that he provides a way of interpreting Ruth that does not favour one over the other. In some critical Marxist work on biblical narratives, it has been argued that the foregrounding of stories about women is in fact a strategy for sidestepping the question of class. However, this creates its own problems in a continuing Marxist debate over gender and class. Eagleton's method, however, enables a different approach. In a reading of the book of Ruth, I argue that these three areas enable an ideological solution to the problem of succession, with the pernicious result that the ruling class becomes the Israelites, that Ruth's foreignness, gender and class status all contribute to her co-optation and effacement in the text. In other words, it is precisely in texts featuring women that sexual difference is avoided: a text like Ruth in fact functions to remove women from the story by the very means of making them central to the story.

Henri Lefebvre is the focus of Chapter 4. Lefebvre, like many of the critics I study in this book, worked in a whole range of areas, such as Marxist activism, philosophy, urban and rural sociology, geography, emergent cultural studies, but he is most well known for his work on the production of space and the fundamental role of the dialectic. The production of space has some profound considerations for the reading of biblical texts, particularly due to the grand scale of Lefebvre's theoretical and practical work on this question. A reading open to the production of space and the way it marks sexual, social, political and economic codes has implications not only for the traditional spatial disciplines, such as archaeology and geography, but also for areas such as hermeneutics, religion and sacred texts. Linked with this is his major work on the practice of everyday life, where the quotidian appears as major category of analysis. Rather than select an obvious spatial text, such as the tabernacle or temple instructions/ descriptions in Exodus, 1 Kgs, 1 Chron. or Ezekiel, or the distribution of land in Joshua, I focus on 1 Sam. 1–2, a somewhat inconspicuous text that relates more to Lefebvre's lifelong concern with everyday lived life. In particular, the opposition between the overt space of the shrine at Shiloh stands over against the covert womb of Hannah. However, in a series of dialectical moves I argue that the shrine at Shiloh is itself marginal in comparison to Jerusalem, which then becomes marginalized in comparison to the imperial centre of Babylon or Egypt. In the end, what appears to be a possible source for an alternative reading— Hannah's womb—becomes the key through which the 'sacred economy' of the text can operate.

In Chapter 5 I turn to Georg Lukács, literary critic, philosopher, political commentator and activist. What interests me is not only Lukács's exercise of the dialectic, but also some key ideas and their influence on the under-standing of the Bible and biblical studies itself. Lukács's literary work included the following interests: the yoking together of analysis and evaluation, and of the text and the social situation to which it responds and speaks (not necessarily that of its original production), a dialectical approach to genre and a commitment to historicism. He also insisted on key historical moments for marking transitions, the traces of a socio-economic period emerging in the form of the literature it produced, as well as the function of an all-pervasive reification and class consciousness in capitalism. My concern with two of Lukács's works, *Theory of the Novel* (1971) and *The Historical Novel* (1983), particularly his discussion of genre, its distinctive features and modes of characterization, as well as contrasts with other genres. Most notably Lukács develops a dialectical theory of genre that I apply to Kings, where I offer a reading of the tension between prophetic and royal narratives in 1 and 2 Kings. I trace the tensions in these narratives between the prophetic material that dominates in 1 Kgs 17–2 Kgs 9.10 and the narratives about kings that dominate the remaining material. Focusing on the questions of narrative rhythm, life and death and characterization I close by asking what is going on with the strange ideological world of Kings, specifically in terms of mode of production.

Ernst Bloch, who appears in Chapter 6, actually used the Bible as one of his main sources for the ideas, language and the concept of utopia itself. Concerned to understand the importance of the Bible for the rural and urban working classes, Bloch's work is notable for the way his vocabulary and syntax are shaped by the Bible itself. Although his work is the source of the widely used hermeneutics of suspicion and recovery, what interests me is the way he develops his utopian hermeneutics. With his search for buried and repressed traditions, Bloch traces the way the language of protest in the Bible has at heart the challenge against Yahweh as ruler and overlord: in other words, there is a deeper logic of protest against Yahweh in the Bible. However, the way Bloch becomes interesting for biblical studies is in the notion of a logic of anti-Yahwism in the texts and their study. Such texts as Ezek. 16 and 23 have featured in recent feminist debates, although I note that time and again such studies avoid the logical outcome of their arguments, preferring to argue that the representation of Yahweh in Ezekiel is problematic and therefore should be discarded or deconstructed in order to remove its misogynist power. Yet there is a noticeable move in studies of such texts that develops an implicit protest against Yahweh. That is, there is a logic of atheism itself within the study of such texts as Ezek. 16 and 23. I then argue that this interpretation cannot avoid the role of the text in producing its own interpretations, especially where it seems to support the overt ideology. Such an implicit criticism appears in Ezek. 20.1-38, where the impossible words of Yahweh emerge from Ezekiel's mouth. Here Yahweh gives laws that are not good, that can only produce sin (Ezek. 20.25), ending with an enforced return from exile and obedience to the covenant.

Chapter 7 brings in Theodor Adorno, one of my favourite critics.

Although Adorno made major contributions to musicology, philosophy, sociology, psychoanalysis and literary criticism, I am interested in his method of interpreting texts, namely, an immanent dialectical criticism. Rather than importing criticisms from outside, this dialectical approach seeks the contradictions of the text through its own narrative patterns and conceptual arrangement. For Adorno, the most rigorous critique is one that emerges from the text under analysis. The example I provide is his critique of Kierkegaard (Adorno 1989). In this light I consider Isa. 5, the so-called parable of the vineyard, arguing within the terms of the text itself that a series of paradoxes emerge—between the social criticism of the ruling classes and the conservative model of society envisioned, the love of the prophet for Yahweh and the justification for punishment, the responsibility of Yahweh for the 'sour grapes', and the complete ideological inversion of the themes of cultivation and wildness—that renders any connection between divine and social justice impossible.

Fredric Jameson, whom I have considered at greater length elsewhere (Boer 1996), returns in Chapter 8. Engaging with a whole range of contemporary methods, from linguistics to architecture, film theory to Russian formalism, Jameson has carried on a programme that both incorporates these methods within Marxism and advocates Marxism's power as an interpretive and political method. He takes Marxism as a set of problems that require constant reworking and is ever open to new developments while always holding to Marxism itself. In this book my interest is in his continual concern with form and its function in a dialectical method that comes from the Hegelian–Marxist tradition. The study of this body of material in the Hebrew Bible may be divided into two major categories: those concerned with the content of the Psalms, whether in devotional, historical or thematic terms, and those concerned with form. In fact, the latter category has dominated Psalms research, in terms of form criticism and the effort to make some headway on the question of Hebrew poetry. However, even the text exhibits a similar tendency, seeking to organize the Psalms in five books, or as the psalms of David, the sons of Korah, Asaph, Solomon or Moses, or in terms of 'musical' directions, or even aligning some of them to moments in the life of David. It seems as though there is an overdetermination of form, so much so that contradictions start to appear. By focusing on Psalm 108, a double over with Pss. 57.7-11 and 60.5-12, as well as 1 Chron. 16.8-36, which overlaps with Pss. 105.1-15, 96.1-13 and 106.47-48, the overdetermination is exacerbated, not only in terms of the repetition of the content, but also in the categories from the superscriptions and those of form criticism. My analysis uses the semiotic square to ask what the problem with the Psalms may be. Is the form a compensation for the content, that is, the overtly 'sacred' language that exhibits its shortcomings or emptiness most clearly in the language of worship and devotion?

Finally, in Chapter 9, I deal with Walter Benjamin. Like Bloch, Benjamin referred to the Bible extensively in his work, although he made use of it in order to develop a method of philosophy and literary criticism that was opposed to the classicism of German theory. I outline his work on both allegory and language in order to raise the question about the tension between the overt political use of language and the blockages to such use that Benjamin himself theorized. I trace a similar tension in the apocalyptic material of Daniel. Working with Dan. 7–12, a tension appears between the allusive and metaphorical language of the vision and a desire both by the text and subsequent scholars to fix the references in this material to particular historical events and times. Moving from Benjamin's positions on language and allegory, I argue that apocalyptic language is anti-referential, a closed system from a very different socio-economic system that is finally undecipherable. However, the dialectical point is that such an anti-referential function is marked by the precise effort to make the referential move. This also puts a question to Benjamin, for whom allegory provided an alternative opening to the future blocked by history. For the effort by apocalyptic language to imagine a future is itself foreclosed by the nature of that language itself.

The focus on major Marxist critics and the sampling of texts from one end of the Hebrew Bible to the other serves an introductory function with a critical bent, for I want to argue for the viability of Marxist literary criticism in biblical studies across a range of texts. The result is series of studies that form some of the pieces of what may be termed the ideological structures of the dominant modes of production under which the Hebrew Bible was written. However, while I think it is futile to offer yet further hypotheses concerning authorship and dating, I do not believe that we should abandon the question of history. In Marxist terms the question of history operates primarily at the level of what has been called mode of production, a term I use at various points in the book itself. The various studies of texts therefore offer a collection of the tensions and conflicts within the ideologies that operated as part of those modes of production. Yet in the conclusion I seek to move the discussion a little further by reflecting on some current work in Marxist economic theory, especially regulation theory, in which the whole question of mode of production becomes one that needs to be rethought for such a different political economic and cultural formation as the one we find in the Hebrew Bible.

Chapter 1

LOUIS ALTHUSSER:
THE DIFFICULT BIRTH OF ISRAEL IN GENESIS

For a time in the 1960s and 1970s Louis Althusser was the central figure of the intellectual left, boldly carving a new reading of Marx that regarded his scientific breakthrough as a unique moment in human history. Through a host of literary critics, such as Pierre Macherey and Terry Eagleton, his work in philosophy made its way into literary and cultural criticism.

Out of the many directions that such a philosophy may take—as a revolutionary weapon, in order to reassess the tradition (Hegel, Kant, *et al.*), the logic of a materialist philosophy etc.—my focus here is with the arguments of a particular essay, 'Ideology and Ideological State Apparatuses (Notes towards an Investigation)' (Althusser 1971: 121-73). My argument picks up the extraordinary congruence between, on the one hand, Althusser's notions of the Ideological State Apparatuses (ISA), especially those of religion, family, the state and culture, along with the definitions of ideology itself and, on the other hand, the patterns of Gen. 25: the heavy weight of religion, family, culture and the state on the question of the promise of a people that is perpetually delayed over against the plethora of peoples who have no promise, the tension between the selection and non-selection that shows specifically in Ishmael and Isaac in Gen. 25, and the way the various ISAs face a profound tension in the barrenness and fecundity of Rebekah's womb. Such an argument is incomplete without an immanent critique of Althusser's own method in light of Genesis.

In Althusser's essay—self-described as 'Notes towards an Investigation', which 'should not be regarded as more than the introduction to a discussion' (1971: 127)—Althusser undertakes a wholesale reworking of the Marxist category of ideology. By and large, ideology in Marxist theory had remained a negative and instrumental category: it designated the various means by which people are kept in exploitative situations by justifying to those people the exploitation as necessary, unavoidable and for their long-term benefit. Ideology was not so much a physical means of enslavement but a mental one, operating in terms of ideas, beliefs, cultural practices and religion. For example, workers in a clothing factory work long hours for low pay, feeling an inchoate frustration at their poor conditions, but working nonetheless under the pressing need to provide food, clothing and shelter for needy families as well as themselves. At work here is the ideology of a family unit, particularly the relatively recent model of the nuclear family with dependent children, for which the parents must work and provide. This pressure comes in the form not only of the immediate physical needs, but with the ideological baggage of parental love, responsibility and greater opportunities for the children than the parents ever had. And then there is the constant expectation, perpetuated through a vast advertising industry, that the workers will spend their meagre income on a whole range of commodities that people 'need' if they are to live at all, ever new needs generated with the emergence of new products. On top of this, the owners of the factory seek to inculcate a team spirit, encouraging the workers to believe they are all part of a collective endeavour to be the best factory. Finally, the promise of promotion, increased responsibility, a slightly higher pay packet and the ability to lord it over those who used to be fellow workers encourage them to work harder. A traditional Marxist ideology critique will seek to expose all of this as the justification for exploitation, the making of profit by means of low pay and long hours, the neutralizing of the workers' rage at being treated so.

Since Marxists have traditionally described the way ideology works to conceal or elide exploitation as mystification, the strategy of ideology critique was described as a process of demystification, of uncovering the techniques by which such ideology operates. Once it was revealed, then the real causes of exploitation could be unmasked and an effort made to overcome them. Further, ideology cannot be understood without the notions of class and class conflict, since another term for ideology, or rather a particular form that it takes, is class consciousness, the various modes by which classes perceive themselves and set themselves over against other classes. I need to stress that the need for such ideological analysis remains, and nothing can be more satisfying than engaging in such an exercise of withering critique.

While recognizing the value of such work and the theory of ideology that formed its heart, Althusser argued that it was also limited. Ideology, he felt, was not something one could unmask and then discard, not merely a means of seeking to legitimate an oppressive situation that would disappear with the overcoming of that situation. However, in order to get to the long and detailed discussion of ideology itself, Althusser begins in a curious fashion, with reproduction. Yet, the expectation that this would feature human reproduction, that is, women and their bodies as central features that had been neglected in Marxist work, is disappointed. For what interests Althusser is the problem of the 'reproduction of the conditions of production', itself ignored within Marxist theory despite Marx's second volume of *Capital*. So he begins with a polemic against the focus on production and productive practice, the productivism of which Marxism has so often been accused.

Althusser raises a whole range of implications from the question of reproduction, most of them reshaping traditional Marxist categories: means of production, relations of production, ideology, the state, now in terms of reproduction, ISAs and interpellation. For my reading of Genesis all of these features are important, and I will deal with them in turn.

As for the means of production, Althusser argues, following Marx, that capitalist production must replace that which has been used up or worn out. The point here is that the system as a whole assists in the 'reproduction' of other parts of the system—the supply of raw materials, machinery repair and replacement, and so on. He is, however, much more interested in the relations of production, or more specifically the reproduction of labour power itself. Here lies the first major silence of the essay, for where I expect a discussion of physical reproduction—pregnancy, childbirth and the labour of women—instead he turns to wages and their function in ensuring the continuation of labour power, in the form of housing, food and clothing. Only a passing reference to physical reproduction appears, although without the mother: 'and, we should add: indispensable for raising and educating the children in whom the proletarian reproduces himself (in *n* models where *n* = 0, 1, 2, etc....) as labour power' (1971: 131). How it is that the proletarian may reproduce himself is left lying, for the choice of words—'in whom the proletarian reproduces himself'—is symptomatic of the exclusion of maternal bodies in notions of labour and reproduction.

Yet despite reproduction itself being defined by the proletarian class struggle, the material conditions for the reproduction of labour power are not sufficient. Workers also need competence and skills, and this is where the institutions of training and education are central—training in literacy,

numeracy, know-how, scientific and literary culture, attitude and behaviour, in short, both skills and 'submission to the rules of the established
order' (1971: 132). Institutions, such as education, church and army, seek
to ensure either subjection to or manipulation of the ruling ideology by its
various functionaries, and this is where the notion of ISAs emerges in
Althusser's discussion. They are the means for the reproduction of labour
power.

In order to arrive at a detailed discussion of both ISAs and ideology
itself, Althusser lays some more groundwork, particularly in regard to base
and superstructure and the theory of the state. But he does so in order to
answer what for him is the key question—the reproduction of the relations
of production (having dealt with the reproduction of the productive forces,
in terms of means and labour power). While the state, ideology and the
ISAs are the major items for my own discussion of Gen. 25, I will also be
interested in the question of the reproduction of the forces of production,
although this appears in narrative form in the biblical text, that is, in an
ideological product.

As far as the Marxist staple of base (infrastructure) and superstructure is
concerned, Althusser reiterates the main points with his characteristic
twists. Base and superstructure is, of course, a metaphor, one that indicates
the reliance of the two levels of superstructure (law and state, and
ideology—religious, ethical, political, legal, etc.) on the base (productive
forces and relations of production). It also indicates what he calls the
'respective indices of effectivity' (1971: 134)—Althusser's well-known
development of Marx's notion of 'determination in the last instance' by
the base. His emphasis is on the last instance, thereby allowing the various
elements of the superstructure a relative autonomy, whose determination is
delayed and mediated. It also means that there is a reciprocal action, an
influence by the superstructure on the base. In this way he avoids the vulgar Marxist move that postulates a direct causal effect of the base on
the superstructure, but the notion of the superstructure's own influence
recognizes the extraordinary power of the ISAs.[1]

---

1.   Even in his later *The Future Lasts a Long Time* (1994), he organizes the text in
terms of the ISAs, beginning with the family. In speaking of the book itself, he writes,
'This seemed to me to be the obvious way of proceeding. Everyone must judge the
results for themselves. Similarly they can judge the powerful role that certain violent
organizations have played in my life. I used to refer to these as the Ideological State
Apparatuses, and I am surprised I have been unable to do without them in understanding what happened to me' (1994: 30).

At the same time Althusser seeks to go beyond the metaphor, and he does so—particularly in terms of the state and ideology—from the perspective of reproduction. As these questions draw near to my analysis of the Genesis text, a lurking question is how Althusser's focus on capitalism may convert into a discussion of a non-capitalist ideological product such as Genesis. Rather than following the path of a Lacanian juxtaposition as the way to see the 'truth' of such a text—although Althusser's interest in Lacan would justify such a move—or even to argue that Genesis is one part of a canonical western text, the Bible, I will stay with Althusser's essay and seek the way his own writing opens up to a reading of the biblical text.

This problem emerges immediately with his discussion of the state, for he speaks initially of the capitalist state. In Genesis the terminology is different—*goi*, *'am* and more rarely *le'om*—translated variously as 'nation' or 'people'. Such a terminology is part of a vastly different function of the state in a distinct socio-economic system. I will return to these terms, but first, Althusser. On the state, he begins with the Marxist insistence that the state is a repressive formation, which leads him to the category of Repressive State Apparatus (RSA). By means of police, courts, prisons, army, head of state, government and administration—various dimensions of the RSA—the state ensures the extraction of surplus value. And yet the traditional Marxist position remains for Althusser largely descriptive. The basic features include a distinction between state power, which may change hands in various ways, and the state apparatus, which tends to remain constant; state power is the objective of class struggle, and the way to the 'withering away of the state' is the seizure of power by the proletariat and then the dismantling of its apparatus.

But Althusser seeks a theory that goes beyond this largely descriptive position, that provides a more comprehensive analysis of the workings of the state. Here he develops the distinction between the RSA and ISAs (taking up some hints from Gramsci). The RSA is singular, comprising the elements mentioned above and it operates by means of violence and its threat. Ideology plays a role here, although in a minor key to direct repression. By contrast, the ISAs appear as institutions, and their distinct characteristic is their predominantly ideological function, a contested and contradictory function on which I will focus in my reading of Gen. 25. The RSA and ISAs, distinguished for the sake of his argument, work together in complex ways. Not only is it a case of predominant and secondary patterns of ideology and repression, but—and this is important for my discussion of Genesis—'very subtle explicit or tacit combinations may be woven from the interplay of the (Repressive) State Apparatuses and the Ideological State Apparatuses' (1971: 145-46).

Out of his list of ISAs, Althusser finds the Church and education the most interesting. My concerns overlap somewhat: religion and family, along with the state itself. Althusser's list includes the following:

- the religious ISA (the system of the different churches)
- the educational ISA (the system of the different public and private schools)
- the family ISA
- the legal ISA
- the political ISA (the political system, including the different parties)
- the trade-union ISA
- the communications ISA (press, radio and television, etc.)
- the cultural ISA (literature, the arts, sports etc.) (1971: 143)

There are two dimensions of the ISAs that are important for my reading of Genesis. First, even though they are disparate, the various ISAs are unified since they operate under the ruling ideology, which, taking up Marx's phrase in *The German Ideology* (Marx and Engels 1976), is the ideology of the ruling class. Here RSA and ISAs work closely together. For Althusser 'no class can hold State power over a long period without at the same time exercising its hegemony over and in the State Ideological Apparatus' (1971: 146).

Secondly, since the ISAs are not directly repressive, the ruling class, with whatever class alliances it makes in order to hold power, faces a continual struggle to assert its ideological dominance. The ISAs are then both the stake and site of class struggle, for those opposed to the ruling ideology wage their battles to undermine this ideology precisely in the ISAs. Although the ISAs represent the ruling ideology, the exploited may make inroads, win a position here and there, by working away at the contradictions within the ISAs.

It is this that interests me with Genesis, for in a text such as this, which is the product of what Althusser calls the cultural ISA, we will expect to identify tensions and contradictions within the narrative itself. 'The ideological state apparatuses are multiple, distinct, "relatively autonomous" and capable of providing an objective field of contradictions' (1971: 149). But there is a further dimension, another layer or two: in this text there is the interplay of the family and religious ISAs (although the form will vary in a markedly distinct mode of production) in connection with the state. Thus, the tensions of the cultural ISA—the text—become much more complex in light of a narrative that concerns religion and family along with the state.

Having outlined a theory of the state in terms of RSA and ISAs, Althusser can now return to his question concerning the reproduction of the relations of production. Here his discussion is notable both for what it does and does not say. What he includes is that reproduction is enabled not only through material processes of production and circulation, but also, indeed mostly, by the two forms of state apparatuses. Whereas the RSA secures the reproduction of the relations of exploitation, the ISAs are the ones mainly responsible for the reproduction of the relations of production in political conditions established by the RSA.

Althusser's example is the shift into capitalism from the feudal mode of production, in which the Church was the dominant ISA, partly because it held religious, educational, communications and cultural dimensions within itself. Coupled with the family ISA, it held sway for the long centuries of feudalism. But the crucial point here is that because of this dominant position, the Church, the religious ISA, was the focus of ideological and class conflict in the long struggle by the bourgeoisie to wrest control from the Church—necessary for its own survival and success—and replace it with the dominant ISA of the capitalist era, education (coupled with the family).

What interests me here is not so much the argument over the transition, nor even the way the educational ISA functions, as the point that all ideological struggle was concentrated in and against the Church. For my reading of Genesis, the search for tensions will have this in mind: that is, the location of the prime form of ideological struggle in the text. The conjunction of family and religious ISAs (which is less the 'Church', although the very sense of this term derives from the Hebrew Bible) focused on the 'state' in a product that is cultural (the text) suggests that ideological tension will appear in the intersection of these four.

Further, with his example Althusser has provided an answer to my earlier question about taking an analysis that was developed specifically for capitalism and adapting it for reading a text that comes out of a very different mode of political economics. His shift into the feudal mode of production, with its focus on religion, the sacred and the Church, indicates that it is possible to apply his work to different modes of production—that is, the method is not specific to capitalism. This is where the possibility for a biblical analysis opens up, allowing for the particular sensitivities as to how ISAs might be shaped in such a context. Of course, my concern is with a text, and this affects the way his analysis may be used as well, for here we have what is already a product of the cultural ISA, except that I will argue later for an elision between the religious and cultural functions that the text itself exhibits.

I also suggested an omission in Althusser's discussion, and the signal of this is the way the family ISA creeps into his example of the transition from feudalism to capitalism. While he writes at some length about the Church (1971: 151-52) and education (1971: 152-57), he mentions in passing that we may also regard it as a transition that includes the family: 'One might even add: the School-Family couple has replaced the Church-Family couple' (1971: 154; see also 157). Such a minor acknowledgment is symptomatic, as Michel Boulous Walker has argued (Walker 1998), of the silence of the maternal body in Althusser's writing. At one other point does birth itself appear: at the close of his discussion of interpellation (see below) he suggests that an individual is an ideologically constituted subject even 'before he is born' (1971: 176). Even here there are two characteristic moves: the first is to dispense with the 'sentiments' of family ideology in its paternal, maternal, conjugal and fraternal forms in order to point out that the identity of the child as subject is marked by bearing 'its Father's Name' (1971: 176). The Freudian echo is explicit, but the 'maternal' disappears in favour of the Father. The second move follows a few comments on the way the child must negotiate the familial ideological configuration as it grows up, and, just as Freud appears, Althusser writes, 'But let us leave this point, too, on one side' (1971: 176). Here again he bypasses the opportunity to consider the connection between material and ideological reproduction in the role of women to bear children. Except that Althusser implicitly limits such a discussion to the family ISA, thereby restricting maternal roles to the family in a classic fashion. For the maternal body is crucial precisely through the various strategies to exclude and to deal ideologically with such an exclusion in the other ISAs, most notably in his preferred examples of Church and Education. In neglecting such an element—especially in an essay that deals with reproduction—Althusser thereby exhibits the dominant ideology of the ISAs. Or rather Marxism unwittingly buys into such an ideology, for one of the effects of the exclusion of the maternal body is that the kind of system of analysis Althusser develops becomes possible. In my own discussion of Gen. 25 I will seek to deal with what is both an omission and an appropriation—both elements are inescapably linked—which will then raise questions about Althusser's method, a method that enables the analysis I undertake in the first place. For Althusser's resolute focus on class and ideology, and the inseparable relation between them, ensures that class does not disappear in any discussion of sexual difference. For this reason Althusser's use of such terminology as ISAs ensures that such questions remain in the discussion.

The repression of the maternal body in Althusser's works comes through more strongly in *The Future Lasts a Long Time* (1994), for his mother features in the long initial discussion of his own family and returns again and again throughout the book. Here her maternal body, which brought him forth with a larger head than normal, is one that is full of projections and fears. Thus, his mother marries the brother, Charles, of the one she loves, Louis, only to be brutalized sexually, have her money taken and career cut short upon their marriage. Althusser represents his mother as filled by fears of being late, of germs, of her sexual body as such, of robbery and of passing her phobias on to him. In particular, it is the image of his mother that stays with him: 'My reason for giving these details is because they have almost certainly helped to shape after the event, and so to confirm and reinforce in me unconsciously, the image I have of a martyred mother, *bleeding like a wound*' (1994: 38, italics in original). This is an extraordinary slippage, one that focuses on rape and martyrdom, as well as the constant association with death, as a way of dealing with his menstruating mother. For her menstruation, 'bleeding like a wound', is the means of representing and yet avoiding her maternal body. The difficult relationship with his father, his own bearing of the name of his dead uncle whom his mother loved, the disgust at his mother's breasts, and representation of his all too masculine grandmother—with a ramrod stiff back, facial hair and brusque manner—reinforce the perpetual repression of the maternal body precisely when he speaks of his mother.

All of this is so much more intriguing with the shift that takes place in *The Future Lasts a Long Time* from the importance of the Church in feudalism and education under capitalism to the centrality of the family. The appeal of his time in the prisoner of war camp during World War II lay in the removal from family, books, classroom and family flat: 'In short, I was free from that most frightful, appalling, and horrifying of all the ideological State apparatuses, in a nation where the State exists, namely the family' (1994: 104). Its power and dominance lies in the way a child is instilled with a combination of fear, upbringing, respect, timidity and guilt, all for the sake of learning respect for absolute authority and the state. 'It is an irrefutable fact that the Family is the most powerful ideological State apparatus' (1994: 105). It would seem that in this work the terrible dominance of the family, as well as the pervading presence of Althusser's mother, are precisely the means whereby Althusser is able to repress the maternal function of his mother's body, and the maternal body as such. For in this text also we find a utopian and homosocial valorization of communities of men—the camaraderie of the prisoner of war camp (1994: 105), the appeal of the celibate monastic life (1994: 96), or the 'hallucination' of his grandfather's mates working, eating and drinking around the threshing machine (1994: 79-81)—that reinforces the repression I noted above. I will in fact argue that the dominant apparatus in Genesis is the family, and this late emphasis by Althusser finds a curious reflection in the biblical text, as do the patterns of repression I have traced in his work. But it is also the inseparable connection between the family and the sacred or religious that Althusser stresses (1994: 105) that brings his work even closer to Genesis.

There is a final dimension of Althusser's argument that is relevant for my own use—the section on ideology that closes the essay. Here Althusser works with four theses: ideology has no history; ideology is a 'representation' of the imaginary relationship of individuals to their real conditions of existence; ideology has a material existence; ideology interpellates individuals as subjects. Each of these is relevant for my reading, although the second one—as with much reception of Althusser—is the most significant.

Ideology for Althusser is ahistorical, that is, whereas individual ideologies have histories, can only be understood within the ISA in which they operate, ideology in general, as a theory, has no history: '...if eternal means, not transcendent to all (temporal) history, but omnipresent, transhistorical and therefore immutable in form throughout the extent of history, I shall adopt Freud's expression word for word, and write *ideology is eternal*, exactly like the unconscious' (1971: 161). Always with us, ideology will be as much a part of any communist society as of the Bible. In order to explicate this a little further, I want to take up the final thesis. This thesis is an effort to deal with the question of the subject. Thus, not only is there 'no ideology except by the subject and for subjects', but also 'ideology interpellates individuals as subjects' (1971: 170). Both statements indicate a dialectical interplay between subject and ideology: the subject as a category is absolutely necessary for all ideology, but 'the category of the subject is only constitutive of all ideology insofar as all ideology has the function (which defines it) of "constituting" concrete individuals as subjects' (1971: 171). Ideology requires subjects to function, but creating subjects is the function of ideology. This also means that 'subject' for Althusser has the specific meaning of an ideologically constituted being, one who lives spontaneously in ideology.

But how is the subject constituted? Here Althusser tells a story, focused on a metaphor that has become as famous as Freud's *fort-da* narrative.

> I shall then suggest that ideology 'acts' or 'functions' in such a way that it 'recruits' subjects among the individuals (it recruits them all), or 'transforms' the individuals into subjects (it transforms them all) by that very precise operation which I have called *interpellation* or hailing, and which can be imagined along the lines of the most commonplace everyday police (or other) hailing: 'Hey, you there!'
>
> Assuming that the theoretical scene I have imagined takes place in the street, the hailed individual will turn around. By this one-hundred-and-eighty-degree physical conversion, he becomes a *subject*. Why? Because he has recognized that the hail was 'really' addressed to him, and 'that it was *really him* who was hailed' (and not someone else). Experience shows that the practical telecommunication of hailing is such that they hardly ever miss their man: verbal call or whistle, the one hailed always recognizes that it is really him who is being hailed. And yet it is a strange phenomenon, and one which cannot be explained solely by 'guilt feelings', despite the large numbers who 'have something on their consciences' (1971: 174, italics in original).

Althusser is keen to stress that the narrative sequence gives a false before-and-after effect, for ideology and the hailing of individuals as subjects is the same thing. That is, individuals are always-already interpellated by ideology as subjects, and so individuals are always-already subjects.

However, what interests me for my reading of Genesis is the way the often forgotten religious 'example' that follows in Althusser's text is crucial to the argument. How does (religious) ideology hail an individual? It calls a particular person, who, created by God, must respond to this call. God speaks to this person through the Bible and Church, and if this subject responds to the law of love he will have eternal life and so on. In order not to be tied into a Christian focus, Althusser's example is the hailing of Moses by Yahweh at the burning bush (1971: 179). In other words the formal structure of all ideology is the same, and since religious ideology has both multiple subjects, a single Subject (God), and a relationship posited between the two, he argues that all ideology has the following features: the interpellation of individuals as subjects; subjection to the Subject (God in this case); the mutual recognition of subjects and Subject, the subjects' recognition of each other, and the subject's recognition of him or herself; the absolute guarantee that everything is really so, and if subjects recognize this everything will be fine.

When this quadruple system is in play, subjects can operate perfectly well, without supervision. Through ideology and the rituals of the ISAs, subjects recognize the existing state of affairs and operate within them. All of which leads Althusser to his final formulation: '[T]he individual is interpellated as a (free) subject in order that he shall submit freely to the commandments of the Subject, i.e. in order that he shall (freely) accept his subjection' (1971: 182). I have spent some time on this, since the religious turn of Althusser's argument allows me to make a direct connection to the function of God in the text of Genesis.

However, I have left until last the thesis that will be most fruitful when dealing with Gen. 25: ideology represents the imaginary relationship of individuals to their real conditions of existence. The key to this definition is that there are two removes from the 'real conditions': the representation and the imaginary relations. Althusser seeks to counter the assumption that ideology is an imaginary way of conceiving one's real conditions of existence. At this level, there is only one stage, one step from reality to ideology: ideology is therefore an illusion, does not correspond to reality (belief in God, justice, etc.), but it does allude to reality. The task of interpretation is then to cut through the illusion, pick up the allusions and locate the reality behind this imaginary representation. Althusser identifies various types of interpretation—the mechanistic (God is the imaginary representation of the king or despot) and the hermeneutic (Church Fathers, Ludwig Feuerbach, Karl Barth, *et al.*), in which the imaginary inversion of ideology need only be set on its feet in order to discover the real source.

As to why people need to do such a thing, that is, make an imaginary transposition in order to represent their real conditions of existence to themselves, there have been two standard answers. First, a group of cynical priests and despots have constructed these lies so that people will serve them in the belief that they are serving God. Secondly, this imaginary representation is a result of human alienation (Feuerbach and Marx): human beings therefore construct an imaginary and alienated realm in order to deal with such alienation in their real lives.

What are the implications for biblical studies? Too often biblical scholars assume that if a text is produced by a religious and scribal elite, it will give expression to the ideological assumptions of that group of writers: priests will then produce documents with priestly concerns, men will produce documents with male interests, political groups will put forward their own propaganda. The result of this is that when material appears, with surprising frequency in the Hebrew Bible, that somehow counters such assumptions, then a number of strategies come into play to deal with it. An older option was to posit different theological agendas for different sources—in Genesis JEPD—so that we end up with differing and overlaid perspectives. Another option was to argue for the presence of a different group of authors, which has been a move in some feminist biblical scholarship: texts that do not exhibit a seamless male hegemony must have been written by women. A third option is to argue for competing political and ideological groups with different agendas, as, for example, most recently Mark Brett, who reads Genesis as a counter text, written by Persian period scribes, to the ethnocentricity of Ezra–Nehemiah (Brett 1999). In each case the significant insights of these approaches have been vitiated by a relatively mechanical or instrumental view of the biblical texts. If I take up Althusser's arguments, then ideology is not the product of a clique, a group of ideological manipulators who seek to dupe their opponents and/or the masses into following them. For the positions I outlined briefly above have an implicit understanding of ideology as the imaginary representation of the real conditions of existence, without any mediation.

By contrast, Althusser shifts the focus:

> it is not their real conditions of existence, their real world, that 'men' 'represent to themselves' in ideology but above all it is their relation to those conditions of existence which is represented to them there. It is this relation which is at the centre of every ideological, i.e. imaginary, representation of the real world' (1971: 164).

In more specifically Marxist terms, the imaginary distortion of ideology represents the imaginary relationship of people to the relations of production themselves and all relations that derive from them.

As for how this might be applied to a text like Genesis, Althusser's work allows me to ask questions not only about the narratives of the text, but also about the status of the text itself. For the text is an ideological product, an item that emerges not only from culture (the cultural ISA, although that is part of the religious ISA), but also one that is subject to Althusser's definition of ideology as the representation of the imaginary relations to real conditions of existence. However, the text is also a narrative—my focus is Gen. 25 with links to other texts—and in that narrative I seek the workings of what Althusser calls the ISAs, especially those of religion and family in relation to the state. What interests me in particular are the way such ISAs are sites in tension and contradiction. So we have two things to keep in mind: that the text itself is an ideological product and that within it ideological tensions may be found. I do not want to apply Althusser's categories in a mechanical fashion, but rather use them as a heuristic device, in a similar fashion to his reflections on the ISAs under feudalism.

In my critical use of Althusser for reading Genesis, I draw upon his terminology of the ISAs, particularly the family and religious apparatuses, their inherent contradictions and their relation to the state. But I will also take up his material on ideology itself, for Genesis is an ideological product, a text, in which these patterns appear. In this respect, I am interested in the definition of ideology as interpellation, as the representation of the imaginary relations to real condititions of existence and the status of Genesis as a political text that has its own place in the political practice it employs. However, I also develop the criticism of Althusser that his system is in part possible by means of the exclusion of the maternal body precisely in his discussion of reproduction and ISAs. For in my analysis of Genesis, the maternal body turns out to be a crux without which the narrative, particularly in terms of the tensions relating to ideology and ISAs, would not be possible in the first place. How this then relates to questions of class and politics is the final turn of my argument.

The Difficult Birth of Israel

Genesis 25 functions as a microcosm of my reading of Genesis, for each of the features in that section of text have echoes throughout Genesis that flow through the boundary of the book with Exodus. Thus, I will draw comparisons with other sections of Genesis through my reading of ch. 25, particularly in terms of the tensions I locate in the ISAs and ideology itself: between the chronically delayed realization of the promise of a people of Israel and the free generation of peoples who are not Israel; the selection of a line that remains unproductive and the productive ones that branch off; the various pairs and twins that appear throughout Genesis; the themes of barrenness and fecundity; the ideological problem that the maternal body causes for Genesis and its crucial role in the construction of that narrative. In fact, Gen. 25 intensifies these tensions to a degree that makes it a crucial text for Genesis as a whole. Such an argument is perhaps a result of the curious conjunction between Althusser and Genesis, and yet what I perceive as the central ideological function of Gen. 25 runs up against a profound disinterest in this text by biblical scholars: they prefer the preceding account of Rebekah's leaving her mother's house to marry Isaac or the following narrative of Rebekah's trickster's agency in ensuring that Jacob receives the blessing over Esau.[2] Is this a sign of the success of the ideological function of the text itself, obscuring precisely that which is central?

Genesis 25 and Genesis as a whole contain a series of problematic items for a text that is both chronically undatable—although this in itself seems to me to be a strategy of the text itself. The material is riven with contradictions that have provided the ground for a whole series of methodological solutions, the most well known of course being the division into sources—JEPD—which seems to solve such contradictions while replicating the text's own concern with origins. My interests run elsewhere with Althusser, but the contradictions teem in the text, ranging through from repetitions such as Seth's birth (Gen. 4.25-26; 5.3) and the wife–sister stories (Gen. 12.10-20; 20; 26) to themes of barrenness, usurpation of birthrights, tensions between twins, deception, thwarted child sacrifice and particularly the problems around women giving birth.

Rather than being a mark of alternative ideological positions, often in terms of sources or editorial overlays, as so many studies of Genesis have suggested, this pattern in Genesis may also be understood as the normal function of ideology, for one expects tensions and contradictions to appear in any ideological product. However, I want to suggest that such tensions, such uncharacteristic material, is precisely the result of the ruling ideology that dominates Genesis, for any ruling ideology perpetually faces the contradictions of its own position. In Genesis the core of this position is a dual one of the possession of land and women, manifested in the infamous 'promise' to Abram of progeny and land, but also in the various stories of creation (Gen. 1; 2–3; 6–8; 9), genealogies and family narratives.

But let me move into the text of Gen. 25 more closely, for here we find elements of the family and religious ISAs. In the same way that Genesis 25 is concerned with the children of Keturah, the *toledot* of Ishmael and Isaac, and the story of Rebekah giving birth to Esau and Jacob, so also in

---

2.   Others who do in fact write on this text, such as Kathleen Norris (1996) in a collection of short stories by contemporary writers in response to Genesis, still fall into the traps of piety, focusing on Rebekah's agency, her direct encounter with God, etc. Hardly necessary, it seems to me, in order to appreciate the story itself.

the whole of Genesis do family interactions dominate the narratives: Adam, Eve, Cain, Abel and Seth; Noah and his sons; Abraham, Sarah, Hagar, Keturah, Isaac, Ishmael and Keturah's sons; Isaac, Rebekah, Jacob and Esau; Jacob, Leah, Rachel, Bilhah, Zilpah and their 13 children (including Dinah); Joseph, Asenath, Ephraim and Manasseh; Judah, Tamar, Perez and Zerah. Although genealogies appear elsewhere in the Hebrew Bible, such as Numbers and Chronicles, the marked difference of Genesis from other narrative texts is the predominance of the family narratives that interleave the genealogies. For these reasons, I will use Althusser's designation of the family ISA as a key feature of the narrative of Genesis.

Genesis 25 is not conceivable without the presence of Yahweh, for he is the one that opens Rebekah's womb, responds to her question, politicizes her womb—in short, exercises rigid control over the narrative. Wider than ch. 25, none of the narratives can operate without Yahweh's clout. At a purely textual level, then, it is possible to speak of a religious ideological dominance in the text, one that, using Althusser's terminology, is part of the religious ISA. I will plot this in more detail in the analysis that follows, as also with the family ideological patterns, but what we have already is an overlay of two ideological systems, two institutional forms of speaking that generate a host of contradictions.

A third major narrative feature on which I focus is what Althusser calls the 'state'. At the risk of covering some obvious points, Althusser's immediate concern is the nation-state, a historical development tied in with the emergence and spread of capitalism—France being the model of the first (bourgeois) nation-state. However, by using *état*, Althusser also signals a wider application of the term, and in political science the state designates any formation of a group of people with institutions for government. In this sense, it is possible to speak of an Israelite state, but I need to emphasize that, as with the religious and family ISAs, such a state is a literary item, an element in the narrative with no immediate connection to any substantive state of Israel.[3] Here, Althusser's definition of ideology

---

3.   The terms used are *goi*, *'am* and *l'om*, of which the first two are the most common: *goi* in Gen. 10.5, 20, 31, 32; 12.2; 14.1, 9; 15.14; 17.20; 17.4, 5, 6, 16; 18.18; 20.4; 21.13, 18; 22.18; 25.23; 26.4; 35.11; 46.3; 47.18; 48.19, and *'am* in Gen. 11.6; 14.16; 17.16; 19.4; 23.7, 11, 12, 13; 26.10, 11; 27.29; 28.3; 32.7; 33.15; 34.16, 22; 35.6; 41.40, 55; 42.6; 47.21, 23; 48.4, 19; 49.10, 16, 29; 50.20. By Exodus, however, *'am* dominates, referring to the Israel that has now appeared. Rather than the misleading 'nation'—with echoes of the nation-states that arose after the French Revolution—I prefer 'people' for all three terms. What interests me in Genesis is the third term, *le'om*

comes into play, for the appearance of family, religion and state remains a representation of an imaginary relationship to real conditions of existence.

For the sake of my discussion I will treat the religious and family ISAs as separate but significantly overlapping apparatuses, both dealing with the question of the 'state', or in Genesis 'people'. The tensions within the family and religious state apparatuses relate not only to each other but also to the question of the people. And all three connect in the central question of the promise of a people that runs throughout Genesis: Yahweh or Elohim (religious) repeatedly makes promises to various figures that a people (state) will arise from a child, always a son (family), of the person in question. Yet already a contradiction arises with this promise: Israel as a people does not appear in Genesis despite the repeated promise. The birth, in other words, is delayed.

This delay in the appearance of Israel as a people is in stark contrast to the continual emergence of a whole slate of peoples other than Israel. These often, although not exclusively, appear in the various genealogies that intersperse the narratives. Thus, Gen. 25 begins with two different genealogies (25.1-4, 12-16) and seems to begin a third (Gen. 25.19) that then shifts into the birth story of Rebekah. The first is that of Keturah, Abraham's wife, who bears (תלד) a series of children. Even though Keturah, not Abraham, is the subject of the verb, it follows the standard formula for when a woman gives birth: she bore for him (see, e.g., Gen. 21.2). The list of names follows a distinct format that appears throughout Genesis, namely, a combination of names of places, peoples and those with no clear identifier: Zimran, Jokshan, Medan, Midiam, Ishbak and Shua; from Jokshan Sheba and Dedan; from Dedan Asshurim, Letushim and Leummim; from Midian, Ephah, Epher, Hanoch, Abidah and Eldah. At a certain point, the list moves from individuals to plurals—Asshurim, Letushim and Leummim. Only a patient eye will pick up the weariness of the list with itself: run out of names, it throws out לאמים (*le'ummim*), 'peoples', which then might be read as the inevitable outcome of every line but the promised one. For the children of Keturah are not of the promised line, so it seems that they can flourish. Any threat to Isaac's status as heir of the promise is negated by the overt statement that every-thing of Abraham's was given to Isaac (although even this is undermined by the mention of gifts to the other sons), and that the sons of his con-cubines (note the plural; Gen. 25.6) were sent east, away from Isaac.

(people), which appears in Gen. 25.3 (*ule'ummim*); 25.23 and 27.29 (*le'ummim*); 25.23 (*ule'om* and *mile'om*) and *'ummah* (tribe) in Gen. 25.16 (*le'ummotam*).

A similar pattern follows with Ishmael, for before the narrative arrives at the struggle in Rebekah's womb, there appears the strange genealogy of Ishmael. It begins with a similar structure to the story of Rebekah: both Gen. 25.12 and 25.19 begin with 'These are the *toledot* of Ishmael / Isaac son of Abraham...' However, whereas 25.19 goes on to say 'Abraham bore Isaac', 25.12 has 'whom Hagar, the Egyptian, Sarah's maid, bore to Abraham'. Here the contrast is sharp, for whereas male begets male in 25.19, in 25.12 this is mediated through a woman weighed down with epithets that provide significant syntactical distance between Abraham and Ishmael. The problem here is that Ishmael too is the subject of a promise, and so this text may read as the fulfilment of that promise. And yet it stumbles. Three times it states, in slightly varying form, that 'these are the *toledot* of Ishmael' (25.12), 'these are names of the sons of Ishmael' (25.13) and 'these are the sons of Ishmael' (25.16). Each has a slightly different function, the first introductory, the second before a list of names itself and the third in a summarizing fashion, but the effect is one of formal overload, a repetition that gives away an ideological tension. For in Ishmael the promise is fulfilled, but the paradox here is that this seems to be the mark, no matter how close he gets, of not being chosen by Yahweh. The names that appear in 25.13 are eponymous; Ishmael has become a *goi*, as v. 16 makes clear in an echo of Gen. 10.5, 20 and 31: 'These are the sons of Ishmael and these are their names, according to their settlements and their encampments, twelve princes according to their tribes [לאמתם]' (Gen. 25.16). Already there are the 12 tribes with princes. So, as with Keturah in Gen. 25.1-4, Ishmael's line unfolds into a *goi*, although his line is replete with the apparatus of a 'state'—settlements, encampments, princes and tribes.

I have already moved on to the whole problem of the promise, since Ishmael is also the subject of one, as a consolation prize for not being of the exclusive line. But before I consider the promise more closely, there are comparable moments throughout Genesis where peoples seem to flourish, except Israel, except the chosen line: Cain's descendants in Gen. 4.17-22; those of Shem, Ham and Japheth in Gen. 10. In each case, the names are often personal names, toponyms and eponyms rolled into one. And the result is a narrative overflowing with peoples in their territories and cities, germinating in riotous fashion, through which the unproductive line of promise wanders its weary way, almost celibate in the singular (or serial) genealogies of Gen. 5.3-32 and 11.10-29. In fact, the text is at pains to point out that what we have here is a comprehensive listing in terms of 'their families, their languages, their lands and their peoples' (10.20, 31; see also 10.5, 32; cf. 25.16).

So also in Gen. 25: in contrast to the flourishing of both Keturah and Ishmael, the select line that runs through Isaac and Rebekah seems paradoxically blessed by its sparseness and troubles. In particular, the pairing of Ishmael and Isaac in Gen. 25 highlights the ambiguities of the promise as well as foreshadowing the struggling twins in Rebekah's womb. But it is a feature that has oft been commented upon in Genesis: Cain and Abel, Abraham and Nahor, Abraham and Lot, Hagar and Sarah, Esau and Jacob, Leah and Rachel, Perez and Zerah, Ephraim and Manasseh. That this relates to the tension over selection and what may be termed, following R.C. Heard (2001), diselection, is something I will trace through, for Isaac is the subject of five promises to Abram/Abraham, pumped up each time in a nervous reiteration of chronic unfulfilment (Gen. 12.1-3; 13.14-17; 15.1-18; 17.1-21; 22.16-18), and Ishmael is the subject of two to Abraham (Gen. 17.20; 21.13) and two to Hagar (Gen. 16.10; 21.18). All of which comes together in Genesis 25 with Ishmael and Isaac compared, acting together to bury Abraham, and then separated.

Ishmael is curiously the recipient of a promise and yet not. For the story of Hagar, Sarai's double, and Ishmael plays with the promise. Thus, Hagar is both recipient of a promise comparable to that of Abram, although without the land component (Gen. 16.10; 21.18), Abraham himself receives a promise of a *goi* through Ishmael, again without the land as an item (Gen. 17.20; 21.13), and this promise is fulfilled in Gen. 25.12-18. Here the pseudo-promise to Ishmael bears fruit in a people, whereas the passage that immediately follows has Isaac and Rebekah in a notable lack of fulfilment. Even though the Ishmael material comes closest to realizing the promise to Abraham, so much so that Gen. 21.13 confirms this as part of the promise, it veers away at the last moment, for only one line is the correct one, and the others, no matter how close, are not. The same applies to Esau, son of Isaac and Rebekah but not the favoured one, from whom the Edomites come (Gen. 36).

What of the promise regarding Isaac, whose sons Rebekah brings forth from her womb with great difficulty? The narrative about Abram in Genesis 12 begins with a promise that involves both land and people:

> Take yourself from your land, from your relatives/descendants [מולדתך] and from your father's house to the land that I show you. And I will make you a great people [*goi*] and I will bless you and make your name great and

a blessing will happen. I will bless those who bless you and those who curse you I will bind with a curse, and all the families of the earth will wish themselves blessed like you' (Gen. 12.1-3).

There a number of things to note with this passage. The word מולדתך (from ילד) is ambiguous, for it can register both relatives and descendants. The usual translation is 'relatives', for it seems to make sense in the immediate context of Abram's departure, but the ambiguity with descendants should be retained, for it is precisely the question of descendants that is at stake in the promise itself. Secondly, the promise concerns land, the generation of a people (*goi*) and blessing: of Abram's name, of the other families through him. Not only does the tension with 11.30 lock into place, only to enable Yahweh's involvement at a later point, but another tension also appears. How is it that the other 'families' (משׁפחת), or perhaps types of peoples, of the earth will wish themselves blessed when they have by and large already appeared on the scene and the *goi* that is the fruit of Abram's loins lies over a distant horizon? As I have indicated, this is a major tension in Genesis, between the delayed *goi* of Israel and all the *goiim* who seem to multiply unimpeded in their lands. For if the blessing to Abram involves both land and people, then it would seem that the other peoples have pre-empted the blessing of which Abram will be a somewhat tardy recipient. The Abram narratives return time and again to the promise with which the cycle begins (Gen. 13.14-17; 15.1-18; 17.1-21; 22.16-18). The detail and length of these versions only draws attention to their lack of fulfilment, exacerbated by Abraham's skepticism.

The incessant repetition of the promise to Abraham then echoes with subsequent figures: Isaac (Gen. 26.3-5, 24), Jacob (Gen. 28.13-15; 35.11-13; 46.3), and then through Jacob to Joseph, although God does not speak directly to Joseph (Gen. 48.4, 16). Yet the chronic delay in the fulfilment of the promise not only stands in stark contrast to the birth of so many others, but also to the numerous flocks and herds of animals, apart from the wealth of silver and gold (Gen. 13.2, 5–6; 26.12-14; 30.43; 36.7; 46.6). It seems as though the promise is about to be fulfilled in Gen. 46.8-27, with its long list of the children of 'Israel', but the number remains restricted to 70 and the people of Israel have yet to arrive on the scene. Even with the phrase בני ישׁראל in 46.8, which becomes the standard term for the 'state' of Israel, this state does not emerge in the genealogical list.

What we find, then, in the narratives of Genesis surrounding ch. 25 is a significant tension between the incessant production of peoples, or *goiim*, and places of anyone who is not part of the line that will lead to Israel, no

matter how close he might come (Ishmael, Esau, and so on). The tension
surrounding the 'state' in Genesis, namely the *goi*, or as it will appear with
great frequency in Exodus and beyond, *'am*, of Israel, is that the promise
of an innumerably great *goi* is delayed for the whole of the text. The sheer
repetition of the promise exacerbates the delay, and yet everyone else has
no problem in becoming peoples, that is, in realizing the promise that is so
difficult for Israel. The key item in this is Ishmael, for unlike the other
eponymous ancestors, both Hagar and Abraham receive a promise for
him that bears fruit within the text of Genesis in distinct contrast to that
of Isaac.

Instead of reading the tension in terms that either seek to locate the
text at a particular moment of authorship or historical and social setting, or
in terms of the theological problem of promise-fulfilment, my focus is
specifically on the way the state becomes a problematic site in this text.
For it is Althusser's material on the state and its contradictions that provides the perimeters of my search. As a text, the narrative shows up a key
tension, but what appears in Genesis is a concern less with state power
than with the state apparatus, that is, with the possibility of establishing a
state in the first place rather than the issue of who controls it. The added
complexity here is that the material on the 'state' of Israel is a text or a
collection of texts, and this is itself an ideological product that will reveal
its own contradictions, the first of which I have identified above. However,
the state for Althusser operates with both RSA and ISAs, and the two that
I have identified in the text of Genesis are the family and religion.

Both the genealogies in their various forms and the narratives of the
promise are concerned with the 'state', specifically the state apparatus, but
there is a significant overlap with the dominant family ISA in Genesis. For
these materials deal not only with the production of descendants and
peoples, but also with the whole question of birth itself. As dominant, I
will also expect that it becomes the site of greatest struggle and tension.
Yet, as I noted in my criticism of Althusser, the restriction of birth into the
family perpetuates the capitalist invention of the distinction between
public and private spheres, with the former given over to men in realms of
religion, politics, economics, and so on, and the private becoming the
domain of women and children. Further, Althusser's construction is predicated upon the exclusion of the maternal body and its appropriation.
However, what happens in Genesis is that such a system breaks down, for
the questions of the production of peoples or states, creation of the world
and the role of Yahweh/Elohim are all dealt with in terms of family

narratives. Thus, the shift in the notion of a family ISA in Genesis is not so much a restriction to a private realm as the ideological dominance of the narrative as such. Yet it is precisely the logic of Althusser's own analysis that raises not only this question, but also the possibility of an analysis of Genesis, such as this one. My discussion will then pick up an important repression in Althusser's own system, which is not merely the critical neglect of the family ISA, but more significantly the maternal body.

The tension between a *goi* and its absence appears with Rebekah herself, for she comes from an existent *goi*—the Arameans, specific epithets of both Bethuel and Laban (Gen. 25.20)—into a family that has no *goi*. Further, she is barren (עקרה). Like Sarah before her (Gen. 11.30; 16.1), and after her Rachel (29.31) and Leah (30.9), the barrenness is a specific device to highlight the direct involvement of Yahweh in the process of birth, or rather, appropriation by Yahweh (see also 20.17-18). Yet it also functions as an ideological device that signals the delay of the birth of Israel, a trope of the narrative itself that is barren, unable to give birth to a *goi* named Israel. It might also be argued that barrenness is in fact a mark of selection, which then itself becomes more a curse than a blessing in Genesis, except that such a promise and selection applies only to the male figures.

As for Rebekah, after Yahweh grants Isaac's prayer regarding her barrenness, Rebekah becomes pregnant (תהר, Gen. 25.21) and there follows a narrative of struggle in birth that differs from the others in Genesis in a number of ways. Those that are born as twins appear only here and in Gen. 38 with Perez and Zerah. Yet Perez and Zerah take little part in the narrative, whereas Esau and Jacob become central. Thus, I suggest that the conjunction of Esau and Jacob within the same womb exacerbates the tensions between the pairs that I have noted above. Further, since Esau and Jacob are patronyms for Edom and a much delayed Israel, Rebekah's womb becomes a site for political struggle. Or, to put it in Althusser's terms, the function of the family ISA finally is to provide ideological justification for the state itself, although it becomes invariably a site of ideological conflict. Thus, we find the backhanded promise of Yahweh in Gen. 25.23, which I will interrogate closely.

It is a promise of struggle, less political than bodily, for its focus is Rebekah's womb; or rather, her womb is a distinctly political item, a site of political struggle. Thus, the text reads 'the sons struggled together in her body [בקרבה]' (25.22); 'two peoples are in your womb [בבטנך], and two peoples from your insides [ממעיך] shall be divided' (25.23); 'and when her days for giving birth were full, behold, there were twins in her womb [בבטנה]' (25.24). In the space of three verses there are four occurrences of a term for womb using three different terms: קרב (inward parts, body), בטן (womb, belly) and מעים (entrails, body, womb). None of these is restricted to the sense of womb, for each word appears elsewhere in a number of ways that take other senses, relating to men, animals, and so on. Significant in itself, my interest here is the way a whole panoply of terms for body, insides and womb appear for Rebekah's womb, for this, ultimately, is the source from which Israel will appear as a *goi*. And is not רבקה, Rebekah, a play on קרבה, her body (Gen. 25.22), in a text full of false etymologies, except that the text's play with her body/womb is deeply sinister. The nervous attention to the womb, in terms of politics (the 'state') and religion (Yahweh's appropriation) signals the instability of the ideological apparatus at precisely this point. Even physiological features of pregnancy and birth take on political appearances: the bodily changes and pains of pregnancy become the mutual oppression or struggle (רצץ in 25.22) of political units, and the birth process itself is but a manifestation of those politics. In fact, Rebekah's womb becomes the site for a heavy investment for everything else in Genesis: the political future of conflict, divine utterances and the possibility of the people of Israel itself. Even the attribution to Abraham of a womb, or at least child-bearing entrails in Gen. 15.4 ('he shall come forth from your body', using ממעיך, from מעים) gives way to a narrative such as this where the womb becomes a site of political, ideological and religious contestation. And Yahweh, the one responsible for the repeated attempts at creation in Gen. 1–11, cannot ensure the delayed arrival of Israel without the womb of Rebekah, or for that matter of Sarah or Rachel or Leah. The struggling sons become the more obvious outward markers over the nervousness surrounding Rebekah's womb that the terminology and its repetition indicates.

But let me return to the 'state' for a few moments, for not only does Rebekah's womb indicate how the family is an ideological apparatus focused on the state, that is, the production of a people, but the terms for people are significant in themselves. The dominant usage in Genesis is both *goi* and *'am*. However, in Gen. 25 another term appears: לאם and its plural לאמים. Apart from Gen. 27.29, where it appears in the blessing of Jacob, precisely one of those born in Gen. 25, all of the other appearances are restricted to this chapter. The singular, לאם, appears twice in 25.23, and the plural in 25.23 and 25.3. The last appearance is syptomatic, for ostensibly this is one of the names of the sons of Dedan, son of Abraham and Keturah, but I would suggest that the narrative gives way in 25.3, not only to plurals as the designator of peoples, but to לאמים as a generic marker for peoples. Yet this is not one of the usual terms, *goi* or *'am*. The related לאמתם, from אמה (tribe), occurs in Gen. 25.16, the tribes of the 12 princes descended from Ishmael. In contrast to both *goi* and *'am*, לאם is constructed out of the preposition ל and the word for mother, אם. Literally 'for a mother', or in the plural 'for mothers', the word itself signals in another way the focus on Rebekah's womb as central to the family ISA. For the people, לאם, can only come forth through the womb of the mother, and here it is Rebekah's womb. That the term is restricted to this chapter, and that the terms for womb cluster here, only enhances my point.

From here the echoes reverberate fore and aft: cave and tent become the ambiguous spaces of mothers, sex and usurpation. The cave in which both Ishmael and Isaac bury Abraham (Gen. 25.7-11) is the same one in which Sarah has been interred in Gen. 23.19. Yet the text fudges between burial cave, mother's tent and the first sex of Isaac and Rebekah—the replacement for Isaac's mother: 'And Isaac brought her, Sarah his mother, into the tent and he took Rebekah and she became his wife, and he loved her. And Isaac was comforted after his mother' (Gen. 24.67). Is 'Sarah his mother' a corruption? Does Isaac bring his dead mother and new woman into the same tent to honour the former and have sex with the latter? Or does the tent double for the cave of burial—less messy, since he wouldn't have to dig her up from Machpelah. In fact the phrase that disrupts, 'Sarah his mother', reveals the logic of the text at the moment of its syntactical breakdown. For tent and cave are drawn into the increasing focus of the text on Rebekah's womb—as also the oblique reference to her mother's house in Gen. 24.28—and I can't avoid the psychoanalytic observation of the warping effect of the Real, the womb, on the symbolic, or text itself. Yet, and here is the first signal of the crucial role of the womb in the economy of the text, Rebekah replaces Sarah's once barren womb, from which Isaac (and by proxy Ishmael) came, entering the space (tent) of the mother so that the son may continue to produce.

Along with both the questions of state and family that connect at the location of Rebekah's womb, the final ideological apparatus that appears in Genesis, the religious, does the same. For Yahweh attempts to direct what happens in her womb: in v. 21, Isaac prays to Yahweh 'on behalf of his wife' since she was barren. But it is not Yahweh who makes barren and fecund? Immediately, Yahweh answers him and she becomes pregnant. A curious threesome in which Yahweh directs the action—even

though Rebekah is the subject of the verb, the syntactical closeness of
Yahweh's answer to Isaac (why does she not ask?) and Rebekah's becoming pregnant places Yahweh firmly in control.

Yet the control of birth is but one element, for Rebekah is constituted as
a subject through the interpellation by Yahweh. Elsewhere, the address by
Yahweh, the hailing or interpellation, to use Althusser's terms, constitutes
the various figures—Cain, Abraham, Isaac, Jacob—as subjects in a political context, as ancestors of a people whose arrival is always over the horizon. The various moments of the promise to Abraham, Isaac and Jacob
may now be reread in terms of interpellation. In Rebekah's case the narrative spins out a little further, for here such interpellation, like that of Hagar,
involves a woman. But before Yahweh speaks, Rebekah asks a question
directed at no-one in particular: 'If so, why then I?' (אם־כן למה זה אנכי,
Gen. 25.22). An extraordinarily cryptic question that is in the mouth of a
woman, but one that also asks, in light of Althusser's theory, the question
about the subject itself, particularly with the personal pronoun, I, held until
the end of the phrase. What constitutes Rebekah as a subject in this narrative? Is it the sons fighting in her womb, or her function as child bearer
for Isaac? But then, in the only occurrence of a woman approaching God
with a question in Genesis, she goes to inquire of Yahweh (Gen. 25.22).
The words of her inquiry do not appear, for Yahweh rushes in with an
answer. Is the preceding question meant to be directed at Yahweh?
Syntactically it appears that Rebekah asks it of herself and that Yahweh
can't be bothered listening, for she must be answered before she can speak
too much. And the answer is the backhanded promise of struggling
peoples in her womb—no longer sons as in v. 22, but peoples. At this
moment of interpellation, when Yahweh addresses her, Rebekah is
constituted as a subject through her political and religious role. As if to
confirm Yahweh's dominance, the text reads, when her days for giving
birth were fulfilled, 'behold, there were twins in her womb' (25.24). That
is, Yahweh was correct, there are two, for up until this point the only
signal of more than one was the plural 'sons' in 25.22. But if we follow
Althusser through, such a narrative gives the impression of a sequence,
whereas ideologically the subject is always already interpellated, always
already constituted. More importantly for my argument is Althusser's
point that all ideology operates in a similar fashion, drawing his conclusions from a religious example. Thus, Rebekah is not merely constituted as
a subject, a distinctly political subject, by the interpellation of Yahweh,
but it necessarily involves the subjection of Rebekah to the Subject

himself, Yahweh. In this process she recognizes her sons as subjects, again political, and recognizes herself. Above all, the function of ideology is to provide a guarantee that it cannot be otherwise, and all Rebekah must do is acquiesce and all will be fine. In other words, Rebekah's constitution as a subject in subjection to Yahweh involves her complete absorption into the narrative of Israel's birth. As a woman who gives birth, she can do no other.

In light of the fact that Gen. 25, especially the narrative about Rebekah's womb, intensifies many of the tensions found elsewhere in Genesis—between pairs, between the generation of peoples apart from Israel and the delay in the birth of Israel, between recipients of promise and those who are not, in the terminology for womb and people—I would argue that it is precisely her womb that becomes the key ideological element in this narrative. For here there is an intersection between the four major elements I have drawn from Althusser's work, namely, the 'state', the family ISA, the religious ISA and the operation of ideology itself in terms of interpellation. Rebekah's womb is the locus through which political 'states' will emerge, where the family narratives of Genesis reach a crux, and where Yahweh must control every aspect of the process of birth, from barrenness, through pregnancy and the struggle in the womb to the birth itself. In other words, the site of the greatest tension and struggle is precisely Rebekah's womb, which breaks out of the categories of family and religious ISAs as well as the state apparatus itself. Yet at the same time, Gen. 25 is a narrative that ideologically co-opts Rebekah's womb.

This is where the other dimension of Althusser's definition of ideology comes into play: for, as a text, this narrative is a representation of the imaginary relationship with real conditions of existence. This goes much further than the general point about genealogies and family narratives—that they reflect ideological concerns over coherence and kinship that are then projected backwards through eponymous figures and genealogical lines (a simple reflection theory of ideology)—to provide an important mediation. Gen. 25 is not itself the imaginary relationship to real conditions, that is, it does not directly give voice to political and ideological questions. Rather, it is a representation of imaginary relationships. And those imaginary relationships, I would argue, are the way political, family and religious ways of constructing the world try to deal with the question of the maternal body itself. And what of the real conditions? One might argue for a range of possible particular circumstances—the perpetual delay of Yahweh's political promises in a context (Babylonian? Persian?) of little promise—but this misses the value of a method like that of Althusser. For it would seem that the real situation that constitutes the problem is the process of birth itself, the ability of women, not men, to become pregnant and bear children. If this is the real condition then the imaginary relationships become those efforts to deal such a situation, and these imaginary relationships are represented in a text like Gen. 25. And it is here that the dual promise of land and progeny works to another logic, for land and women's bodies are two sides of the same coin. Yet as Althusser would argue, in the representation itself all the tensions and contradictions show up, in terminology, grammar, syntax, speech and narrative.

Yet if I follow Althusser's method, then my discussion is incomplete without the questions of politics and class. In a text that is itself an ideological product I identified and traced the various intersections of the family and religious ISAs that interact with the question of the state. In following the various tensions of such an interaction, with a focus on Gen. 25, it seems to me that the womb of Rebekah and the narrative of the pregnancy, struggle and birth of Esau and Jacob provide the key point at which family, religious and political concerns come together. Rebekah's womb is the site of an intense religious, political and familial ideological investment, even an overdetermination (to use another term of Althusser's), that generates a whole series of tensions and contradictions, ranging through from specific terminology to that of the themes that run through Genesis. At the moment that it becomes possible to identify Rebekah's womb as the location of these tensions, since the maternal body forms the real conditions for which imaginary relations are developed that in turn appear in the text as a representation, it also becomes possible to identify the various processes of appropriation. And this takes place, not in ostensible fashion through the religious, familial and political ideological investment in her womb, but through the narrative of her interpellation, which renders her not so much an excluded item in the narrative, but as one that is absolutely necessary for the narrative of Israel's birth to exist at all. I would suggest that this also is a representation of imaginary relations, namely, the economic and class conditions within which women, specifically maternal bodies, can be co-opted into a system of political economics, here explicitly identified as those of land and a people. However, I stopped at 'imaginary relations', for the real conditions of such an appropriation may be quite different.

How, finally, does the narrative resolve the problem of the birth of Israel in Genesis? It is only when we cross the boundary of books, between scrolls, that Israel may appear, for in Exod. 1.7 it takes place, in Egypt: 'But the sons of Israel were fruitful and increased greatly, they multiplied and grew exceedingly strong, so that the land was filled with them.' Five verbs appear here, all dealing with the growth of Israel into a people, and in Exodus the vast number of *'am*, people, signals their arrival. Paradoxically, it is only outside the land that is so much a part of the promise, in Egypt, that the promise of a people is fulfilled. The ambiguous promise of a land, one to be possessed and dominated in the same fashion as the maternal body, must wait for a much longer stretch of time, but why is the difficult birth of Israel possible only in Exodus? This can only happen outside the zone of the land itself, the setting for most of the family narratives of Genesis, in the same way that the men who desperately desire progeny in Genesis must go outside their own bodies to do so. Both Egypt and the maternal body are then the necessarily excluded elements that can realize the narrative drive of Genesis, but that is the subject of another argument.

Let me turn back to ask Althusser a final question or two. My argument rests on making the most of what I signalled as an omission in Althusser's own theory, namely, the maternal body in his discussion of the reproduction of the relations of production in general and specifically in the family ideological state apparatus. It seems that Althusser's own omission or elision brings him closer to Genesis than may at first appear to be the case, for he partakes of a similar ideological pattern to the one I traced in Genesis. For, if we take his argument that ideology is ahistorical seriously, then it seems that both his theory and the narrative of Genesis function in similar ways—the exclusion and appropriation of the maternal body that then becomes crucial for Althusser's method and Genesis itself. Yet this happens in different ways. The narrative tensions in Genesis over women's wombs, specifically Rebekah's womb, and the investment in her womb of politics, family and religion, contrast with Althusser's concern over the reproduction of the relations of production, which is itself a political and economic investment in that which remains unnamed, except as an item of the family ISA. However, is it not then a case of the text setting the agenda for its own interpretation, by a process of transference for which David Jobling (1998) has argued in more detail?

Chapter 2

ANTONIO GRAMSCI:
THE EMERGENCE OF THE 'PRINCE' IN EXODUS

Like Lenin and Lukács, Antonio Gramsci lived as a politically active intellectual, with the impeccable credentials of dying at the hands of Mussolini's fascist regime. Apart from towering over the history of the left in Italy, he has had a profound influence on the way some newer disciplines conduct their work, particularly cultural studies and postcolonialism. But those with a slightly longer tradition than a decade or two have also dipped into Gramsci's legacy—sociology, philosophy, political science, literary criticism and feminism. Apart from his deepening of the Marxist categories of ideology and class consciousness in terms of hegemony, Gramsci also contributed to understanding the role of intellectuals, ideology, the state, politics, civil society, the philosophy of praxis, reformation and revolution.

In this chapter, I want to read the figure of Moses in Exodus in terms of Gramsci's reflections on Machiavelli's *The Prince* (1988). Taking up Machiavelli's own admiration for Moses as the epitome of the ideal ruler, as well as Fontana's suggestion (1993) that the interaction with Machiavelli provided many of the concepts that Gramsci himself was developing, it seems to me that, as with my reading of Genesis with the help of Althusser, there is more than a passing acquaintance between Exodus and Gramsci's work. Behind the main work of theoretical and textual reading, there lurks also the question of the nature of Exodus, and the whole Pentateuch, as a political myth, a foundational political document that can only be written in mythical form. Moses attracts to himself two specific areas of Gramsci's writings—those concerned with the state and ideology. For in Exodus we not only find the literary construction of a 'state', an *'am* that is finally born after the boundary with Genesis (and the promised land) has been breached, but also distinct signs of ideological conflict, for which Gramsci coined *egemonia*, hegemony. Always a contested zone, the stories of revolt or opposition in Exodus become crucial, for they indicate not merely a textual nervousness about the uniformity of an ideological position, but also a more complex strategy of incorporating opposition within such an ideology. For this reason the key text will be the story of the golden calf in Gen. 32.

It is one of the ironies of the great body of Gramsci's literature that had it not been for his imprisonment he would not have been able to carry out such a huge intellectual project, nor would he have been killed off by an exponential multiplication of diseases and ailments. From July 1926 until his death on 27 April 1937, at the age of 46, Gramsci was a political prisoner, although he had been officially free for two days before he died. Moved from prison to prison, the right to write was granted in January 1929 only after a struggle, although he had already outlined a plan for what became the Prison Notebooks in March 1927. So, for a decade he wrote, in cell after cell, communicating with his family—Julia Schucht and their children, Delio and Guilio, resident in the Soviet Union from July 1926—and his prime contact, Tatiana Schucht, the sister of Julia, as well as writing the extraordinary Prison Notebooks. The story, however, that needs to be written is that of Julia Schucht, on her own with the children in Moscow and suffering from mental illness.

It is impossible to avoid the biographical dimension of Gramsci's work, martyr that he is to Marxism. The danger is that, like Benjamin, the biography with its spectacular death becomes the window through which any understanding of the thinker in question must pass. I have of course done precisely this with Gramsci, but perhaps recognition of the process is one way of neutralizing, in part at least, its influence. For Gramsci's ideas, his reshaping of Marxism in light of the struggle in Italy, have been widely influential. Taken up by the left everywhere, from Hanna Arendt to Gayatri Spivak, Edward Said to Raymond Williams, Gramsci is the name that still appears in theoretical discussions.

The Prince

Rather than discuss Gramsci's thought in the absence of the text he exegetes—Machiavelli's *The Prince*—I prefer to run the two together, backtracking perpetually in order to show how close they touch the material on Moses in the Pentateuch. As for Gramsci, his initial observation on *The Prince* reads as though it were written of Exodus itself: 'The fundamental characteristic of *The Prince* is that it is not a systematic treatment, but a "living" book, in which political ideology and political science are fused in the dramatic form of a "myth" ' (Gramsci 1957: 135). The almost scriptural invocation of the living book takes an unexpected turn towards the political myth, for this is precisely why it is such a book, full of breath and pulse and vitality. Do I speak of The Prince or the Bible? Both, I would suggest, for the continuing power of a text like Exodus—in fact the whole stretch from Genesis to Joshua—is as a political myth, one that fuses political ideology and political science, as well religion and ritual, social and familial organization, in short, that deals with the question of the state whatever the particular details might turn out to be. Specifically, fantasy and art, argues Gramsci, are the forms in which Machiavelli expressed such a myth, forever altering the practice of political science that had until then been characterized by 'disquisitions and pedantic classifications of the principles and criteria of a mode of action' (1957: 135). And the key to all of this is the way he draws everything into the figure of the *condottiere*, the 'qualities, characteristic traits, duties, necessities of a concrete person', who both represents the collective will and excites the 'artistic fantasy of those he wants to convince and give a more concrete form to political passions' (135). Is not Moses partially concealed behind Machiavelli's ideal prince?

Yet there is a utopian dimension to *The Prince*, one that derives from his ideal nature:

> The utopian characteristic of *The Prince* lies in the fact that the Prince did not exist in historical reality, did not present himself to the Italian people in a directly objective way, but was a purely doctrinaire abstraction, the symbol of a leader, the ideal *condottiere*; but the emotional, mythical elements contained throughout this small book, with very effective dramatic movement, are recapitulated and come to life in the conclusion, the invocation of a 'really existing' prince (Gramsci 1957: 135).

If Machiavelli was clearer about the identity of this really existing prince (Lorenzo de' Medici), Gramsci does not mention his name. The one Machiavelli exhorts to be Prince remains anonymous in Gramsci's text. So also, it would seem, with the unnamed biblical authors, for if there were a specific audience, a 'prince' that required exhortation to lift himself to the heights of Moses, then he also lacks identification. But this is part of the mythical and utopian function of both *The Prince* and Exodus, even though one should always ask, a utopia for whom? As for Machiavelli, he is for Gramsci a passionate partisan who seeks to bring about new relations of forces, to work to what should be rather than what is. It is not

Gramsci's version of Mach.

a hopeless wishing or a 'yearning for the stars' (Gramsci 1957: 163), but rather a concrete will based on an analysis of effective reality.

In his inexorable drive to interpret the contemporary political situation in Italy, Gramsci seeks to bring Machiavelli into the present of pre-war communist and fascist politics. My reading moves in the opposite direction, at least initially although even here there is an illusion, since the biblical material itself has had its own influence on Machiavelli and beyond.

Gramsci is selective in applying Machiavelli's guidelines to what he calls the 'modern Prince', but there are two fundamental points from which any concrete suggestions must emerge in a dramatic rather than pedantically reasoned fashion. The first is the 'formation of a national-popular collective will of which the modern Prince is at the same time the organiser and active working expression' (1957: 140). The Prince's very status as a 'myth-prince' renders him the first sign of this new collective, which turns into its most potent form in the political party. In the bulk of his notes he applies Machiavelli's observations upon his 'Prince' to the political party, especially the revolutionary communist party, 'that particular party which, at different times and in the different internal relations of the various nations, aims (and is rationally and historically founded for this end) to found a new type of State' (1957: 146). Just as the Prince is the means for establishing a new and unified Italian state, so also the party will produce the conditions for a socialist society, uniting the collective will of the proletariat. For Gramsci, in the same way that Machiavelli becomes, in the rousing conclusion to *The Prince*, the embodiment of the people to whom he has addressed his tract, a political myth such as this can only realize itself if it becomes the ideology, the drive behind and content of the political programme of the party.

The second basic point is the need for a reform of religion or world outlook, for which the modern Prince 'must and cannot but be the preacher and organiser of intellectual and moral reform' (1957: 139), which itself provides the basis for a national-popular collective will whose desire is a better and higher form of civilization.

Must I part company from Gramsci here, arguing for a different logic in the text of Exodus? I suspect not, for not only should Exodus be read as the myth behind a particular political programme or programmes, but it is precisely here, in Exodus, that the 'state' or *'am* of Israel, the *bene Yisrael*, emerges within the text at the same time that Moses rises to prominence. He is nothing other than that preacher and organizer of intellectual and moral reform so necessary for the emergence of the collective will. I don't want to return to the old argument in biblical studies over the collective individual; rather, 'Moses' is the necessary precondition for the mythical emergence of the state, or *'am*, of Israel. In a way comparable to the connection forged between the new Prince and the people through Machiavelli's new knowledge—the people and the Prince come into being simultaneously through the new political knowledge—so also Moses can only emerge with the people of Israel by means of the mythical narrative, the 'new knowledge', of Exodus itself. Moses and the people become, therefore, a necessary fiction of the political myth of the first books of the Hebrew Bible, one that carries through the patterns I traced in Genesis, as the male 'mother' of Israel without which Israel would not have been born (hence the birth story of Moses).

This is all very well, although Gramsci could well be accused of following a liberal agenda of seeking a change in attitude or consciousness as the key to any reform. But he is a Marxist, and any such change would not be possible without the seismic shift in political economy that is basic for any new form of civic and cultural life. Not only is any intellectual and moral reform tied to economic reform, but the programme of 'economic reform is precisely the concrete way in which every intellectual and moral reform is presented' (1957: 140). In this respect Gramsci is on firmer ground than the biblical critic, for the economic situation of the recent past and present is far more easily known than those of the biblical texts, at least in its details. The problem with a text like Exodus is that the temptation to locate it at a particular historical moment—the exile in Babylon, or perhaps the later Persian era in the lead-up to the Hasmonean state—is so strong, and yet the text is notoriously impossible to date. That Exodus speaks of fundamental moral, intellectual and religious reform—in the structure of a political myth—I will assume, but the economic reform is a little harder to locate, except in the way the text generates its own image of such reform.

But what does resonate between *The Prince* and Exodus is Gramsci's observation that the 'Prince takes the place, in the conscience, of the divinity or of the categorical imperative' (1957: 140), for in Exodus the elision of the figure of Moses with God is one of the features of the text, one that runs through to his 'assumption' at the end of Deuteronomy.

Thus far I have outlined some of the ways in which Gramsci's reading of *The Prince*—as political myth, the fictional nature of the Prince, the concern with collective will and moral and intellectual reform—applies not merely to the urgent task Gramsci faced in the politics of the Italian communist party but also to the role of Moses in Exodus and the books that follow. I am less interested in the analysis of the situation in Italy, in which Gramsci follows a pattern of analysis inspired by Machiavelli's own. Rather than pass through the details of this material—guidelines for leaders as long there are ruled and rulers, the role of the army, of the political party (the 'modern Prince') and parties, current economic theories ('economism'), crisis, bureaucracy, representative domocracy, division of powers and law—it is far better to take up the deeper imperative of Gramsci's own text and interrogate Gen. 32 in a similar fashion. In fact, I would argue that it is through such an application that the possibilities of reading Moses in this way emerge, except that there is something more in Machiavelli's own text that removes any sense of coincidence.

To begin with, along with Cyrus, Romulus and Theseus, Moses is a prime example of one who has come to be ruler through his own ability (*virtù*) rather than through luck or fortune (*fortuna*), on account of which rulers must remain flexible and change with the times. Having included Moses in the list, he remarks laconically, 'And although one should not discuss Moses, because he was merely an executor of what had been ordained by God, yet he should be admired even if only for that favour which made him worthy to speak with God' (Machiavelli 1988: 20). The censors and piety satisfied—later he will describe Moses and the others as 'only human' (1988: 88)—he immediately brings Moses back into the list as the first exemplar of those '[n]ew principalities acquired by one's own arms and ability' (1988: 19). Such principalities are of the highest order, in contrast to hereditary, mixed and ecclesiastical principalities. And the combination of ability and fortune is better than acquiring states with the favour or assistance of others, by means of crime, through being chosen by one's fellow citizens, or election by the pope. Each is viable, but only the first reveals the true character of its new leader. So Moses is at the head of a list rulers of the most desirable form of the state, a new principality.

Further, Moses, like the others, made the most of both his great ability and the opportunity presented him, finding the people of Israel in a state ready to follow and serve him out of a situation of servitude and oppression by the Egyptians. In fact, the Israelites had to be enslaved, suggests Machiavelli, in order to reveal his ability (see 1988: 88). The difficult part is attaining power, but it is held easily when this hurdle is overcome:

> The difficulties encountered in attaining power arise partly from the new
> institutions and laws they are forced to introduce in order to establish their

> power and make it secure. And it should be realised that taking the initiative
> in introducing a new form of government is very difficult and dangerous,
> and unlikely to succeed (Machiavelli 1988: 20).

Another factor, which will be important in my reading of Exod. 32, is that the opponents of innovation are often stronger than the lukewarm enthusiasm of the supporters of the Prince. Thus, the struggle becomes even more intense, and the opponents of change will attack vigorously whenever possible, throwing the Prince and his supporters into danger.

Given such a situation, armed supporters become absolutely necessary. Machiavelli is scornful of mercenaries and auxiliaries, stressing the need for an army comprised of one's own men (a Prince should always arm his own subjects), for only these soldiers will remain firm in battle, neither fleeing nor leaving one at the mercy of another power. In the same way, he suggests, that David was unable to fight Goliath with Saul's armour but required his own weaponry, so also must the Prince secure his own forces (see 1988: 50). Thus, the 'armed prophet' (Machiavelli 1988: 21)—and here he has Moses directly in mind—is always more successful. Why? Force is always required against one's external enemies, but also those within: 'People are fickle; it is easy to persuade them about something, but difficult to keep them persuaded. Hence, when they no longer believe in your schemes, you must be able to force them to believe' (1988: 21). Again I have Exod. 32 in mind, although Machiavelli's assessment may as well have been drawn from the biblical text's focus on the perpetual murmuring of the Israelites against Moses. For the Prince of a new principality, then, the dangers and difficulties are therefore immense, but when the long haul of attaining power and instituting reform is over, rulers like Moses become secure, honoured and successful.

At the close of the work, Moses returns in the impassioned call to Lorenzo de' Medici to become a new Prince by following Machiavelli's precepts. Italy, he writes, is in desperate straits, 'more enslaved than the Hebrews' (Machiavelli 1988: 88), and it is in this situation that one with ability could unite Italy to become a great state. In fact, he attests, there have been favourable events, 'signs from God': 'the sea has opened; a cloud has shown you the way; water has flowed from the rock; manna has rained down here' (1988: 89). Many have commented on the contrast between the exhortation at the close of the book, where these words are found, and the terse style of the preceding pages, but it is only when he gets carried away that the biblical allusions sprout forth.

While the discussion of various principalities has a certain appeal, the controversial and intriguing parts of the *The Prince* are those that deal with the characteristics of the ideal Prince, exactly those that have given the adjective 'Machiavellian' its ambiguity. I am going to run through the desirable features of the Prince, for not only does Machiavelli provide his suggestions in an unembellished prose, overturning an entire tradition of political advice that ran back to Seneca's *De clementia* and Cicero's *De officiis*, but it will also serve as a checklist for my own reading of Exod. 32.

A ruler should never, he argues (ch. XVI), exhibit lavish generosity, for this will deplete his resources and force him to tax his subjects. Para-doxically, such generosity will lead to hatred. Rather, he should be miserly, for eventually people will see that he is in fact generous, always holding enough resources for war and other expenses without having to burden his subjects with taxes. The only exception is with what belongs to another: a ruler must be generous with, for instance, loot and booty, but not with his own money, since 'meanness is one of those vices that enable him to rule' (1988: 57).

Similarly with cruelty (ch. XVII), for a proper mercifulness can only be achieved through cruelty. A little well-directed cruelty—the occa-sional beheading or imprisonment—is far more merciful than ill-thought clemency: 'by punishing a very few he will really be more merciful than those who over-indulgently permit disorders to develop, with resultant killings and plunderings' (1988: 58). Machiavelli pushes the paradox: the ideal is a prudent and humane cruelty. This means, he suggests, that although it is best to be loved and feared, a ruler will do much better by being feared rather than loved or indeed hated.

As for the virtue of honouring his word, the ruler should set little store by this. Cunning deception, where required, is far better. Again, the reason is that people are treacherous and faithless and that a ruler will fall foul if he doesn't exercise prudence in this matter: he should keep or break his word when it is to his advantage. With the guile and perceptiveness of a fox and the strength and force of a lion should the Prince rule (Machiavelli 1988: 61). This argument has direct implications for Gramsci's notion of hegemony, to which I turn in moment, and my reading of Exod. 32.

In the remainder of his tractate, Machiavelli offers direct advice in order to rule effectively. To begin with, he argues that the best rulers are those who show all of the virtues—merciful, trustworthy, humane, upright and devout—even if he finds that the circumstances require acting in other ways. Machiavelli stresses that the Prince should at least 'seem' to have these virtues, he 'should not deviate from right conduct if possible, but be capable of entering upon the path of wrongdoing when this becomes necessary' (1988: 62). This is the new virtue (*virtù*). Further, he considers the ways to avoid hatred and contempt, and the best way to do so is to ensure that everyone under his rule is kept respectful and content: 'Well-ordered states and wise rulers have always been very careful not to exasperate the nobles and also to satisfy the people and keep them contented; this is one of the most important things for a ruler to do' (1988: 66). By displaying grandeur, courage, seriousness and strength, taking strong positions and steering clear of neutrality or vacillation, keeping a small circle of serious advisers and shunning flatterers, and avoiding the seizing of property and women he will ensure that he is not hated or despised, for these are worth far more than fortresses built as a security against one's own people.

A purely Machiavellian reading of Moses is entirely possible, and part of what I undertake below may be seen in this way. But what I find intriguing about Machiavelli's book is the way in which Gramsci, as well as Althusser, appropriate Machiavelli for Marxism. It is not so much the opportunism, the Jesuitical means justifying the end, but the extraordinarily practical nature of the treatise that is most appealing. Thus, Machiavelli writes that it would be desirable if rulers could display all the virtues, as so many had argued before him, but because he wants to focus on what is useful, 'it seems to me better to concentrate on what really happens rather than on theories or speculations' (1988: 54). Since people are corrupt and unscrupulous, a ruler who wishes to maintain his power must be prepared to 'act immorally when this becomes necessary' (1988: 55). And yet Gramsci can claim Machiavelli as the Italian Luther, one who provides the way to enact change in political economics as well as in moral and intellectual terms. Did not Luther himself say, when you sin, sin boldly? In the end Machiavelli is not caught up in the past, reiterating what others before him written: he offers a vigorous way and positive alternative that actually focuses on the *volgo*, the people (Althusser [1999] argues that this is a crucial feature of *The Prince*).

For Gramsci, *The Prince* is misread as a treatise on morals: Machiavelli is a man of action who urges others to action. The book is therefore a 'manifesto', a work with revolutionary implications. For, like Marxism, Machiavelli writes for those who are not accustomed to rule, not in the know, and his advice is for the newly emergent and politicized people, the citizen democracy. And what this new force requires is an awareness of its own independent personality that constitutes a break from traditional ideology. Couched in the language of practicality and action, full of details and examples, *The Prince* becomes an enabling ideological force, one that provides impetus to a new political direction. And indeed Exodus may be read, not without some qualifications, as a comparable revolutionary document—the emergence of a collective will out of the escape from slavery—replete with its own precepts and laws, whether for the tabernacle or for living, that are to be read prescriptively rather than descriptively.

At one level my reading of Exodus, especially the thirty-second chapter, seeks to read Machiavelli and Gramsci *back* into the figure of Moses. Straightforward though this might seem, I have already suggested another pattern in which Moses and the texts in which he appears becomes a necessary partner (not merely a precursor) to the features that are apparently new in Machiavelli. But there is a further element, perhaps the most widely known of Gramsci's work, that insists on its own presence in my interpretation, namely, hegemony (*egemonia*). Not merely a significant advance on Marxist deliberations over ideology and political practice, hegemony is also intrinsic to Gramsci's encounter with Machiavelli. For me, hegemony is an extraordinarily useful concept for charting the workings of political myth, of which Exod. 32 forms a snippet.

Gramsci's reconsideration of ideology has been as influential as that of Althusser, the two often working side by side with each other, except that for Gramsci hegemony is very much a class concept, concerned with the relations between the rulers and the ruled, between the owners of the means of production and the non-owners, those who work for an income and those who do not but live off the work of others. For Gramsci, the concept of hegemony recognizes that ideology is never seamless, that it is never a given, but must be struggled over. It is constantly under threat of losing ground, collapsing, of being undermined as a lie. It is not so much that the classes develop their own comprehensive ideological systems, forever opposed to the other class, yet somewhat consistent within themselves. Rather, Gramsci takes Marx's point that the ruling ideas of an age are the ideas of the ruling classes a huge step further by pointing to the gaps, inconsistencies, the inability of such ruling ideas ever to be completely dominant. That is, the ruling ideas need constantly to be reasserted, ever new ways have to be found to ensure that they hold onto their somewhat tenuous status as ruling ideas. Ideas, beliefs and feelings, such as the value of the nation-state, nationalism and patriotism, the value of competition, the inviolability of private property and the individual person (to which the bulk of the judicial system is devoted), the foundational role of the nuclear family in social organization and reproduction, the gene-ration of self-esteem by selling one's labour power in working, the right to render anything for sale, and so on, are not so much givens as items of struggle that need to be reasserted time and again. Hence the crucial role of advertising, of political propaganda, of sustained intellectual arguments in their favour, of the role of competitive sport at all levels, of the perpetual need for the various judicial systems to punish those who do not hold these values. Like Althusser, Gramsci also recognized the role of such institutions as education (now covering the bulk of childhood and the emergence into adulthood) and religion as crucial factors in ensuring that the various dimensions of such a hegemony are inculcated into new generations or incorporated into religious belief systems.

Why is it that any hegemony is so unstable? Since one of the means by which ruling classes hold onto power is through the key components of ideology, the instability of hegemony points to the instability of those ruling classes themselves. In other words, there are always oppositional forces, tendencies that undermine the power of the ruling class, ensuring that there is always a struggle for power itself. Such power is never certain, and so one of the ways to hold onto power is to assert a particular hegemony over those who are ruled.[1] The source of this instability lies within those who are ruled, who always sense that the rule over them is unjust, that they have been denied power in some way. At the root of the concept of hegemony, then, is the idea of class conflict.

Apart from accounting for class conflict itself, by hegemony Gramsci refers to an intellectual and moral leadership (*direzione*) that operates primarily through consent and persuasion. Thus, a dominant hegemony, usually that of the ruling class, works by articulating and spreading a

---

1.   Let me use a couple of examples from the Olympic Games, held in Sydney, Australia in September 2000. After travelling through many countries from Athens, the Olympic torch finally arrived in Australia, passing through the length and breadth of the country. The hegemonic idea of the torch was to 'bring the nation together', to celebrate Australian patriotism and so on. The media duly reported this day after day, bypassing counter-hegemonic acts, such as the repeated efforts by people to douse the torch with water-bombs, or the occasional person who snatched the torch from the designated runner. And then there was the 'fat-arsed wombat', an alternative mascot marketed over against the official mascots of the Kookaburra, Kangaroo and Koala. Sales of the fat-arsed wombat began to eclipse the official mascots, so the International Olympic Committee banned the fat-arsed wombat from stores. Small examples, to be sure, but one that indicate how carefully hegemony is asserted and policed.

specific set of cultural assumptions, beliefs, ways of living and so on that are assumed to be 'normal', accepted by people as the universally valid way of living. Here intellectuals, the 'organizers' of ideology, culture, philosophy, religion, law and politics are central to the idea and operation of hegemony. Hegemony runs deeply through any social and political formation, for the structures of knowledge and values, the filters through which society acquires form and meaning, are precisely those that are constructed and maintained by the leading class or party. The intellectuals mediate between ruling and subaltern groups and classes, universalizing the values of the ruling class through this 'organization of culture'. Leadership, a continuing concern of Gramsci's along with the intellectual, thus takes place when a particular social class can transform its own ideas into a universally assumed understanding of the world. As Fontana writes:

[margin handwritten note: or-mediate mainly amongst themselves]

> Hegemony is thus conceived as the vehicle whereby the dominant social groups establish a system of 'permanent consent' that legitimates a prevailing social order by encompassing a complex network of mutually reinforcing and interwoven ideas affirmed and articulated by intellectuals (Fontana 1993: 140).

In his study of the relationship between Machiavelli and Gramsci, to which I am indebted here, Fontana traces the importance for understanding hegemony of the interaction between teacher and pupil (the Bible becomes *the* item that mediates such a relationship), as well as the relationship between moral and intellectual reform, brought about by the democratic philosopher. But what I want to draw from Gramsci is the way he carries on the long Marxist tradition of analyzing the existing (capitalist) forms of ruling and control so as to be able to find not only the contradictions that may be exploited but the means for overcoming it. I am therefore interested in Exod. 32 as a hegemonic document, full of its own contradictions.

[margin handwritten note: Intellectuals are? professional students trained in "right" forms of criticism.]

Yet the means of attaining consent through cultural organization is but one side of the notion of hegemony. Intellectual and moral leadership (*direzione*) must be combined with domination or coercion (*dominio*), especially over against antagonistic groups. By contrast, those with whom the leading group in is alliance and association work together by consent:

> The supremacy of a social group is manifested in two ways: as 'domination' and as 'intellectual and moral leadership'. A social group is dominant over those antagonistic groups it wants to 'liquidate' or to subdue even with armed force, and it is leading with respect to those groups that are associated or allied with it (Gramsci Quaderni del Carcare 3.19; quoted in Fontana 1993: 141).

These two elements of leadership by consent and coercion emerge in Machiavelli's image of the centaur:

(Centaur as political allegory)

> You should know, then, that there are two ways of contending: one by using laws, the other, force. The first is appropriate for men, the second for animals; but because the former is often ineffective, one must have recourse to the latter. Therefore, a ruler must know well how to imitate beasts as well as employing properly human means. This policy was taught to rulers allegorically by ancient writers: they tell us how Achilles and many other ancient rulers were entrusted to Chiron the centaur, to be raised carefully by him. Having a mentor who was half-beast and half-man signifies that a ruler needs to use both natures, and that one without the other is not effective (Machiavelli 1988: 61).

Gramsci comments on this passage:

> Another point to be decided and developed is that of the 'double perspective' in political action and state life. There are various levels in which the double perspective can be presented, from the most elementary to the most complex, but they can be reduced theoretically to two fundamental levels, corresponding to the double nature of the Machiavellian Centaur, savage and human, force and consent, authority and hegemony, violence and civilization, the individual stage and the universal stage ('Church' and 'State'), agitation and propaganda, tactics and strategy, etc. (Gramsci 1957: 161).

Here Gramsci has imperceptibly moved from hegemony to the question of the state: not so much a coercive instrument, as Marx and Lenin would have it, of the ruling classes that needs to wither away, it must be seen from the double perspective of coercion and consent (Althusser's RSA and ISAs) and all of the pairs that flow from this. And the ideal figure, the mix of force and consent? The 'armed prophet'. According to Machiavelli, 'all armed prophets succeed whereas unarmed ones fail' (1988: 21). Yet, in the end, as Christine Buci-Glucksmann argues (1982), the purpose of Gramsci's analysis of the contemporary state in terms of hegemony is to indicate how such a situation might be transformed into communism: hegemony is both a tool of analysis and of revolution.

We are back where we began, with Machiavelli's reflections on principalities, but above all with political myth, for such myth concerns itself with all of the various dimensions of the state. This will run through my reading of Exod. 32, for in this small slice of text we find not only a hegemonic document per se, albeit more on the side of persuasion and consent (although the Bible has been used as a justification for coercion more than once), but also a narrative of hegemony in Gramsci's sense. That is, in the story of the Golden Calf and comparable accounts of rebel-

RSA = Repressive State Apparatus
ISA = Ideological   "   "

lion, the narrative provides a fantasy and model of the hegemony in which it sought to take part. Gramsci sees Machiavelli's Prince as the harbinger of revolutionary politics, as the hegemonic innovator and reformer that now becomes the collective party. I will leave the decision as to Moses' revolutionary credentials in Exodus until later, although they have been asserted time and again, but it is the figure of innovator and reformer, the Centaur who blends persuasion and force that emerges from the text.

The 'Armed Prophet' of Exodus 32

What follows is a Machiavellian reading of Exod. 32 that passes into a fully Gramscian interpretation by its close. I begin with the paradoxical virtues of the Prince—cruelty and clemency, generosity and meanness, keeping one's word or not. This will allow me to slide into the pair of force and consent, that is, arms along with intellectual, moral and religious reform; in short, hegemony. It turns out that this is a story about the hegemonic force of the law, for the law cannot operate with the consent of the people; yet this consent can be achieved only by force of arms. And then I find myself concerned with the state, already implicit in the earlier discussion. But here, where Gramsci interprets Machiavelli's Prince as a mirror of the people, or rather that the Prince and the people cannot exist without the other—which then enables his move to arguing for the modern Prince as the political party that unites the people in order to move forward to the new society—we encounter a problem. For the interaction in Exod. 32 involves Moses, the people and a third player, God. The whole issue of Moses' *virtú*, or ability, and *fortuna* is relevant now, since not only does God comprise in large measure the function of fortune, but Moses must craft his leadership by managing God as well as the people. What are the implications for understanding the state and hegemony when Moses mediates between Yahweh and the people? All of this brings me back to political myth, only to ask the question, What should be? Is Exod. 32 the fragment of a much larger piece, utopian and revolutionary, or dystopian? I will ask the question of Gramsci as well.

It always surprises me, even in light of a certain propinquity of biblical texts and the methods with which I work, how closely text and method connect with each other. Is it that Moses is thoroughly Machiavellian, or that Machiavelli's new Prince is thoroughly Mosaic? Let me begin with the paradox of cruelty and clemency in Exod. 32. In contrast with Moses, Aaron is the figure of clemency and humaneness. With not a whisper of criticism or refusal, let alone anger, he responds to the people's complaint by suggesting they bring *him* gold from which he can then be generous. But Aaron's easy-going character, giving the people free reign, is in stark contrast to Moses' anger. But how does Moses' cruelty become the true means of mercy? Yahweh swings into action, calling for the annihilation of the people. Not merely a contrast to Yahweh's rampaging vengeance, which now becomes the inevitable consequence of Aaron's action, Moses actively intervenes with a limited brutality that curtails mass bloodshed. Thus, in the scene with the Levites (Exod. 32.25-29), Moses calls for loyalty first (v. 26) before demanding that the Levites kill brother, son, friend and neighbour. Not only does Moses secure the Levites' loyalty— for they now must stick with him in light of the murder of those closest to them—but the 3,000 dead produces a mere handful of corpses in contrast to what Yahweh had in mind. And Moses points out the implications should any of them remain unclear (v. 29). As far as this story is concerned, Moses comes through as the wisely cruel leader, in contrast to Aaron's initial clemency that threatens greater cruelty.

The other paradoxes play in a minor key. As for generosity and meanness, the fatally generous figure in Exod. 32 is Aaron, who, in response to pressure from the people, gathers all their gold in order to make the calf. The twist in this text is that Aaron is not strictly the generous one. Instead, he acquiesces to the people's request, asking them for gold. In fact, he insists on a tax so that he can be generous, a formula that will only lead to discontent as far as Machiavelli is concerned. Aaron's later excuse to Moses—'Do not let the anger of my Lord [*adonai*] burn hot; you know the people, that they are bent on evil. They said to me, "Make us gods, who shall go before us; as for this Moses, the man who brought us up out of the land of Egypt, we do not know what has become of him". So I said to them, "Whoever has gold, take it off"; so they gave it to me, and I threw it into the fire, and out came this calf!' (Exod. 32.22-24)—with its dissembling shuffling and shifting of responsibility so that it appears as though he could not but help be leader in light of 'events' (compare 32.1-6) suggests an alternative leadership. If we read in Machiavelli's vein, leadership is the issue: Aaron gives in, seeking to rule by consent, allowing the people to set the agenda, attempting to be generous at the people's expense. It would not be the last time he opposes Moses (see Num. 12, this time with Miriam). Moses, by contrast, has none of the popular generosity of Aaron, bringing instead the tablets of stone to which he expects obedience. As far as he is concerned, the false generosity of Aaron can only lead to destruction. His immediate response is to throw down the tablets, burn and pulverize the calf and force the people to drink the heady brew of idolatrous gold dust and water (Exod. 32.19-20).

Finally, on the question of whether a ruler should be loved or feared, Moses is a classic Machiavellian Prince, preferring that the people fear rather than love him. The various punishments meted out to the people, from the slight rap of enforced imbibing of liquids to the selected slaying of about 3,000 people, as well as the command to the Levites to kill brother, sons and friends, leads towards fear rather than love. Of course, for Machiavelli, only the ruler whom the people fear can be loved, for fear is a far better basis for stable rule.

Above all, Moses succeeds in avoiding both hatred and contempt. Like Machiavelli's model Prince, he is neither rapacious of the people's goods, nor does he take their women and form a harem. In fact, Moses studiously avoids taking Israelite women, making first a Midianite, Zipporah, his woman/wife (Exod. 2.21) and then a Cushite (Num. 12.1). If anyone is rapacious, it is Aaron: he requires gold from the people in order to provide his own form of largesse. He is, as it were, already at the stage of taxing the people in order to be generous, a paradox that Machiavelli argued could only lead to hatred by the people.

Moses, it would seem, exhibits many of the signs of a Machiavellian Prince: his cruelty functions not only to secure his leadership, but also to avoid the greater cruelty of mass annihilation (a paradoxical mercy); he neither taxes the people nor takes their women; his meanness comes out in contrast to Aaron's taxing generosity. The image of Moses that emerges from the text is of a wise, capable and strong ruler, an example that Machiavelli could hardly avoid as a primary model.

Yet a Machiavellian reading will take us only so far (how is Moses an ideal model?). Gramsci's Marxist interpretation of Machiavelli makes his work far more interesting and complex, particularly on the whole question of hegemony and revolutionary leadership. Let me begin with the question of arms: for both Gramsci and Machiavelli the organization and nature of armed force was an important aspect of the Prince's work, whether that involved the acquisition and maintenance of a new principality, or the revolution required for communism to be victorious. Moses fits the bill: he relies neither on mercenaries nor on auxiliaries, drawing his troops from within the people, as he does throughout Exodus–Deuteronomy, drawing from the most loyal of groups, the Levites. Or rather, he ensures their loyalty by ordering them to kill those to whom they may have felt an alternative loyalty. Now Moses has a loyal militia who cannot but help stay with him, given the enmity and fear they have instilled among their families and friends.

However, Exod. 32 is not merely a narrative of force of arms: there is no armed insurrection that Moses must quell, for the people are too busy partying, full of dancing and revelry. Even Moses' fear of 'war in the camp' (Exod. 32.17) turns out to be unfounded, as Joshua points out (v. 18). Why then are the arms necessary? Apart from avoiding Yahweh's rampaging fury, the arms are necessary in order to ensure consent. The narrative of Exod. 32 begins with Moses' absence: he is on the mountain, apparently on his way down with the tablets of law in his hands. The stern, puritanical and killjoy side of Moses shows through, for he does not expect the pure enjoyment of worship that the golden calf seems to provide. But the act of destroying the tablets effectively indicates not only the well-known motif of Moses' anger but also the absence of the law among the Israelites. Moses brings down the law to find the Israelites already disobeying a law they have not yet received. Exod. 32 is then a story about the law. Not an earth-shattering conclusion, except that if we follow Gramsci then it is also a narrative about consent to the law. The law cannot operate, cannot come into being without consent, without the agreement and obedience of the people, and yet such consent, the narrative indicates, is impossible without the force of arms. In this intertwining of arms and consent we have Gramsci's notion of hegemony. To write that it is a narrative of the law is to write that it is a narrative concerning hegemony. Yet even this conclusion is not enough, since it is not merely a story of hegemony, but one that enacts with the narrative itself—and here I take Exod. 32 as a microcosm of the Pentateuch as a whole—the hegemony of the text over those who read it and hear it. The text itself is torah, law, and Moses carries with him the text that is to be read. Tauto-logically, a key figure within the story gives, through such texts as Exod. 32, the hegemonic authority of the text. There is then a certain logic— hegemonic—to the notion that Moses is the 'author' of the Torah, the Pentateuch.

I have withheld another feature of hegemony until now, namely, intellectual and moral reform. A niggling suspicion is that my discussion of Exodus 32 describes very well the workings of any repressive regime, any state's manufacturing of consent, no matter how reactionary or progressive. Gramsci stresses Machiavelli's concern with moral, religious and intellectual reform, reading Machiavelli as a forward-looking writer, one who points to what ought to be rather than what is. For Gramsci the great model of such reform is the Protestant Reformation, yet Luther and Calvin modelled themselves not only merely on Jesus Christ and the early Church, but also on such figures as Moses.

Thus, Exod. 32 is about law and hegemony, yet hegemony understood as a force of change rather than describing the status quo. As far as the story is concerned there is a sharp opposition between what seem to be the regressive activities of Aaron and the people—gold contributions, golden calf, burnt offerings and sacrifices, revelry, in short a falling back to old practices—and the reforming direction of the newly minted law that Moses brings with him. Thus, in the descriptions of the calf we find words of extravagance, pleasure and celebration: gold rings, images, festivals, sacrifices of well-being (שׁלמים), eating and drinking, revelling. When we turn to Moses and Yahweh there is none of this, for the language reverts to austerity, control, obedience and punishment: command, anger, disaster, tablets of the testimony, engraving on stone, punishment and death. And the acts of the people become perverse (שׁחת), sinful and disobedient. Yet rather than curtailing the pleasure of the Israelites, a Gramscian reading notes that the text is cast in terms of reform, a change in intellectual, moral and religious sensibilities, through force of arms if necessary.

Rather than lamenting the closure of a polytheistic impulse (is polytheism indeed any better?), or pursuing the possibilities of an alternative mainstream religious practice in relation to the other calf stories of 1 Kgs 12 and 2 Chron. 10, I am interested in the internal ideological machinery of the text. And what emerges is that Exod. 32 concerns more than the virtues of Moses as a leader, or indeed more than the mechanisms of hegemony. The issue that runs through it, backwards and forwards, is that of the 'state', which has been a hidden element in my discussion so far. In the end, the moral, religious and intellectual reform that Moses brings about through the law, that is, through consent and force, can only be understood in terms of the 'state', the distinct political entity of the *'am* with which Exodus as a whole is overloaded. Indeed, following on from my discussion of terms for people in the first chapter on Althusser and Genesis, there is a marked shift in Exodus from the mixed usage of *goi* and *'am* in Genesis, along with the smaller group of terms in Gen. 25, to a predominant usage of *'am*. For in Exodus the promise of a people is finally realized, although in the absence of the fulfilment of promise of the land (is the fulfilment of the former predicated on the absence of the latter?), and this realized promise is marked by the use of *'am*, which I will

translate as 'state' over against the 'people' of Genesis. If I restrict myself
to Exod. 32, then *'am* appears 14 times (vv. 1, 3, 7, 9, 11, 12, 14, 22, 25,
28, 31, 34, 35) even to the point of Yahweh and Moses alternatively
designating them as 'your state' when they act perversely (see Exod. 32.7,
11-12). To put it in a rather utilitarian fashion, Exodus 32 is one text that
explores some of the features that are required for a 'state'. But, at one
level at least, I have described the function of political myth.

I am not yet done with Machiavelli or Gramsci. One of the latter's
astute observations is that the new Prince is a popular leader, one who
unites a dispersed and disaggregated population to become a people as
such. The people, in other words, cannot gather together without the
Prince; he is a singular expression of the popular and collective will. But
the converse also applies, for the Prince himself would not be possible
without the people; the one requires the other. For Gramsci this is
Machiavelli's great discovery, and it enables him to develop his own
argument concerning the political party. But is this not the case with
Moses also? Only in Exodus does the term *'am* become the privileged
designator for Israel, at the same narrative moment that both the collective
entity of Israel emerges and Moses is born (the 'beginning' of the book
itself). *And* the people escape from Egypt only at the instigation of Moses,
who is himself ambiguously Egyptian.

I want to suggest that such a narrative mirror also operates between
Moses and the people in Exod. 32? Let me pick this up via a circuitous
route: a major player absent from both Machiavelli's or Gramsci's deliberations (except in the argument that ruler should use religion in a way that
enhances his rule and as part of a revolutionary hegemony), but one that
appears as a major character in Exod. 32, is God, more specifically
Yahweh.

On a general level, a crucial locus of hegemonic activity is with the
figure of Yahweh and how one perceives the deity operating in the text.
Science fiction has shown us that the crucial value of characterizing
Yahweh in the Hebrew Bible elides the role of the writer. For the text has
succeeded in its hegemonic strategy of the depiction of Yahweh, or for
that matter Jesus and God in the New Testament, in whatever form, when
he is taken as in some way a representation of the deity or person in
question. When I taught in a theological college, although this problem is
not restricted to seminaries, the unacknowledged step was to consider
representations of God or Jesus as in some way theological statements
about the nature of God as such. Yet in the same way that the worlds

and universes constructed by science fiction authors, with their own, immutable 'laws of nature' are produced by those writers themselves, so also with Yahweh or God in the Bible. In other words, there is always one thing more powerful than God in these texts and that is the author or authors who construct this character in the first place. The point, of course, is that this 'God', this character within the text, is the most strongly contested site of hegemony. For, if the authors can efface their role in that narrative or poetic construction, then their own particular ideological positions will be taken as those of God, an extraordinary elision that adds immense weight to those positions, that is, enables a particular hegemony to roll into place. So, with regard to my textual example above, when we remind ourselves that Yahweh's role in the text is one of hegemony, then the text takes on a different hue, for the hegemony sought becomes contested within the representations of Yahweh.

At the specific level of this text, rather than a twofold play in a mirror between Moses and the state, Yahweh is a crucial third figure. The narrative moves between the activities of the people (Exod. 32.1-6), the dialogues between Yahweh and Moses (20.7-14, 31-34), between Moses and the Israelites (20.15-20) and between Moses and Aaron (20.21-24). Never do the Israelites engage directly with Yahweh; only Moses is the common denominator. Although one might suspect that Yahweh is the Prince in Exodus 32, the one whose leadership (a theocracy) is at stake, he is in fact the bulk for this story of what Machiavelli calls *fortuna*. The vagaries of fortune are those factors beyond the control of the Prince, which he must nevertheless manage to the best of his ability and to which he must adapt if his leadership is to remain intact. Hardly the most consistent of operators, Yahweh perpetually throws crises at Moses. In Exod. 32 these crises are the twice-uttered threats of the annihilation of the people (vv. 10, 43). Moses responds by attempting both to manage Yahweh—he calls on Yahweh to 'turn from your fierce anger' (32.12) or forgive their sin (32.32) and suggests that Yahweh take Moses' life (32.32)—and adapting to the situation—the measured cruelty of the Levites in order to stave off Yahweh's wrath. Through his various responses to fortune—Yahweh—the narrative highlights Moses' *virtú*.

Gramsci also argues that the Prince and people cannot exist without each other. In Exod. 32 Yahweh brings about both and controls the narrative. There is something more in Moses' challenge to Yahweh to take his life instead of the people's, to blot his name out of the book (Exod. 32.32). Too quickly has the whiff of the atonement sacrifice wafted over this text—Moses offers to take on the sin of the people—but the point lies elsewhere: Moses himself would disappear without the people. Yahweh's promise is to make another 'state' from Moses (Exod. 32.10), but this will not do, for Moses *must* ensure that the people survive if he is to survive. This means that Moses' request in Exod. 32.32 is not an either/or option; it is two sides of the same coin. The destruction of the people or of Moses would result in the pair disappearing from the narrative. That is why Moses throws down the challenge to Yahweh: if you destroy them, you destroy me, so take me first.

There is a further twist in Exodus, picking up Gramsci's point that Machiavelli himself becomes the voice and personification of the people, especially at the close of *The Prince*. Machiavelli merges with his Prince and becomes the united people about which he writes. Moses exhibits this even more seamlessly than Machiavelli's text, for he is both a character within and 'writer' of this narrative, the one through whose hand both he and the '*am* of israel come to be.

All of this means that the 'ultimately determining instance'—to gloss a Marxist phrase—of Exod. 32 is the 'state' of Israel. In its own way Gramsci's work brings the discussion back to this point. But it is a new state, for which a new hegemony is required, namely, that of the law in the hands of Moses. In this respect, Gramsci does in fact appear to be correct: hegemony is a forward-looking concept, one that seeks out what ought to or should be. Exod. 32 exhibits all the workings of both Machiavelli's and Gramsci's desire for change, the former into the nation-state of capitalism, the latter into the new state, led by the party, of whatever communism might be. For me, the curious fit between Gramsci and Exod. 32 appears in the details: the paradoxical virtues of Moses, the necessity for consent and force in hegemony, the necessary binding together of Moses and the people, and the interplay of fortune and virtue. But this is why Gramsci's description of Machiavelli's *The Prince* also applies to Exod. 32 and the texts that surround it: they are political myths. And that myth functions by playing out the ideological possibilities and necessary conditions for a new state. The initial function of such a myth is to create a fantasy image of the new 'state', one that has not existed up until then. However, once that state is realized, the myth becomes both a legitimation and critique of the actually existing form of that state.

I will explore these questions further in a new project—'Political Myth and the Bible'—but I close with a question Gramsci leaves hanging. Is such a state utopian or not? Gramsci's daring move was to claim Machiavelli as a utopian man of action, that *The Prince* is a political manifesto of the calibre of Marx's and Engels's famous tract. And Gramsci did so in order to work through a programme for the realization of communism.

As far as Exodus is concerned, particularly the story of the escape from Egypt, there has been as much debate as to its revolutionary credentials as there has been over Machiavelli's book. While liberation and political theologies have used Exodus as paradigm of revolution, a biblical source and justification for revolutionary action in the present, the Exodus model has also come under significant criticism, beginning with Edward Said's response (1988) to Michael Walzer's *Exodus and Revolution* (1984). In his criticism of Walzer's effort to appropriate the Exodus narrative as a non-Marxist alternative for social change—what Walzer calls an 'Exodus politics'—and the use of the narrative to justify Israeli oppression of Palestinians, Said argues for a close connection between the Exodus from Egypt and the invasion of Canaan, all under the command of a God who orders the destruction of the local inhabitants. Following Said, others have carried his arguments further, suggesting that the Exodus functions as an ideological justification for appropriation of Canaan in the same way that the Holocaust of the Second World War is used to justify the establishment of the state of Israel (Shohat 1992: 137-40); or that the myths of Eden and Exodus have been combined in some situations, such as Australia, to create an ambivalent image, one that sees the new land as that to which Adam and Eve were banished from the garden and the other that takes the land as one of promise and hope (Curthoys 1998: 177); or that the Exodus narrative must lead to dispossession of another people since it cannot be separated from monotheism, with its demand for one land for one people under one God (Docker 2001).

A more utopian reading of Exodus relies on the disjunction between the escape from Egypt and the invasion of Canaan. Focusing on the former, and coming from a very different political climate than that of the Middle East, liberation and political theologians have taken a long tradition in which Moses is the liberator (for instance, with African American slaves) and connected it explicitly with Marxism (see Pixley 1987; van Iersel and Weiler 1987; Croatto 1981; Fierro 1983). In this case Exodus becomes a lasting paradigm, no matter how mythical, of a revolutionary and utopian drive that is profoundly biblical in origin.

Whereas I feel that there is no necessary connection between the narratives of Exodus and conquest (agreeing with the liberation and political theologians), that does not render Moses and the Exodus any more appealing (here I agree with Said *et al.*, but for different reasons). However, I want to shift the terminology slightly to the question of utopia, although, following Jameson, I take it as a code word for socialism. In suggesting that Machiavelli is a utopian thinker, it seems to me that Gramsci takes a similar tack, for it is the revolutionary possibilities of Machiavelli's work that Gramsci identifies and takes up for his reflections on the role of the communist party. And in one respect I agree: the model of the merciless revolutionary who does what it takes to get the job done is the most appealing part of the images of both Machiavelli's new Prince and of Moses. Further, if I take the line that the very effort to imagine a different world, no matter how dystopian the content of that imagination might be, is in itself utopian, then Exodus, particularly ch. 32, does count as a utopian text. However, it seems to me that Gramsci's problem, brought into sharp relief by the narrative of Exodus and its subsequent appropriation, is that he relies on a past model. Machiavelli's genius was to see through the contradictory trends of his own time and forge an ideological position that became constitutive of the nation-state under capitalism. All the same, it is a model of revolution based on the bourgeois revolution. In a similar way, Moses and Exodus have been understood as a narrative of past events and thereby the source of a particular model (reinforced by its biblical authority) of social change and state formation to which we are still tied, for better or worse. Apart from the fact that imagining change can use only the various bits and pieces of language, thought and history available at the time, the problem is one of utopia itself: in the same way that (pace Adorno) it is not possible to construct a blueprint for a society we do not know, even down to its language, so also the change itself can only be hinted at rather than prescribed. For if the model of change is tied too closely to existing models, then the patterns of social and political interaction, class and gender relations, economics and ideology have a habit of replicating themselves in the new society. Thus, the figure of Moses as the brutal reformer or revolutionary, the representation of Yahweh as the validation of the new state, the systematic exclusions that the notion of the *'am* Israel implies, the usages to which Exodus has been put—in other words, the apparatus of the state whose workings appear in detail in the political myth of Exod. 32—indicate a few hurdles too many for such models of change and the state to be utopian.

Chapter 3

TERRY EAGLETON: THE CLASS STRUGGLES OF RUTH

What is most noticeable about Terry Eagleton is not only the immense readability of his prolific writing, but the catholicity of his interests. He writes both complex critical texts and readable introductions, essays and monographs, plays and novels, poetry and speeches, film scripts and musicals, even travel books in his newly recovered home of Ireland, as well as a whole range of items that have never made it into print, at least with his name attached to them. But Eagleton is also a Marxist, occupying, at least at the time of writing, the chair of Cultural Theory at Manchester.

Coming from dirt poor Catholicism, with a solid dose of Irish genealogy, in the Lancashire Mill Town of Bacup, Eagleton arrived at Cambridge to work with Raymond Williams and quickly became his most famous student. From early on he wrote for the sake of writing, or rather, to develop a craft on which he still works. A fellowship at Cambridge gave way to Oxford, where, after being fellow of Jesus College, he took on the Warton chair before moving to Manchester. Such an extraordinarily conventional career, from Cambridge to Oxford in the old imperial centre, has led finally to rediscovery of an Irish heritage in the moment of postcolonialism, an echo perhaps of an earlier, brief moment in which the priesthood seemed a good career move, as well as his central role in the Catholic left that resulted in two books on radical Catholic theology and the journal *Slant*.

Yet it is as a Marxist that Eagleton has made his name. His Marxism insists on the central questions of class, ideology and ideology critique and, above all, a revolutionary politics. So much so that, in the midst, or perhaps as part of, his prolific writing, he has engaged and continues to engage in various forms of political activism, ranging from protests in the Catholic Left, through university politics to political interventions in the Irish rebublican struggle, especially through his plays—*St Oscar, The White, the Gold and the 'Gangrene', Disappearances* and *God's Locusts*

(Eagleton 1997)—with the Field Day Theatre Company in Derry and the Doublejoint Theatre in Belfast.

Class and Gender

My usage of Eagleton is quite specific, a focus on a particular issue within the catholicity of his work: the intersections between class, gender and ethnicity. Class, and the closely related class conflict, are staples of any Marxist criticism worthy of the name, although Eagleton has made it a central feature of much of his literary criticism and creative writing. As if the question of class were not interesting enough, he has been involved in debates in feminism, especially materialist and psychoanalytic feminisms that have insisted on the category of gender, or preferably sexual differ-ence, in Marxism itself. In light of these debates, and especially Eagleton's attempts to deal with both issues—class and gender, or class conflict and sexual warfare—in his work, the book of Ruth becomes an extremely interesting text. As with the previous chapters, I will also offer some criticisms of Eagleton's own work.

The bulk of the debates within Marxist or materialist feminism, and between Marxism and feminism (where such a division is possible) concerns the so-called irreducibles of class and sexual difference. Conventional Marxists, if squeezed sufficiently, will not renounce class, however much else may have been relinquished on the way. Post-Marxists may be as ready to give up the faith as any quisling, but Eagleton is hardly one of those. For feminism the unrelinquishable and untranscendable horizon is sexual difference, or as some prefer, gender. If sexual difference goes, then so does feminism.

I do not find either option—the assertion of one or the other as the primary category, as though we need a philosophical first principle or prime mover—any use whatsoever. One response to this impasse between class and sexual difference is to include the other hitherto forgotten or neglected category within one's critical and political inventory, assuming that such an inclusion is necessary for two overtly political forms of literary or cultural criticism. But even the inclusionary move, in some form of common front, doesn't get us very far. So a substantial part of my discussion will watch for the way Eagleton himself deals with this question.

But how is all this relevant to Ruth? I will certainly not be declared the most perceptive of biblical scholars by writing that these few chapters in the Hebrew Bible concern sexual difference, nor even that ethnicity (however qualified such a term might be) is central to the narrative. But class? If we remember that division of labour is both the pre-condition and necessary machinery of class, then Ruth, it will turn out, is very much concerned with class as well.

However, before considering Ruth in more detail, a few observations from Eagleton on class. He has insisted time and again that Marxists at least keep the question of class in the foreground, particularly in light of attempts to shift the focus to various political micro-groups that operate in terms of identity politics—gender, race, sexuality, indigeneity, religion, ecology and so on. I am thinking here of the reconsiderations set in motion by the influential *Hegemony and Socialist Strategy* of Ernesto Laclau and Chantal Mouffe (1985). For Laclau and Mouffe, the poststructuralist critique of master narratives and essentialism must lead to a re-evaluation of older forms of political theory and action from the left. This 'micro-politics', the development of a host of small political pressure groups, is a sign of a new political scene in which various groups move into alliances based on their drive for radical equality. Class is therefore suspect since it operates with essentialist assumptions, but so are the older identity groups who now need to reconstitute themselves in an anti-essentialist fashion. In many ways Laclau's and Mouffe's work foreshadowed the newer ways in which the massive protests came together at the World Trade Organization meeting in Seattle (November 1999), or at the World Economic Forum in Melbourne (September 2000). While Eagleton seeks not to dismiss such political groupings, he insists that class, specifically the Marxist notion of class, cannot be excluded so easily, that it has not in some way been superseded, but that it remains a crucial and viable category of thought and politics. In fact, it is dangerous to so, for an absence of the awareness of class conceals its operation all the more effectively.

This emphasis on class operates at a number of levels for Eagleton. First, the fundamental division between the bourgeoisie and the working class is part of the structure of capitalism. This particular division of labour is crucial for the operation of capitalism, based as it is on the rational organization of the means of maximizing profit. A more specific description is between those who work and those who do not work but live off what is known as the surplus labour of the workers. The system can operate only if workers are not paid the full value of their work: there is something left over, a certain amount of labour power (which the worker sells to the employer), that is then appropriated by the employers so that they themselves can live. Rather than a mythical category—as it is so often dismissed by liberal economists—surplus labour has a material existence (surplus value) in the commodities the worker makes: when sold the workers receive only a portion of the money, much of it goes to the employers, wholesalers and retailers. Hence the notion of 'surplus value', in a myriad complex of overlays, on which capitalism relies. But such a division of labour also relies on a number of other divisions, many of which are older than capitalism: between manual and intellectual labour (the first 'real' division for Marx and Engels), between country and city, or rural and factory work, and between male and female. Although listed last, the division of labour according to gender is the crucial division for my discussion, particularly because Marx and Engels identify it as the primary division that is not yet a 'real' one.

Eagleton's insistence on class, then, is inseparable from the notions of division of labour and surplus labour/value. But this has implications for the kind of politics in which one engages: rather than activism within the various pressure groups seeking to influence the ruling forces of capital, politics must be class based. That is, political work against capitalism must take place within the context of the working class, creatively mobilizing the deep, inchoate rage of this class against systematic exploitation. Specifically, such political effort must keep awake the sense that the various modifications of the working class—minimal increases in standard of living, incomes, commodity fetishism and so on—are merely there to counter the awareness of deeper patterns of exploitation, seen baldly in the maintenance of an army of unemployed people ready to take jobs at lower rates, in the pressure to increase working hours or give up hard-won benefits.

Eagleton's insistence on class may also be seen as the result of his living and working in the same society that was the basis for Marx's analysis in *Capital,* albeit some 150 years later. For here class is an obvious feature of social relations, marked out sharply in terms of language, culture, politics, and above all in working conditions. That is not to say that class does not exist elsewhere; yet in England, and in other places in Europe with a longer history of the shift from feudalism to capitalism, one can make a class identification the moment someone opens his or her mouth, if not before. So Eagleton in his funeral oration for Raymond Williams:

> I found myself marooned within a student body where everyone seemed to be well over six foot and brayed rather than spoke ... Williams looked and spoke more like a countryman than a don, and had a warmth and simplicity

of manner which contrasted sharply with the suave, offhand style of the upper middle-class establishment (Eagleton 1989: 1)

It is no surprise then that Eagleton's political commitment to the super-session of capitalism is based on class politics, a revolutionary politics if necessary, whose viability remains, he observes, when it is widely asserted that such a process was no longer possible. For Eagleton the explosion of the largely non-violent revolutions in Eastern Europe in the late 1980s and 1990s are evidence that revolutions are indeed possible and happen with alarming regularity, at least for capitalism and its liberal apologists. But it is also no surprise that class and class conflict are the central categories of his literary method. An Eagletonian reading—except that such a term suggests a literary movement—remains incomplete if the dynamics of class do not appear in a particular interpretation. Thus, in my major exam-ple 'Heathcliff and the Great Hunger' (Eagleton 1995: 1-26), the final issue becomes the way class is both crucial to the organization of the text *and* how it is concealed through various strategies.

Eagleton engages in a large-scale allegorical reading of *Wuthering Heights* in terms of the Great Famine in Ireland. At times the suspicion creeps in that the novel is but an excuse for vast stretches on the historiography of the famine, or of the tension between Nature and Culture (Ireland versus England) and so on. But what soon becomes apparent is that Eagleton is concerned with the question of ethnicity, along with economics and class, as part of the mix of British colonialist capitalism. For Heathcliff becomes an allegorical personification of the Irish, especi-ally working Irish peasantry, even though it is unclear whether he is Irish in the novel, or indeed whether the timing of the writing of the novel with the Famine will pass close historical scrutiny (see 1995: 3). The plot itself runs through the tensions, class alliances and final triumphs and losses of the various classes and class fractions of the remnants of feudalism and a rampaging capitalism.

Yet the class dynamics are peculiarly English: the Lintons at Thrush-cross Grange are the largest landowners in the district, the landed gentry, whereas the Earnshaws at the Heights are not squires—employing others to work their land—but yeomen, or at least a remnant of the yeomen, who prefer to dirty their own hands in their own soil. Central to the dynamics of class are the very materialist categories of law, property, kinship and inheritance that govern plot and narrative. Before we worry too much about the staple class categories, Lockwood turns out to be the middle-class figure, and Heathcliff represents all that comes with the working class, especially the Irish. It is not for nothing that he is taken in at the Heights, where Nature dominates, for he is earthy, filthy, starving and dark. But the allegory runs deeper: 'Heathcliff starts out as an image of the famished Irish immigrant, becomes a landless labourer set to work in the Heights, and ends up as a symbol of the constitutional nationalism of the Irish parliamentary party' (Eagleton 1995: 19). Unable to break the class boundaries that keep Catherine and he from ever connecting, Heathcliff sets off to appropriate the outer bearing and weapons of the ruling class (at heart he remains a boor, although there is nothing intrinsically wrong with that) in order to take over the Heights and the Grange, only to die before he can enjoy it all. He is, in the end, both oppressed and oppressor rolled into one, except that this is not such an uncommon situation within capitalism, the current oppressor using a former oppression to justify his or her own species of brutality.

Not merely transformed rural working class, Heathcliff is for Eagleton also the threat of the middle classes on the landed gentry, as well as the embodiment of the ruling class fear of revolution: he must be beaten off, the landed gentry or squirearchy, the 'oldest landed capitalist class in Europe' (Eagleton 1995: 19), must defeat the yeomanry, so that Catherine may take up her rightful place as heiress of the Grange. In all its complexity, Eagleton settles for Heathcliff as the allegory of the rural (i.e. Irish) revolution, in both its right and left forms, in its failure and near miss at triumph, archaic and modern:

> From the gentry's standpoint, the novel recounts a tale of catastrophe just averted; from a radical viewpoint it records the loss of revolutionary hopes, now projected into a mythologized past but, like the ghosts of Catherine and Heathcliff, still capable of infiltrating and disturbing the present (Eagleton 1995: 21).

Yet Eagleton remains with the conventional items of character, plot and narrative to argue for a class reading and attempted 'resolution' of class conflict, interspersed with reflections on the Famine as in some way the context for the novel. The class reading is distinctly materialist and it traces the complexity of class, especially in terms of colonialism and ethnicity, but only with regard to Heathcliff: the other characters, as well as plot, remain as ciphers. However, I will want to take up Eagleton's insistence on class and ethnicity for my reading of Ruth, arguing that it is not merely one concerning gender.

With all that Eagleton's argument has going for it in terms of class and ethnicity, there is a crucial absence that Eagleton himself marks, describing the relationship between Heathcliff and Catherine as 'genderless'. A strange comment, even if he is speaking descriptively, from one who has insisted on the importance of feminist criticism. And this after the long initial consideration of the opposition between Nature and Culture in terms of England's colonial domination of Ireland. In contrast to England, the economic appears without the aesthetic in depictions of Ireland. Thus, Nature appears in the novel as both the English domain on the Heights, a vast region of land acquired through the enclosures by the first capitalist class, the landed gentry and Heathcliff himself. (Culture is then the transformed Nature of the Grange.) But, in contrast to the English Nature of the Heights, Heathcliff is hardly aestheticized in the novel, bearing all the uncouth and filthy wildness of Irish Nature that can only be aestheticized through his connection with the Nature of the Heights. Yet is not Nature a conventional code for woman, in both aspects? If—and here I move beyond Eagleton—the Heights provide the more aestheticized side of Nature, in all its untouched beauty, does not Heathcliff emerge as the wild and arid other side of woman in this text? In the same way, I would suggest, as the Irish were characterized as effeminate, dissolute and yet untameable. We could then read the impossible relationship between Catherine and Heathcliff as the failed effort to mediate this contradiction within Nature/Woman.

But what I want to do is turn to another study by Eagleton to see what he does when sexual difference is at the centre of discussion. *The Rape of Clarissa* (Eagleton 1982), a brief monograph or long essay on Samual Richardson's *Clarissa*, as well as *Pamela* and *Sir Charles Grandison*, is an innovative as Eagleton's interpretation of *Wuthering Heights*. Eagleton's main thesis is that Richardson's three novels were central to the emergence of a dominant bourgeois ideology. In the long transition from feudalism to capitalism the bourgeoisie—regarded at the time as crass and uncultured—enacted an ideological shift away from the overt power and violence of public male relations. Richardson was instrumental in this shift through leading what Eagleton calls the feminization of male relations. If *Pamela* is the first experiment, *Clarissa* foregounds the moral and ideological bankruptcy of the older aristocracy, embodied in the libertine violence of Lovelace. Clarissa herself, at least as far as Richardson was concerned, exhibited all the desirable feminine virtues—tenderness, purity, kindness, piety and so on. Her rape and murder by Lovelace is the last gasp of an old order, for in *Sir Charles Grandison* the full appropriation of feminine qualities by its protagonist, Grandison, takes place.

Eagleton is also interested in how Richardson's activity of writing itself intermeshes with his three texts, *Clarissa, Pamela* and *Sir Charles Grandison*, among the most influential cultural and ideological texts in nineteenth-century England. This practice operates with a profound contradiction that appears in its own way with Ruth as well. In a process comparable to the paradoxical way in which the 'new' values of love, choice of partner (by a woman) and companionship both enabled women to pick out their own husbands *and* rendered them completely dependent and bound to such a man within the emerging nuclear family, so also Richardson's practice of circulating drafts of his novels among a circle of educated women, for extended comment and revision, served to fetishize women as 'technicians of the heart' (Eagleton 1982: 13) through granting them a more authoritative and public voice. Undercutting the older forms of patriarchy, in which marriage was arranged and men assumed they knew what women wanted, was a newer form that was simultaneously better and worse. Richardson writes at the time when the transition from an open and vigorous patriarchy to its subtler bourgeois forms is under way. He exploited 'his literary powers to tighten his hold over women' (1982: 13), fashioning an alternative to the patriarchal family. In short, the contradictions of Richardson's literary practice are those of the newly dominant bourgeoisie: a new father–daughter relationship that challenges older forms of sexual domination through comradeship; the canonization of women as 'specialists in sentiment' (1982: 13) at the moment of a substantial feminization of the mores of male bourgeois public relations. Not merely a reflector of social and cultural change, Richardson's small but highly influential press on Fleet Street, along with his novels, were major agents in that change. Eagleton wants, at least for the moment, to keep the contradictions open, as he does with his reading of *Wuthering Heights*, in order to identify the regressive and emancipatory potential of the work in question. But the suspension of ethical assessment cannot hold off forever:

> The 'exaltation' of women, while undoubtedly a partial advance in itself, also serves to shore up the very system which oppresses them. For the eighteenth-century woman, as indeed for women of any epoch, the pedestal is never very far from the pit (Eagleton 1982: 15).

As far as Ruth is concerned, my suspicion is that the foregrounding of women has a very similar agenda.

Unlike the interpretation of *Wuthering Heights*, Eagleton gives considerable space in *The Rape of Clarissa* to a feminist reading. I will consider the details in a moment, but what is noticeable in his interpretation is that he moves from a deconstructionist concern with writing, *écriture*, focused on the letters sent between Lovelace and Clarissa, through a feminist reading that is also heavily psychoanalytical, to a Marxist interpretation concerned with class and ideology. In these methodological shifts he unwittingly replicates the association of women with the personal and private and men with the public and political. Although he would not want to argue for the supersession of one by the other, the superiority of a Marxist to a feminist reading, that is in the end the effect. For all his concern with sexual difference—and he cites Luce Irigaray at certain points—class is the ultimately determining instance.

Although the integration of feminist and Marxist questions is impressive, it is still ultimately a Marxist narrative that incorporates feminism. Thus, Eagleton makes the connection between deconstruction and psychoanalytic feminism by means of writing: Clarissa's is masculine, fully in control of her meaning, whereas Lovelace's is feminine, uncontrolled, exuberant and diffuse. As soon as he has established the point, however, the differences fade away. Here Freud comes to Eagleton's aid, so that he may interpret the letters and Clarissa's body via the categories of narcissism, eroticism, the letter as body, faeces, gift and exchange, in short as fetish—the detachable items of the human body that are both personal possessions and public objects. Citing Irigaray—incorrectly it seems[1]—he picks up the suggestion that the prime object of exchange is not faecal, like money, but women. Thus the letter signifies not merely female sexuality but Clarissa herself as the exchange object that is crucial for male dominance. If Clarissa, especially her body, is the major item of exchange in the novel, then it functions for Eagleton as the transcendental signifier, the phallus, detachable and exchangeable. Yet Eagleton's reading of Clarissa as phallus misreads Irigaray, for woman is not the phallus, but that which ensures the abstract phallus its place as transcendental signifier. Phallic woman, fetish, Lacan's Law and Name-of-the-Father—all of these variously describe Clarissa, even though her body resists representation. This is why Lovelace rapes her, the act itself upon which Richardson's text revolves and which cannot be represented—Lacan's Real and lack, an empty space that is the source of meaning.

---

1.   He cites 'Des marchandises entre elles' ('Commodities among Themselves'), which first appeared in French in 1975 (see Irigaray 1985: 192-97). However, this essay develops the points of her key essay on Marx, 'Women on the Market' (1985: 170-91), which appeared in French in 1970 as 'Le marché des femmes'.

As intriguing as the argument is, it falls short of a full integration of feminist and psychoanalytic approaches. Perhaps Eagleton's well-known refusal of dialectics is at fault here, as also his somewhat superficial discussion of feminism and psychoanalysis—Clarissa cannot fill so many of the Freudian and Lacanian categories, such as fetish, phallus, faeces, Name-of-the-Father, Real, lack and so on. The surest signal is, however, the way Marxism comes in to provide the most comprehensive argument: Clarissa's death, in all its meticulous detail, unwittingly offers a critique and refusal of bourgeois ideology that 'is made to stand shamefaced and threadbare in the light of its own doctrines' (Eagleton 1982: 77). And this in spite of the best intentions of Richardson to provide a model for such an ideology. I suspect that many biblical critics fall into the same trap with Ruth, seeing it as women's story that runs against the grain of the Hebrew Bible without noticing the systematic effacement of women throughout the text.

Richardson is hardly a willful agent in this critique of bourgeois ideology: his detailed defence of puritanism, itself an indispensable element of that ideology, over against the feudal-cavalier behaviour of Lovelace shows up, through its intensity, the contradictions of the very position Richardson espouses: 'his pen exceeds his expectations, conjuring a levelling sub-text from beneath the carefully policed script of his novel' (Eagleton 1982: 77-8). Yet I want to give Eagleton his due, for it seems to me that a faithfulness to Marxism as the most comprehensive and insightful of critical and political approaches is the correct position to take. Eagleton does argue that sexual difference is not the displacement of class conflict, but in the end he assumes that sexual difference is the code in which such conflict registers in Richardson's text, the medium through which class conflict is conducted. But cannot the alternative work just as well: that class conflict is the code through which sexual difference is articulated? It seems to me that this approach does not advance the discussion any further. For in the end the novel is about inter-class tensions, between the bourgeoisie and landed aristocracy—the Harlowes and the Lovelaces— who need to form alliances rather than bicker among themselves. Here the logic of *Sir Charles Grandison* appears, for in Grandison such an alliance is forged, an alliance that shows up already in the complicity between Clarissa's parents, who forced her into the relationship with Lovelace, and Lovelace himself.

At this Marxist level, all of the various elements of *Clarissa* may be read in terms of the tensions and alliances between the aristocracy and the bourgeoisie: Clarissa's pacifism is an onslaught on the whole social system; her death is the violence of the system let loose on Clarissa herself, an inversion necessary for the patriarchal class alliance of bourgeoisie and aristocracy; Clarissa's forgiveness of Lovelace is a signal of the bourgeois need to make peace with the existing ruling class; and in abjection Clarissa signals the profound tension of this new class alliance between Richardson's Christian piety and social aggressiveness.

What Richardson sought in *Clarissa* he achieved in the magnificent failure of *Sir Charles Grandison*. Here he realizes the feminization of public male relation: the criticism of Lovelace's aristocratic values, with all their public violence, which is carried out through the feminine figure of Clarissa—embodying the virtues of meekness, chastity, sentiment and benevolence—comes together in Grandison. For Eagleton, Grandison is a cipher for the class alliance of aristocracy and bourgeoisie in which the ideology of the latter—a mollified and subtler form of ruling class and patriarchal domination—wins through. Yet for Eagleton *Grandison* is a failure, showing all the contradictions of middle-class ideology: chastity, altruism, piety and pacificity produce a new male subject who subtly alters the structures of sexual oppression so that they remain in place, as powerful as ever: 'The contradiction of *Sir Charles Grandison* is that its blending of genders in inseparable from a synthesis of classes which simply reproduces sexual oppression' (1982: 101). And the mark of this contradiction is that Grandison cannot but be removed from everyday life. Grandison is remote, pontificating on society, a womanly man who connects power and tenderness, and because of this emerges as 'a prig of the first water' (Eagleton 1982: 96). He is 'Jesus Christ in knee breeches, a dreary paragon of goodness' (1982: 96), whose unreality signals an ideological failure: Grandison can only be tender because he has power and riches, a patriarch who can, like Boaz in the story of Ruth, freely dispense moral and financial largesse. In such an unbalanced connection between public and private elements, he becomes more a private than a public figure, an aristocrat well past his time. The contradiction is that Richardson's ideal male is nothing more than a social throwback, for virtue and success cannot blend so easily in public life. The harmony of Grandison in his remoteness shows up the tensions of Richardson's ideological effort. In the end, however, it matters little whether Grandison the patriarch is chaste or not, for he has power and can use it as he chooses: morality has nothing to do with power.

Although Eagleton's argument has its difficulties—it structurally incorporates psychoanalysis and feminism within Marxism—my criticism should not detract from the fact that his analysis foregrounds the important questions of any effort to bring together feminism, psychoanalysis and Marxism. Any consideration of class, class conflict and ideology is inadequate without the dynamics of sexual difference and conflict. This much Eagleton takes as a given: his discussion is an effort to show how the three approaches work together without recourse to a dialectical argument. As far as my reading of Ruth is concerned, I follow Eagleton's lead in a resolute focus on class and gender. The persistent constructivist objection that it is extremely difficult to speak of either in such a vastly different time and place is of course valid, except that it ignores the Marxist origins of constructivism itself. And Marxism is certainly not afraid of historical continuities and the occasional irreducible category.

One of these is class, Eagleton's most consistent Marxist category. Even with the work of Gottwald, Sneed and Horsley, a most urgent task in biblical studies is a consideration of class in the texts of the Hebrew Bible and New Testament. This requires not only the effort to reconstruct what forms class took in the contexts from which the Bible emerged, and not only an engagement with the theoretical work done on class under the Asiatic and Ancient modes of production outside biblical scholarship, but it also requires an investigation into the way class operates in the form and content of the texts themselves.

The Effacement of Women in Ruth

Like Eagleton I will watch in my reading of Ruth for the contradictions and tensions that the shifting patterns of class and sexual dominance produce in the text. For all the space that women occupy in the narrative, what function do they fulfil? And what of the Moabite/Israelite distinction that has been discussed so much? Finally, does not Ruth occupy the lowest rung in the structure of work, gathering the leftovers after the reapers have been through the fields? Eagleton's reflections on the intersections between class and ethnic difference appear in his focus on Heathcliff in *Wuthering Heights*, whereas the issues of class and gender are the focus of his treatment of Richardson's novels. What I want to do is bring together all three—class, gender and ethnicity—in a way that is thoroughly Marxist and yet does not enable class to become the ultimately determining instance.

The path I tread bears the prints of those who have written on Ruth before me. Athalya Brenner has argued that the model that best describes

Ruth is that of the foreign woman worker, common in Israel today (Brenner 1999). Women come into Israel to work at the lowest-paid jobs—usually domestic—from countries where there is little work at all: because they are women and foreigners they fill the lowest class stratum of unskilled workers. This is a finely balanced argument, much better than her earlier valorizations of Ruth as a woman's story (Brenner 1993),[2] for the questions of ethnicity and gender provide greater complexity for an implicit class analysis, and yet ethnicity and gender are not the determining factors of class. Except that Brenner does not offer a class analysis (hence my use of 'implicit'), and is notable more for her feminist criticism than any Marxist categories.

David Jobling, in his commentary on 1 Samuel (1998), which I will consider more closely in the next chapter on Lefebvre and Samuel, divides his book into sections on class, gender and ethnicity. While this is one of the best and most astute commentaries I have read, partly because Jobling is interested in similar questions to mine, and while there is a distinct value in the three sections of the book, studiously avoiding the favouring of one category over another, he curiously makes similar moves to Eagleton. The middle section on gender is where the most sustained use of psychoanalysis appears. The sections on class and ethnicity are less taken with psychoanalysis. In other words, where gender is an issue, psycho-analysis seems most appropriate, for they both speak of the individual and private, specialists in sentiment, to use Eagelton's phrase for the women of Richardson's circle. When the questions of class and ethnicity come to the fore, the modes of analysis move from the private to the public. And it does not seem to me that Jobling provides an adequate reflection on the interrelation between the three areas.

Before attempting precisely such a dialectical reading, I need to ask how class, gender and ethnicity work in the narrative of Ruth. Even though one should hesitate to apply the notions of gender that work today, in late capitalism, the question of sexual difference is one of the oldest divisions for both Marxism and feminism. In this respect, as Eagleton argues in regard to Richardson's texts, the story of Ruth attempts to deal with a problem, although the problem in Ruth is quite different from the one Eagleton identifies: whose mother is Obed's? He is not simply Ruth's child, for the story has with the women of the neighbourhood saying, 'A

---

2.   In fact, most of the essays in the first *Feminist Companion to Ruth* (1993) follow this line, some suggesting female authorship (Bledstein 1993; Van Dijk-Hemmes 1993).

son has been born to Naomi' (Ruth 4.17). And then the narrative closes with a male genealogy from Perez to David in which Boaz and Obed feature. In other words, the story faces the problem of succession, of transition from male to male, when there is no male to continue the line. What happens when only women are left?

As for ethnicity, the ambiguity of 'Moab' runs through the text and beyond. The Moabites are, for the Hebrew Bible, the descendants of Lot and his first-born daughter (Gen. 19.32-3, 37). In this denigrating tale the Ammonites come from Lot and his younger daughter (Gen. 19.34-6, 38). Ruth is therefore one of this incestuous brood, a secondary part of the lines that tie in with Abraham. In Ruth itself the ambiguity of Moab—a sign of textual nervousness concerning Israelite identity? (see also Boer 2001: 120-49)—continues. Ruth and Orpah are Moabite wives of now-dead Israelite men, Mahlon and Chilion. Ruth, whose Moabite identity is so much part of her character that it becomes an epithet, follows Naomi back to Judah, but it is she who marries Boaz and produces a child in the curiously 'impure' genealogical line that leads on to David.

Class, Eagleton's most favoured category, is less obvious in Ruth, but only because it has been less of a focus in criticism than questions of gender and ethnicity. Yet the narrative, especially in ch. 2, cannot be understood without a notion of class. As I outlined earlier, class is one of a cluster of terms in Marxist theory that explores the relations between productive and non-productive labour: those who control the means of production extract, in order to live, the surplus product, or value, from those who work for them but do not own the means of production. Within this basic description a host of particular variations exist in any one political formation (see Marx's famous analysis in *The Eighteenth Brumaire of Louis Bonaparte*), so much so that the Marxist category of class becomes the name of a problem that must be addressed afresh on each occasion.

Like Eagleton in his discussion of *Wuthering Heights* and *Clarissa*, class emerges as a inescapable category for the story of Ruth; in fact, Eagleton's own insistence on class hardly lets me avoid it in any reading that begins with his work. Thus, the return of Naomi and Ruth to Bethlehem takes place at the 'beginning of the barley harvest' (Ruth 1.22), a crucial temporal marker that sets up the sequence that follows. Ruth begins, at her own suggestion, the task of gleaning after the reapers of the harvest. In the hierarchy of labour she is a long way from the wealthy Boaz, owner of the means of production: between them come the young man in charge of the reapers and the reapers themselves. Ruth follows the reapers in the field (Ruth 2.3). As far as the story is concerned, there is but one field in which the reapers work, for the text mentions that part of it belonged to Boaz. The word for reapers is masculine plural (הקצרים), although this does not necessarily refer exclusively to men. The suggestion is strong, however, that the young men (הנערים, Ruth 2.9) are the reapers, but the mention of 'my young women' (נערתי) by Boaz (2.8) points to female workers in the field. Are they reapers also? Ruth 2.23 suggests most clearly that the young women glean rather than reap. The alternative term, שפחה, that designates menial service, concubinage and connection to a female master, is one that indicates that for this story the women workers occupy the lowest rung in the work hierarchy (see 2.13). However, the ambiguity over נערת/נערים, young men/young women, requires alternative signals in the text concerning any division of labour according to sexual difference. For the sexual difference of the נער/נערה is ambiguous elsewhere in the Hebrew Bible—for instance in Gen. 34.3, 12 where Dinah is הנער in Ketib and הנערה in Qere (see Kelso 2003)—and the masculine plural is no sure sign of gender identification. Is it the case, then, that the gender distinction between young men and young women only takes place in the Hebrew Bible when the division of labour becomes an issue? As for Ruth, she is also הנערה (Ruth 2.5, 6), clearly one of the labourers, yet she is one step down from the lowest group, a female servant (שפחה) who is not like one of Boaz's female servants (see 2.13). Only after Naomi's instruction does she join the group of young women gleaning (2.22-23).

In this class microcosm, the mediation between the reapers and gleaners on the one side and Boaz on the other is but one 'young man'—often glossed as 'servant'—who is in charge of the reapers (Ruth 2.5). But Boaz himself is the singular male, like Grandison in Richardson's novels, who controls the means of production and for whom the rest labour. His wealth, the public activities of commercial exchange at the 'gate' (4.1), his age, the eating and drinking at the threshing floor (3.3-7), and the instructions given to his reapers as to how they should work (2.15,16), all indicate a man in charge of the means of production and labour. Only in this context can he, like Grandison, utter pieties—'Yahweh bless you' (2.4) or 'May you be blessed by Yahweh' (3.10; a more indirect phrase for Ruth)—and appear incongruously generous (see below). But the most obvious signal is that nowhere does Boaz engage in any work as such, nowhere is he involved in the production of the necessary items for human existence. In other words, he lives off the surplus labour of those who do work. The only thing he does is tell others what to do: note the variations on the imperative and jussive in nearly all of his reported speech in the text.

A complication to this whole structure of social class lies with Naomi, for she is not factored into the economic equation of the narrative. She remains in domestic space once back in Bethlehem. And her role for the rest of the story is to give Ruth directives (3.1-4: like Boaz, Naomi is given to imperatives and jussives), encourage Ruth in her decisions (2.2), utter pieties (2.19, 20), question Ruth's daily activities (2.20), urge her on in the back-breaking work of gleaning (2.22), gain ownership of Ruth's child (4.16), which is then recognized by the other women (4.14, 15, 17). Both Naomi and Boaz use the familiar 'my daughter' (1.11, 12; 2.2, 8), a distinct place marker in the hierarchy of kin structures. Naomi is then most like Boaz in this story, for she also does no work: she controls Ruth's actions, directing her to go out and glean, seduce a man on the threshing floor and bear a child. This legitimate Judahite is another who lives from the surplus value of those who work.

Yet is not the representation of Boaz and Naomi fraught with difference? A valid objection to my reading is that the absence of Naomi's work is characteristic of the repression of women's work in domestic space. Surely Naomi engages in tasks of cleaning and cooking while Ruth is outside the domestic sphere, doing the work that does register in the text. And is not Naomi the one who cares for the son after he is born? Boaz, by contrast, controls the means of production to which and to whom Naomi herself is subject. At one level this absence in the text signals that Naomi is yet another enabler of the necessary patriliny with which the story closes. There are, however, other signals in the text that indicate the deeper complicity of Naomi and Boaz.

To begin with, there is the question of kinship, which will itself devolve into that of patriliny. The story begins with the Judahite credentials of Elimelech, Mahlon and Chilion, 'Ephrathites from Bethlehem in Judah' (1.2). The issue returns in the narrator's note in 2.1: 'Now Naomi had a relative [מידע, Qere 'relative', Ketib 'acquaintance']³ of her husband's, a powerful man [גבור], of the family of Elimelech, and his name was Boaz.' After this note, Ruth's encounter with Boaz is predetermined, although the economic factor of the division of labour becomes crucial in order to allow the connection to be made. Time and again the kinship of Naomi and Boaz

---

3.   Although both words come from ידע (to know), the Ketib is interesting here, for it designates merely someone known, an acquaintance, rather than a relative.

recurs (2.3, 20; 3.2, 12) until the whole question needs to be resolved by the transaction at the gate with the unnamed 'redeemer', who is closer to Naomi than Boaz.

However, the connection of blood is but the mark of a deeper allegiance, of which the dealings in ch. 4 are the first element. Here the public transactions of men over property and women enable the first steps towards a narrative resolution. The issue here is who will act as גאל (redeemer) for Elimelech. The concentration of various forms of the verb and noun that form part of the semantic cluster of גאל (3.13; 4.1, 3, 4, 6, 7, 8)—to redeem lost property or inheritance—indicate a distinct economic transaction as the solution to the narrative problem of inheritance. Yet when Boaz and the 'redeemer' in question have sat down together with other men, the surprise in store is that the key issue is a parcel of land (חלקת השׂדה) that belonged 'to our brother Elimelech' (4.3). The negotiations begin and the dealings remain at the level of land. But when the nominated 'redeemer' agrees to buy the land, Boaz finally mentions Ruth: 'On the day you buy the land from the hand of Naomi and from Ruth, the Moabitess, the wife of the dead, you buy to restore the name of the dead to his inheritance' (4.5). At this the 'redeemer' withdraws his offer and allows Boaz to become the 'redeemer' of Elimelech, thereby relinquishing the legal duty of the next of kin to take the wife of the one who died so that he would not compromise his own inheritance.

There are a couple of things worth noting in Ruth 4.5. To begin with, the text stumbles at a couple of points, suggesting the problem that Ruth causes for the transaction. Her syntactical place in the sentence is unclear: while the phrases 'from the hand of Naomi and from Ruth' (מיד נעמי ומאת רות) appear balanced as the indirect object of the infinitive construct 'on the day of your buying' (ביום־קנותך), the מאת before 'Ruth' is different from the מיד, 'from the hand of', before 'Naomi'. Of course, the problem, as the following verses make clear, is that Ruth is not the one from whom the property must be redeemed. And so commentators suggest, following the Vulgate, that the full ומאת should be as in v. 10: וגם את, 'also (you buy... Ruth)', rendering Ruth the direct object of the next verb. The syntactical ambiguity hints at a possible inheritance from Naomi to Ruth, outside the control of men, and it is this threat that must be closed down by the convoluted transaction at the gate. Further, the Qere/Ketib for the second verb, קניתי—'you buy' or 'I buy'—disrupts the sentence yet further. Is it that when the 'redeemer' buys the land from the hand of Naomi and from Ruth, Boaz buys to restore the name of the dead to his inheritance? Or does Boaz buy Ruth and the nominated redeemer buy the land? Or is it as the Qere has it, that the one who redeems the land, along with Ruth, redeems the inheritance of the dead? Once again, Ruth disrupts the syntax of a sentence in which she is an object of exchange.

My second observation is the secondary status of Ruth to the 'parcel of land' (חלקת השׂדה), found in both Ruth 2.3 and 4.3. It is as though her inadvertent wandering, while gleaning, onto Boaz's 'parcel of land' (2.3) inextricably ties her to the exchange of land, now that of Elimelech's in 4.3. So close is the connection between women and land—as producers of children and food that men perpetually seek to control—that a metonymy creeps in, suggesting that Ruth herself is the 'parcel of land' over which the men haggle. What is being exchanged here? Obviously a woman, her status as afterthought to the land overturned by the surrounding narrative in which she is the prime object of exchange. The ritual of the sandal, with which Boaz walks on the land and at which Ruth sleeps, makes explicit the purchase of both (4.9).

Again, Naomi, does not seem to fit the equation. Although the exchange of land and woman takes place between men, Naomi is the one who sells. On three occasions (4.3, 5, 9), each time in the reported speech of Boaz, Naomi is mentioned: once as subject of the verb (4.3) and twice as indirect object (4.5, 9). In the presence of the elders the exchange takes place between Naomi and Boaz, even though the former is absent. From Naomi he buys 'all that belonged to Elimelech and all that belonged to Chilion and Mahlon' (4.9). And this, as v. 10 elaborates, includes Ruth: he has not, as the usual formula would have it, 'taken' (ויקח) her; rather, 'and also Ruth, the Moabitess, the woman of Mahlon, I have bought [קניתי] as a woman', says Boaz (4.10). In the end Naomi sells Ruth and the land: in fact it now becomes all (כל) that belonged to Elimelech, Mahlon and Chilion (4.9).

Naomi, it appears is one of the men with whom he exchanges various items, including the foreign woman. But not quite, for at this point the question of ethnicity—or more preferably, social boundaries—makes it clear that this is not merely exchange between (honorary) men. I am going to argue that such economic activity may take place, as far as the narrative is concerned, between Israelites, all of whom appear in this text as non-workers, as those who live off the surplus value of others and exchange it among themselves.

Before I consider this more closely, I want to return to ch. 2, where further complicity between Naomi and Boaz takes place. I have already noted that they act in a similar fashion, controlling and directing Ruth's actions. But what interests me now is the apparent generosity of Boaz. It begins with his order to Ruth to remain with his own 'young women' (2.8), his report of the instructions to the young men not to molest her—as though this was the norm—and to drink from what the young men have drawn (2.9). Ruth herself comes to the party, uttering her thanks: 'May I find favour in your eyes, my lord, for you have comforted me and spoken kindly to your female servant, though I am not one of your female servants' (2.13). Not only does Boaz, in all his largesse, talk to her directly and offer her food (2.14), but he orders the young men to give her as much help as possible, allowing her to glean among the sheaves instead of after them, and to pull out some grains from the bundles so she can gather more (2.15-16). This incredible generosity—a virtue only for the wealthy, as Eagleton points out with respect to Grandison—finds ready support from Naomi, who responds to the information that Ruth has gleaned in Boaz's field: 'Blessed be he by Yahweh, whose kindness [חסד] has not forsaken the living and the dead' (2.20). The elision between Yahweh's and Boaz's 'kindness' is not fortuitous in light of my comments about class earlier (is not Boaz closest to God?). But what we miss in the uniform chorus of Boaz and Naomi, as well as the smoothness of the narrative that lines up such generosity with Yahweh, is the sheer effrontery of the acts and support of both Boaz and Naomi. Not only is Ruth already engaged in the most back-breaking labour, but both Boaz and Naomi enhance the working conditions—within strict limits—in order to make her work harder. Thus, as the 'young man' in charge of the reapers says: 'she has continued from early morning until now' (2.7). And all this before Boaz shows any 'generosity'. Her work credentials are clear, so that by the time Boaz provides more incentive to work 'she gleaned in the field until evening' (2.17), after which she beats what she has gleaned into an ephah of barley. This work is for one day only: after Naomi's encouragement, Ruth gleans for the whole season 'until the end of the barley and wheat harvests' (2.23). This is hardly benevolence, but more like pure exploitation.

It seems, then, that Naomi and Boaz have multiple ties, in terms of kinship, economic exchange and the exploitation of labour. But to what end? A hint of this purpose comes already in ch. 2, when Boaz offers Ruth bread and wine in which to dip the bread: 'So she sat beside the reapers, and he passed her the parched grain, and she ate and was satisfied, and she had some remaining' (2.14). If this grain that is left over is ambiguous, the 'gift' after their night together makes it a little clearer. Boaz orders her to hold out her mantle (הַמִּטְפַּחַת), places in it six measures of barley, and 'laid it upon her' before she goes out into the city (3.15). Apart from the play on garments (see 3.3, 9) and uncovering (3.4, 7)—would not a deconstructive reading make the most of such items?—is this to be understood as a bridal price—if so, a poor one—or a signal of her more significant productive role later? I would suggest that here the connection between the 'part of the land' and Ruth in 2.3 and 4.3 has its sense, for the relation between women and land is not merely that they are exchange items. Rather, the left over parched grain and the six measures of barley placed in her mantle (so that she was virtually naked) signal a deeper association between the productivity of land and women: both produce 'fruit' for others to appropriate. Ruth labours on the land for the gleanings of barley in a way comparable to her production of a son, both burdens and 'gifts' from Boaz.

There remains the final narrative of the book itself. The blessing of 'all the people'—note the expansion from the ten elders of 4.2—'who were at the gate' (4.11) concerns productivity, now in terms of child-bearing. But not any form of child-bearing: the bearing of sons like Rachel and Leah (although Leah also bore Dinah), 'who together built up the house of Israel' (4.11), and, of all people, the house of Perez, born of the somewhat dubious union of Tamar and Judah (Gen. 38), like that of Ruth and Boaz. Nevertheless, the result is what counts: 'because of the seed [זֶרַע] that Yahweh will give you from this young woman' (4.12). Ruth's purpose in the narrative is to produce 'seed', both the son to be born, Obed, and as the closing genealogy shows, *his* descendants. Note the word used again for Ruth: she is no longer the Moabitess but the 'young woman', the gleaner and worker from 2.5, 6 (where only those who work are designated as 'young men' and 'young women'). Linguistically, at the moment of her immanent son-bearing, the terminology links her inextricably with her role as field-worker and gleaner.

However, in the narrative of conception and birth (a perspective from Boaz, for these moments neglect the long period of gestation) there is a curious twist. Boaz, now in conventional terms, 'takes' (לָקַח) Ruth and she becomes his wife, Yahweh enables conception (not Boaz!) and she gives birth to a son (4.13). The narrative has, of course, been moving to this point, but Naomi has not had her last word. In a reversal or rescue of Naomi's bitter words in 1.20-21 at the dereliction by Yahweh, the women point out Yahweh's blessing for Naomi by means of Ruth: 'He shall be to you a restorer of life and a nourisher of your old age; for your daughter-in-law who loves you, has borne him' (4.15). Not only is the blessing for Naomi, for she takes (לקח) him with the same word that is used for Boaz's taking of Ruth (4.13), and puts him in her own bosom (בחיקה), becoming a wet-nurse to him (4.16). With the words of the women—'A son has been born [ילד] to Naomi'—the appropriation is complete, although Ruth's status lingers in his name, Obed (עובד).

Like Clarissa in Eagleton's analysis of Richardson's texts, Ruth becomes a pure ideological means to an end: the resolution of an ideological anomaly. For Richardson this is the feminization of bourgeois relations, whereas for this narrative the disparate identity of Israel and its patriliny is ensured through the appropriation of Ruth's labour and body. And the narrative closes with the lineage of Obed through Jesse to David, backtracking to Perez (now his appearance in 4.12 makes sense) only to finish with the same final three.

In my exploration of the working out of this ideological anomaly the three concerns I have taken up from Eagleton—ethnicity, class and gender—all draw together. As far as ethnicity is concerned the epithet 'Moabitess' is crucial, for Ruth's foreign status is reiterated over and again. She is and remains a foreign body within Israel, so much so that, despite all her protestaions of loyalty (1.16-17), she cannot be the mother of the son. In the narrative Obed belongs to Boaz and Naomi: Ruth is merely the vessel by which the son in born. For what it is worth, this nervous concern over the dynamics of social boundaries appears to be relatively late, when the identity of 'Israel' was very much an obsession. How can an older woman, Naomi, beyond child-bearing age, and a man without a son have an heir? Or rather, how can a threatened inheritance, that of Elimelech, be rescued? But the whole question of ethnicity in this text concerns the establishment of the clearest boundaries between legitimate Israelites and those who are not.

As for gender, only a woman can fill the narrative role, for Ruth must both work in the field and give birth to a son who becomes crucial for the unfolding patriliny. Yet, what happens to Ruth is that she must both work the fields and produce a son, only to diappear when her tasks are done. Thus, after the short narrative of her giving birth to a son, the characteristic yet anomalous formula of men giving birth returns: 'Perez caused to bear [הוליד] Hezron, Hezron caused to bear…' (4.18-19). The indirect object—the woman—disappears and men give birth to men. Ruth's effacement is complete. As for Naomi, she becomes an honorary male, operating in the world of men, trading land and living off the surplus labour of Ruth. Like Ruth, she also disappears, although in a somewhat different direction.

But we must bring class back into consideration, for neither Naomi nor Boaz work in this story. They, the Israelites, do not labour but appropriate the surplus labour and value—the grain from the fields and the son from Ruth's body—of one who does work far too hard. The terminology here is, I have argued, class driven: if the 'young men' who reap, overseen by another 'young man', are at one remove from Boaz, the owner of the means of production, then what status have the 'young women' who follow the reapers and glean after them? While the young men and women may be Israelites, the only named worker in the narrative is Ruth, the 'young woman'. And the term appears both when she works in the field and when she is about to give birth. This means that the pernicious economic picture that emerges in the book of Ruth is that the Israelites— above all Naomi and Boaz—are those who do not work, who exploit and live off the surplus labour of others. Naomi, then, disappears into the world of Israelite men, owners of the means of production, whereas Ruth, Moabitess, woman and worker, is gone when her body has been used up.

As for Eagleton's final arguments in his analyses of both *Wuthering Heights* and Richardson's novels concerning the class transitions that these texts both mark and enable—class alliances between an older landed gentry and the new bourgeoisie in the former or the feminization of bourgeois public relations in the latter—it seems to me that Ruth is both a text of an ideological status quo and that it also sees the emergence of an ideological position that identifies Israel's superior status, as 'chosen people', in terms of class. That which distinguishes Israel from other states is not merely ethnicity, but also as a class of the owners of the means of production. Impossible economically, it is nevertheless an ideological position that is but one aspect of the contested ideologies we find in the Hebrew Bible. I will return to this question in the conclusion, save to note here that such a class identification of Israel neatly removes women from the picture, especially in stories that concern women.

Chapter 4

HENRI LEFEBVRE: THE PRODUCTION OF SPACE IN 1 SAMUEL

Henri Lefebvre, Marxist philosopher and social scientist, one-time member of the French Communist Party, parent of numerous offspring, director of the Institut de Sociologie Urbaine in Paris (Nanterre), intellectual inspiration for May 1968 in France (at the tender age of 67), author of no less than 66 books, remains one of the under-translated giants of the great tradition of French intellectual life from the 1930s to the 1980s.

I undertake here a rather specific task, which is to engage in a critical discussion with Lefebvre's *The Production of Space* (1991a) in order to consider the construction, or, as Lefebvre insisted, the production of space in the ancient world, specifically in this case the Bible. The book was the final product of an intense investigation, as David Harvey points out in the Afterword, into urbanization and the question of space between 1968 and 1974, the year the book first appeared in French, after a number of others from the same project.

Various Spaces

Before I plunge into the stream of his work, I need to make some comments about method. Lefebvre operates with a few crucial moves, strategies that are distinctive marks of his dialectical Marxism.[1] To begin with, he constantly seeks to link the abstract realm of theory with the concrete reality of praxis, speaking of the connections needed between mental and social space, describing in detail such features as urban traffic and human dwellings and then moving into theoretical discussions of habitus, flows and so on. But there is also the retrospective-prospective dialectical habit he assumes, running back, sometimes to his favoured Greece and Rome, to

---

1.   For this reason I prefer Lefebvre over the non-Marxist although valuable developments of his work in Edward Soja (1996) and James Flanagan (1996, 1999, 2001).

pick up a certain topic and trace it through to the contemporary situation, only to cast a view into the future.

Dialectical thinking, Hegelian or dialectical Marxism, has been a characteristic feature of western Marxism, and one finds it in operation, and explored, in the work of the Frankfurt School, especially that of Theodor Adorno, and those closely connected with the school, such as Walter Benjamin and Ernst Bloch. It is also central to the methods of others, like Georg Lukács, Fredric Jameson and, of course, Henri Lefebvre. The dialectic has not necessarily been restricted to Western Marxism (although that term, a product of the Cold War, is now falling by the wayside); for dialectical thinking, termed dialectical materialism, was also central to the intellectual endeavor of the old Eastern European communist countries. The taint of Stalin always meant that many Western Marxists trod warily, seeking out less mechanical and deterministic forms of the dialectic. A few have indeed sought out a non-dialectical Marxism, among them Louis Althusser and Gilles Deleuze, whose thinking may provide one of the ways forward for a post-Cold War Marxism.

Another may indeed be from Lefebvre, whose Marxism runs to the left of the French Communist Party, from which he was expelled in 1957 after a 30-year membership. Calling his dialectic a 'dialectical materialism' as well, but finding the Stalinist line of the French Communist Party too restrictive and stifling, Lefebvre developed a Marxism profoundly touched by situationism and surrealism, but also with a deep sensitivity for human living. He wanted to take up what he felt was Marx's unfinished project in so many ways: he saw that work less as a fixed body of texts to be exegeted with the reverence accorded sacred texts and more as the beginning of much larger programme of intellectual and practical work. The introduction of the question of space is but one of the ways in which Lefebvre undertook to expand Marx. (For instance, he argued that the tendency to reduce society to questions of economics and politics in both Marxism and liberalism was incredibly restrictive: the issue of space was one of the ways of shifting away from such a fixation.)

Less a process that, like Hegel, called for *Aufhebung*, a supersession that kicks the whole problem, the impossible contradiction or antinomy, onto another level in which the problem in question suddenly becomes a much smaller issue in a wider context, Lefebvre's dialectic is one that plays with the opposition or contradiction in question. Toying with it, looking at it from myriad perspectives, and inevitably favouring the lesser term of the opposition in order to move through the whole problem, Lefebvre kept his dialectic open and running. At times he picks up the threefold dimension of a more conventional dialectic, speaking of, for instance, energy, space and time, or of truth, beauty and rhythm, or, as I have already suggested, economics, politics and space. They might be analyzed separately, in conflictual pairs, or on an entirely different tack (see 1986: 42), bringing in an item from elsewhere with which to raise questions about one of the terms under discussion. He does this effectively in *Critique of Everyday Life* (1991b: 141, 145-47, 226), where he connects the notion of the quotidian with religion, especially the popular, half-conscious practices of religion (for Lefebvre, traditional French Catholicism). One distinctive feature of Lefebvre's dialectic is that it produces a profound destabilization of the received notions concerning particular terms and their relationships, which is distinctly reminiscent of the practices of a certain poststructuralism that arose at the time Lefebvre was himself doing his most influential work.

A dialectical reading of the construction of space in the ancient Near East might run in a number of directions, seeking out the play and flow between rural and urban, contrasting the production of space in seats of religious and political power and that of the peasants, or tracing the interaction between the crucial commerce of the sacred and that of space, or contrasting texts from the MT and the LXX in order to read for their different productions of space. In fact, I have found, due to a spasmodic practice of what might be called spatial reading over the last decade or so, that many of the texts of the Hebrew Bible, my specific focus of expertise, give over to spatial analysis.

A distinct form of Lefebvre's dialectic appears in his discussion of space. It is perhaps best to refer to Lefebvre here on the conceptual triad that recurs time and again in the book:

1. *Spatial practice*, embracing production and reproduction, and the particular locations and spatial sets characteristic of each social formation. Spatial practice ensures continuity and some degree of cohesion. In terms of social space, and of each member of a given society's relationship to that space, this cohesion implies a guaranteed level of *competence* and a specific level of *performance*. This is space perceived (perçu) in the common sense mode.

2. *Representations of space* (*représentations de l'espace*): the discourses on space, the realms of analysis, design and planning, which are tied to the relations of production and to the 'order' that those relations impose, and hence to knowledge, to signs, to

codes, and to 'frontal' relations. In other words, the conception of space (*l'espace conçu*).

3. *Spaces of representation* (*espaces de la représentation*): the deeper presuppositions behind plans and definitions. Coded, recoded and decoded, these spaces embody complex symbolisms, linked to the clandestine or underground side of social life, as also to art. It provides partially concealed criticism of social orders and the categories of social thought, and may happen through bodies, aesthetics, gender, and so on. As the third part of a dialectic it offers, as lived space (*l'espace vécu*), as historical sediments or glimpses of the new, utopian possibilities of a new spatialization of social life (see Lefebvre 1974; 1991a: 33, 245; Shields 1999: 160-70).

As ever, Lefebvre's descriptions leave one simultaneously puzzled and illuminated. There are in fact a number of other terms used in relation to space that I want to touch upon in a moment—social space, absolute space, abstract space, contradictory space, mental space, natural space and so on—but the above distinctions are in fact crucial, not only for Lefebvre but also for my reading of some Hebrew texts that will appear in the next parts.

In order to make sense of these three central categories of his spatial dialectic, there is some philosophical legwork to be done. Although it seems like a commonplace now, the idea that certain givens of human experience are social and economic constructions rather than immovable and eternal, natural, objects was an argument that still needed some work in the early 1970s. The constructionism that now reigns across the humanities and social sciences owes a large debt to the work of Marx and Marxists like Lefebvre, so that it has become possible to see how bodies, genders, sexualities, apart from the more common targets of religion and the family, are constructed in certain ways in certain social formations. But in Lefebvre there is a crucial difference that I want to emphasize. He speaks not of the 'construction' but of the 'production' (*la production*) of space. In the first point of his spatial dialectic, production is closely tied in with reproduction, the perpetuation of the means of production in question.

More than a linguistic quibble is at issue here, for 'production' evokes the crucial Marxist category of mode of production, into which I need to diverge for a moment or two. For Marx and Engels (and I draw here from *The German Ideology* [Marx and Engels 1976]), human beings both produce and are produced: they are produced by the conditions in which they live but they also produce those very same conditions. The production of the means of subsistence through the organization of physical resources affects their social and cultural life, but it also acts to remake the material life of the people in question. That is, their very being and nature as human beings are produced by their production of subsistence in relation to nature.

In other words, for Marx mode of production is the way human beings produce their means of subsistence in relation with nature and the existing mode of production. It is the means required for the production of the necessary and luxury items of human existence. Marx identified two dimensions: the forces or means of production, which designates human interaction with nature in terms of raw materials, technical knowledge and the uses of labour; and the relations of production, which refers to the patterns of human interaction and allocation of labour.

At this point we find some of the terms in the first two categories of Lefebvre's spatial dialectic—(means of) production in spatial practice and relations of production in the representation of spaces. Indeed, the ultimate category for any Marxist criticism worthy of the name is mode of production, a notion simultaneously abstract and concrete, since it deals directly with the understanding of history.

Let me provide a few examples that will return in some form in my discussion of the biblical texts. In capitalism, the great focus of Lefebvre's work, the means of production involve industrial (a euphemism for capitalism is sometimes the 'industrial revolution') and now electronic or cybernetic technologies, the extraction of minerals, the massive farming process of agribusiness, unequal wages and the mobilization of masses of low-paid workers, especially women, children and workers in the 'Third World'. The social relations of production involve the fundamental distinction between bourgeoisie and working class, which is now thoroughly globalized. The ideologies of such a mode would include liberalism and the oppositional Marxism. Its culture is marked by the growth of popular and media culture over against high culture, as well as the all-pervasive presence of commodification. Its politics involves the rise of the nation-state and democracy, and a legal system whose prime focus is the protection of private property, whether that be the individual person or non-human objects. Along with commodities, money and capital itself, Lefebvre argues that a particular form of space has also been produced: the city, as successor to the mediaeval town, has become the centre for finance, government, human and social living. In relation to this the rural has been transformed into an area for the capital production of food and other raw materials, supplying the cities from whom it expects its money;

and human dwellings have been produced in terms of the bourgeois family, 'boxes for living in' on private lots.

Or, at the other end of the scale, the so-called Asiatic mode of production has as its means of production the various techniques for widespread hand-tooled agriculture with domesticated animals. Any new developments in technology are directed towards agriculture (improved quality of implement metal, or irrigation, and so on). The relations of production involve a multitude of small landholders that pay tribute to various layers of a significant bureaucracy, at a local, 'national' and imperial level. At the top of the bureaucracy is the imperial centre—Babylon, Egypt, Asshur, Beijing, etc.—where the tribute is lavished upon a standing army (used to ensure the regular payment of tribute and increase the empire), buildings of imperial government and religion and the relatively large number of officials required to keep the system running. Culturally and ideologically religion or the sacred was the central language for expressing political, philosophical, juridical, political and other matters (except that it is a little anachronistic to put it this way). The production of space in the Asiatic mode of production depended upon the layering of tribute payments enforced upon the peasants: very few centres of bureaucracy (the ancient 'city') towards which all tribute was directed, and then the subservience of even these spaces to a larger centre, of which the smaller centres seem like various points on the spokes of a wheel. The spatial practice was then focused upon the flows towards and away from the centres, and this was inextricably tied up with the religious centralization in the places of power and the destination of tribute. If the language and ways of thinking could operate only in the sacred, then the spatial direction always looked towards the point of tribute payment. Domestic space was then ordered in terms of the need to maintain such a system, and the family unit was a much larger affair focused on ensuring that there was produce to survive and pay tribute: many generations, as many children as possible, small dwellings in which humans and animals all spent the night, if not a good part of the day as well.

With these kinds of descriptions, bare though they are, one gets a sense of the difference between modes of production—something Marxist criticism is able to highlight. Of course, the problem with any approach that seeks to periodize history according to one pattern or another is how to account for longer patterns, the carry through of one item into other modes of production, whether they are sacred texts or the status of the peasant. So, in Marxism a growing awareness has arisen of many overlaps, foldbacks and glimpses of new forms found at any one moment, but the assumption is that one mode of production will end up being dominant.

This is basic Marxist theory, but it provides the background necessary to understand Lefebvre's insistence on the 'production' of space. One of the results of a shift to 'construction' over against 'production' in the more recent development of the idea is that 'construction' conjures up the notion of social construction, the social context that constructs the individual, bodies, genders and so on. What are lost in the transition are both the specific historical dimensions of a Marxist theory of modes of production, and its connection with economics, politics, ideology and so on.

I have also been speaking, albeit somewhat briefly, of the whole issue of the spatial practice that is produced in different modes of production. But Lefebvre points out that a mode of production needs to perpetuate itself, to reproduce itself, a process carried out at all levels from the macro-economic (the investment of capital and the deployment of finance capital), to class (the reproduction of the labour power of the working class) to the personal (a point close to home for Lefebvre and his many offspring from a series of partners). Indeed, the reproduction of modes of production is a distinct way of introducing the sexual into the most fundamental of Marxist categories, for Marxism has not been noted for its ability to deal with Eros in a positive fashion: the ability to do so has usually been imported. Lefebvre shifts gear and argues that production and reproduction cannot be separated, taking a tip from the traditional Marxist notion that the basic means of production (technology and resources) also includes the numbers, patterns and distribution of human population. But in order to think about this adequately one needs to think about sex, not just the processes of breeding, but the libido itself.

Yet the spatial practice of which Lefebvre speaks, and the space that is produced, refers primarily to social space, the space created by humans in their interaction with nature, each other and former modes of production. Social space appears in relation to, and over against, physical or natural space, the space of a nature in which human beings increasingly have the upper hand. Since capitalism is now rampant, Lefebvre, while admitting that natural space remains the point of departure for considerations of space and the social process, argues that social space under capitalism now has nature at its mercy: everyone wants to preserve nature, yet everything now seeks to undermine such a desire. Natural space for Lefebvre disappears rapidly over the horizon, for the very 'nature' upon which we now look has been produced by human beings (see 1991a: 30-31).

But there is one final distinction of the categories of space listed above that I have not explored: that between frontal and hidden, the overt and the covert relations of production. For this is the key to his distinction—an odd one on first reading—between the representations of space and spaces of representation. Not only does each mode of production produce specific types of social space (as well as all sorts of other forms from other modes that are subsumed as subvariants), but it also has a specific type of relations of production (the organization of human resources in terms of class, division of labor, and so on). But the issue here is how those relations of production operate spatially. In order to trace this, Lefebvre invokes all the complexity of his dialectical materialism. Under capitalism, he identifies three types of interaction between reproduction and the social relations of production: biological reproduction, the reproduction of labour power, and the reproduction of the social relations of production. Each of these three interacting layers is displayed symbolically, simultaneously exhibited and displaced, that is, concealed. Such a symbolic system works with relations of production that are both out there and not, in the forefront and clandestine, explicit and repressed. The former, overt type appears in the forms of monuments, public art and buildings, especially those of state and business: this is the realm of the representation of space, the frontal, obvious node of the relations of production. The more covert and clandestine version, the shadowy realm of spaces of representation, is interested in what is hidden, closed over, spaces that represent in wayward and diverse fashions.

Lefebvre's oft-repeated example is one he in fact loathed—the bourgeois family home. The overt dimension of the house, facing the street (and do not all detached houses have to face the street?), is its sitting room or formal lounge room, where considerable expense is outlaid: lounges and tables and exquisite chairs, with expensive curtains and pieces of art either on the walls or standing. The public realm of the bourgeois house is one of decor, money and repression. Perhaps the only other room allowed such visual presence is the formal dining room, usually leading off from the lounge room. But there is another realm of such boxes for living in that marks a whole series of repressions: the preparation of food takes place out of sight, as do toilet functions, both evacuating and washing. If these are relegated to the back of the house, the most hidden is sex itself, restricted to night time in the parents' bedroom, with a locked door and when the children are asleep, or, if older, out of the house.

To return once more to the distinctions between spatial practice, representation of space and space of representation, it seems to me that any application of such categories must recognize that the distinction Lefebvre makes between biological reproduction, the reproduction of labour power, and the reproduction of the social relations of production is one that applies to capitalism. As he notes:

> It should be pointed out that in precapitalist societies the two interlocking levels of biological reproduction and socio-economic production together constituted social reproduction—that is to say, the reproduction of society as it perpetuated itself generation after generation, conflict, feud, strife, crisis and war notwithstanding (1991a: 32).

All the same, the powerful distinction between the representation of space and space of representation remains in place, since the lack of distinction between reproduction and production applies directly to the realm of social practice. The notion of covert and overt, of hidden and clear, comes of course from the Marxist perception of class conflict as crucial to historical processes. And it is not for nothing that Lefebvre locates the opposition in the realm of relations of production, where class and class conflict operate in Marxist thought. The frontal class, the one of monuments and impressive buildings and the clear marks of power, stands over against that class which is repressed, beaten down and exploited. Lefebvre's innovation is to widen this to the symbolic field of relations of production, of class relations.

And since it is a symbolic field that is his primary concern, it seems to me that such an approach may be taken up in the reading and interpretation of texts as well. While spatial practice in the ancient world may be more difficult to trace in the texts that derive from it, the representation of space and space of representation are far more amenable to the consideration of texts, including texts from the Hebrew Bible.

There is one final issue before I turn to the Hebrew Bible. A substantial portion of *The Production of Space* seeks to refashion Marxist periodization in terms of space. This is a grand plan that involves a prior commitment to periodization as a viable way of considering history itself. Of course, if one is, like Lefebvre, persuaded by the power of Marxism and Marxist analysis, then historical periodization is an issue and a problematic that needs some thinking. And if space and its production are inescapably tied to mode of production, as I have argued above, then there will necessarily be different types of space for different modes of production. What is interesting about all of this is that the substantial part of *The Production of Space* is given over precisely to such a periodization; Shields, in his advocatory study of Lefebvre (1999) remains unimpressed by the larger system-building dimensions of Lefebvre's Marxism— to which he remained committed throughout his life—preferring the freer, playful, erotic and lived radicalism of this indefatigable writer. For me, however (and this may be symptomatic of a much larger dimension of my physical and intellectual life), the sheer imagination and ability to sustain thought in this way is one of the most impressive dimensions of Lefebvre's work. So, in the following table I have outlined in the first two columns the received Marxist periodization of history in terms of modes of production and what might be called the cultural dominant—a particular way in which culture, and in fact the superstructure as a whole, might be characterized. In the third column I have lined up the various productions of space as Lefebvre follows them through in the bulk of his book.

Table 1. *Mode of Production and Space*

Mode of Production	Cultural Dominant	Space
Hunting and gathering, agriculture and husbandry (tribal society, primitive communism or the horde)	Magic and mythic narrative	Absolute space (nature)
Neolithic agriculture (the gens or hierarchical kinship societies)	Kinship	Absolute space
Asiatic mode of production ('oriental despotism' and divine kings)	Religion or the sacred	Sacred space
Ancient or classical mode of production (the *polis* or oligarchal slave-holding society)	'Politics' in terms of citizenship of the city-state	Historical space (political states, Greek city-states, Roman empire)
Feudalism	Relations of personal domination	Sacred space
Early capitalism (classical and monopoly forms)	Commodity reification	Abstract space (politico-economic space)
Late capitalism	Commodity reification	Contradictory space (global capital v. localized meaning)
Communism	Original forms of collective and communal association	Differential space (future space revaluing difference and lived experience)

What I have done here is take the periodization of space in Lefebvre's work, linked it with Shields's discussion and tabulation (1999: 170-72), and then fine tuned a number of points where I think that Shields misses the point somewhat. I find it odd, for instance, for him to argue that such a periodization is linear and undialectical, for Lefebvre himself argues that each of the types of space is contained, albeit in subordinate or hidden forms, in each of the modes of production. Further, each mode of production and of space cannot exist without dialectical connections to those forms around it, especially the ones that precede and follow. Finally, in periodizing space, Lefebvre carries out the grandest dialectical move with space and time themselves, the inescapable categories (thanks to Kant) of thinking in the modern, capitalist world.

I need to close my theoretical section with a closer look at the realms of absolute space and sacred space, for they are relevant to the biblical material I want to visit next.

The original moment is the space of nature itself, absolute space, pure space. In this context the first social space of the tribe inscribes itself, specifically the semi-nomadic tribe of a hunter-gatherer society, with its seasonal paths, temporary camps and border zones. Whether hunting for game, engaged in limited agriculture or even in the first farming settlements, absolute space dominates. The production of space is here analogical, conceiving of the camp, settlement or village—that is, human society—in terms of a mythic body, with the layout of such settlements narrativized in mythic and magical narrative. There is a distinct anthropomorphism in the representation of space, the settlement and its environment, with settlement and its outside understood in terms of the body and its beyond.

Sacred space, that which follows absolute space temporally and logically in Lefebvre's schema, is produced with the emergence of the city-state, which he finds in the ancient Near East, traditional Asian societies, such as that of China, and also the early stages of the Greek world. Rome and its empire comprises a new stage, that of historical space. In other words, over against the more conventional division that begins with Greece and the reliance of such a mode of production on slave labour—a system whereby the very economic and social, let alone the cultural, possibilities of the Greek and Roman worlds are enabled by the labour of slaves—over against this characterization, he posits the emergence of the city-state and then of the Roman imperial system as the points of transition. This is a larger argument that I don't need to pursue here, but it is symptomatic of Lefebvre, for whom the city was a vital dimension of his lived experience, as well as much of his writing and research, that the emergence of the first cities should be central.

But this is not capitalism (for which he reserves his most sustained analysis and critique): in the new city-state the sacred and the political are inseparable. The location of palace and temple in the one location, side by side and often connected as one building, marks the possibility of the city-state. The sacred city—Babylon, Beijing, Egyptian cities of the Pharaohs, Jerusalem itself—supersedes the village and the semi-nomadic tribe to constitute the new, central sacred space. Despot, city and the gods are inseparable: the despot is, in many cases, god, a descendant of a god, or in a relationship much closer than any other citizen; the city is where the god-despot dwells. In exacting tribute, such cities dominate the rural regions surrounding them, pushing back nature, the realm of absolute space, through the technologies of political, economic and sacred power. This form of the city mutates into the Greek *polis* and even dimensions of the Roman *urbs*, in which the sacred space of the city, as *imago mundi*, is set over against the barbarian outside, that realm beyond the power of the city-state.

Ironically, in light of my own particular use of Lefebvre, he is at his weakest with these early productions of space. His energy was of course directed to capitalism and its emergence and dissolution, but the realm of absolute space, although suggestive, is too much shot through with European, especially French, conceptions of the primitive and prehistoric. He is on better ground with sacred space and the emergence of the city-state, although, as some have argued, it is very much gendered in terms of heterosexual binary, with the realm of the city-state characterized as active and masculine and the outside as passive and feminine. Apart from the fascinating connection with the vast programme of Deleuze and Guattari in *A Thousand Plateaus* (1987), especially the *urstaat*, what is sorely needed for this kind of work is a detailed consideration of earlier modes of production and their construction of space.

My use of Lefebvre, then, while bouncing off this spatial schema, is more interested in reading for the production of space, specifically in terms of the threefold dialectic of spatial practice, the representations of space and the space of representation.

Biblical Spaces

How much can we really learn, for instance, confined as we are to Western conceptual tools, about the Asiatic mode of production, its space, its towns, or the relationship it embodies between town and country? (Lefebvre 1991a: 31-32).

The texts I might discuss are legion, but I restrict myself to one, namely, 1 Sam. 1–2. Here we have a rather inconspicuous text that touches more with Lefebvre's lifelong concern with the quotidian, everyday lived life. I should make it clear that whereas Lefebvre assumes the representational function of texts, from architecture through human bodies to written texts themselves, the kind of representation he works with is not of the sort that is second nature to most biblical scholars, namely, the specific history of a people or a period, the acts of states, groups of people or individuals from day to day and year to year. Historical research remains focused on locating texts in such a history and reading them for reference to it. In this respect the energy now directed at the Second Temple period, arguing for very late dates, works with the same set of assumptions; it is only the period that has changed.

So, while the referential function of a text like 1 Sam. 1–2 can tell us little about any figures, such as Samuel or Eli, or the events surrounding them, or even the moves of story-tellers and scribes who may have told or penned such a story at an indeterminate later period, it can tell us some- thing about the production of space, of broader economic and cultural patterns in a much larger time frame that beggars any effort at more specific dating.

Since 1 Sam. 1–2 is a written text, it speaks, according to Lefebvre's schema, of the representations of space and spaces of representation: that is, as a text it functions in some representational way. It can then speak only in a secondary manner about spatial practice; or rather, there is a spatial practice of the text that refers to the spatial practice of whatever social formation it comes from. As far as the representation of space is concerned—the 'frontal' discourse of space, the logic, ideology and conceptual depictions of space in relation to modes of production—we need to begin with the last verses of Judges, which may be read as an introduction to this text:

> And the people of Israel departed from there at that time, every one to his
> tribe and family, and they went out from there every one to his inheritance.
> In those days there was no king in Israel; every one did what was right in
> his own eyes (Judg. 21.24-25).

Following the suggestion of David Jobling, I read these verses as not so much a condemnation of the chaos just depicted, a conclusion to the story of the Benjaminites, but rather as the possibility of a desirable state of affairs, without a king to rule over them and exact tribute and so on. In this case, the verses set up the spatial possibilities of 1 Sam. 1–2.

So there is a man from his own inheritance—Ramathaim-zophim of the hills of Ephraim—and from his own tribe and family—Elkanah the son of Jeroham, son of Elihu, son of Tohu, son of Zuph, an Ephraimite (1 Sam. 1.1). The representation of space here is a dispersed pattern of living, each person living in a particular geographical and tribal place, what Lefebvre would designate as a *habitus*. The issue is one of the relations of production, specifically the distribution of human beings and their relations to each other in the production of what is required for human existence. The naming of the two women of Elkanah, Hannah and Peninah, is part of the same logic, as is the crucial statement, 'And Peninah had children, but Hannah had no children' (1 Sam. 1.2). The problem as it unfolds in this story is the barrenness of Hannah, which, as the story makes clear, is distinctly *her* problem since Peninah had sex with the same man as she. This touches on the question of the reproduction of the means of production, as well the spaces of representation, to which I will turn in a moment. But what we have here is an economic unit, given that families of whatever shape are at basis economic units in particular modes of production. David Jobling, following Norman Gottwald, has argued that under the monarchy we find what may be termed a 'tributary' mode of production, a revised form of Marx's famous Asiatic mode of production. Prior to this, under the ideal of judgeship that appears in Judges and 1 Samuel, he prefers, following Marshall Sahlins, the notion of a 'household' or 'familial' mode of production, one that is somewhat more egalitarian in terms of sexual difference than what follows under monarchy, to Gottwald's 'communitarian' mode of production. He also makes explicit use of Karl Wittfogel's *Oriental Despotism* (1963) to argue that the:

> transition from a more egalitarian to a tributary mode is typically accompanied by shifts from female-based to male-based patterns of kinship and social organization, from a low-level agriculture dominated by women to an intensive agriculture organized by men, and from the extended family to the nuclear family (Jobling 1998: 146).

Apart from the reactionary nature of Wittfogel's argument (it is directed against the Soviet Union) and the technologism (changes in mode of production have to do with uses of water and irrigation), what lies behind it is the fantasy of Bachofen and Lewis Henry Morgan, with their arguments for a prior matriarchy before patriarchy took over. Jobling's is a more gentle version, but it still assumes such a background. As will become clear in what follows, such a position is difficult to sustain.

But let me stay with the representations of space: the immediate narratological event is the annual journey to worship and sacrifice at the sanctuary at Shiloh. This journey, the path taken from a small space in the hills of Ephraim to Shiloh, is one of those flows of which Lefebvre speaks time and again, open to what he also calls 'rhythm analysis' (see Lefebvre 1996: 219-40). The annual journey frames the story itself, determining its rhythm: at the end of this particular trip 'they rose early in the morning and worshipped before Yahweh; then they went back to their house at Ramah' (1 Sam. 1.19). But then, after conception and birth, the family, minus Hannah and Samuel, travel to Shiloh again (1.21). Eventually Hannah goes up after weaning the child in order to dedicate him to the shrine (1.24), they return home (2.11), and then return year by year with a robe for Samuel that Hannah makes for him and gives to him at the time of yearly sacrifice (2.19) The annual journey to the major shrine of course indicates the importance of the shrine itself, with its priestly family, Eli, Hophni and Phinehas. In contrast to Ramah (רמה), the shrine, the place of worship, no matter how modest or grand, is a key representation of space, a frontal dimension that orders the lives of the smaller economic units of the extended families and tribes. The spatial pattern is like a wheel with unequal spokes leading in all directions from the centre, or perhaps like an asterisk with lines leading out and coming into the point at the middle, the sanctuary. What we have here, then, is the production of sacred space and its organization of the social and economic patterns of human life.

The spatial patterns of the sanctuary itself, while not laid out explicitly as in so many places (the tabernacle of Moses, Solomon's temple, Ezekiel's temple plans and so on), appear as well. Eli, semi-retired (Hophni and Phinehas are the priests—1 Sam. 1.3), sits 'on the seat beside the door post of the temple of Yahweh' (1.9), able to observe Hannah praying. The line of sight is important here as well, for, apart from suggestions of voyeurism, Eli commands the sanctuary with his sight, although his insight itself is lacking with regard to Hannah.

What of the spaces of representation—the clandestine or underground side of social life, the sediments of lived space, of gender relations and family patterns, and the possibilities of something new? The annual journey to Shiloh moves from Ramah (רמה) and back again. Ramah emerges as one of these of spaces of representation, from which Hannah, Peninah, Elkanah and then Samuel emerge. Elsewhere in 1 Samuel (7.17; 8.4; 15.34; 16.13; 19.18-23; 20.1; 25.1; 28.3) it is the exclusive domain of Samuel (see Fokkelman 1993: 7). The journey itself is occasion for rivalry between Hannah and Peninah, for the latter taunts Hannah over her barrenness. Peninah provokes and irritates, so Hannah responds with weeping and refusal to eat. An ineffectual Elkanah, who 'loves' Hannah, can only ask questions restricted to the space of representation—weeping, eating, her heart and her barren womb (1 Sam. 1.8).

It is these kinds of family dynamics that have led Carol Meyers to argue for the importance of the public/private divide in this and other stories. The curious turn of the Meyers's argument is to search for the active presence of women in the biblical narratives, a presence screened by the effects of theological and male dominance in biblical studies, in terms of the domestic or private sphere: thus, Hannah's sacrifice in 1 Sam. 1.24 becomes a private ritual, an aspect of 'family religion' (Meyers 1994: 101) that is more apparent in the MT. The catch here is not only the problematic public/private distinction that it assumes but also that any attribution of female agency in ritual remains in the private sphere—hardly a gain in an assumed world of public male dominance. It seems to me that Lefebvre's distinction between spaces of representation and representations of space are much more subtle and workable, for the whole public/private distinction is tied too closely with capitalism itself.

Thus, apart from the family dynamics, the bodies of the women function as the major spaces of representation, specifically their wombs (רחם), the matrix of the story (for which Ramah, רמה, as a veiled pun, itself becomes a cipher). It is as though the wombs are set over against the sanctuary, the other pole around which this story oscillates. Both hidden, and fore-grounded, Peninah's fertile womb contrasts with Hannah's barren womb. It is the cause of their conflict, a marker of her economic superfluity (Elkanah gives her but one portion), and the focus of her prayer in the sanctuary. Her vow—to dedicate the son born as a Nazirite to Yahweh at the shrine—focuses again on her womb, for she seeks Yahweh to open her womb in reverse to the divine closure (1 Sam. 1.6). Then it is time, after the blessing pronounced by Eli, for Elkanah's seed to find its way into her womb, where a son is conceived and born (1.19-20). Hannah's body is now the location of sex and impregnation, and it remains fecund, particularly after the dedication of Samuel and the annual blessing from Eli (2 Sam. 2.20-21). I will return in a moment to the pattern whereby various males—Eli, Elkanah and Yahweh—all ensure Hannah's fertility.

Hannah's body works in one other way in this text, apart from empty womb, source of anguish, and then blessing, divine visitation and sex. I refer here to Eli's singular lack of perception: he observes her mouth and her lips moving. This is the realm of representations of space, for Eli, the priest in the sanctuary of Yahweh, is in that realm. It is also, for Lefebvre, the zone of perception, space that is perceived. Spatial practice breaks in here, percieved space, for Eli perceives her lips and her mouth, but that is all, given his spatial role in the story, that he can perceive. She, however, speaks in her heart, but her voice is not heard. The very use of heart in this sense, very different from the observed heart of medicine, or (to avoid too much anachronism) an open dead body, is in the realm of the symbolic and the mythic. The heart as lived is very different from the heart as thought and perceived. Desire, Hannah's desire, her anxiety and vexation (1 Sam. 1.16), and mythification appear here. The contrast between Eli and Hannah could not be sharper in terms of space: the one comes from the representation of space, the other from the space of representation.

Eli sees her mouth and lips, but does not hear her voice. Hannah's heart acts as a metaphor for her womb, but her womb cannot be mentioned directly. In a perceptive *tour de force*, Eli concludes she is drunk. In response to Eli's rebuke, she admits not to pouring drink into her body, but pouring out her *nephesh* to God (1 Sam. 1.15). Yet even though her womb draws the prayer from her, she reveals to Eli none of the content of her prayer. Other parts of her bodily self, internal and external, have been revealed, but not her womb and its vexations. The spaces of representation in this case are not as myopic as Eli, for in the realm of the shrine, the external and frontal representation of space, it is not possible for her womb to be mentioned, seen or referred to. It is a realm both crucial to yet suppressed by the overt structure of space in this text. Hannah's womb remains unspoken and unperceived within the sanctuary, since sanctuary and womb are at odds with each other in spatial terms. If we pick up Lefebvre again, we find that in the production of sacred space, the realm of nature and of women's bodies is suppressed and removed from the domain of shrine, temple and also city. But this space, what he calls absolute space, does not disappear; rather, it retreats into the interior, into the enclosed spaces of caves, nooks and crannies, alleyways, and of course bodies. The womb becomes a prime site for such an investment of alternative space, outside the bodies of males, of sanctuaries and cities, it yet remains crucial to the pattern of sacred commerce: hence the roles of Eli, Elkanah and God in relation to her womb. So here, it seems, we find the intersection of absolute space and sacred space, an overlap that Lefebvre himself was keen on locating.

Is there a utopian possibility in these spaces of representation, specifically with Hannah's womb and the way that it is the focus of the story? If we follow the work of Butler (1993), Grosz (1995) or Blum and Nast (1996), as well as Lefebvre, then bodies, especially female bodies, spatially exceed our representations and images, twisting away from patriarchal signs and controls. It would appear, on one reading at least, that the militant anthem of 1 Sam. 2.1-10 fits the bill. It celebrates the strengthening, by God, of the weak and lowly, the bringing down of mighty kings, powerful, proud and arrogant men. The hungry, feeble and barren find food, strength and pregnancy (see especially Jobling 1998: 166-68). And barely a critic who wishes to oppose more conventional commentaries can resist, especially when locked into a severely limiting analysis of the characters themselves, the argument that the narrative gives (limited) range to Hannah's agency: Meyers speaks of the 'validity and autonomy' of her actions (1994: 102); Amit of Hannah's 'delicacy', 'virtue' and 'sensitivity' in protest, when one is more sympathetic to Hannah's perspective rather than, as with a legion of male commentators, Elkanah's (Amit 1994: 75); Klein (1994) of her move from being the victim of mimetic desire to a social redeemer who refuses such a logic; and Jobling argues for a deliberate strategy of recuperating Hannah's initiative for an ecclesial context in which such women are few and far between (Jobling 1998: 131-42). For Jobling, however, Hannah's initiative seeks to forestall the arrival of kingship and restore the traditional order of judgeship (which is, for Jobling, at least a little more egalitarian), although the irony is that it is precisely Samuel who becomes king-maker and ends the older order.

Only Klein and Jobling recognize that despite Hannah's initiative, she is finally co-opted back into the larger (mythic) logic of the narrative (Klein 1994: 92; Jobling 1998: 165). My argument is a little more dialectical: Hannah's agency cannot be gainsaid. However, it is not so much that she is co-opted, reluctantly, back into the narrative: it is through her agency, her initiative, that she becomes a key to the deeper logic of the system itself. And a major signal of that logic is the interactive of space, for here we find the dominant mode asserting itself time and again.

What of Lefebvre's final category? Spatial practice appears at certain points that reflect an economy of the sacred, a sacred commerce in which issues of production and reproduction can only be perceived in terms of the sacred. So it is that Peninah taunts Hannah on the annual journey to Shiloh, specifically after the allocation of portions to each member of the extended family, for Hannah would be given only one portion (1 Sam. 1.4; see also 1. 7). Why not at other times in this story? At this moment the role of the divine in reproduction is highlighted: on the journey, or rather at

Shiloh, after the sacrifice, sacred commerce comes to the fore.

In order to maintain a mode of production it is necessary to reproduce labour power, that is, human beings. In different modes of production this may happen in different ways. For instance, in slave-holding societies the slaves who do the work for the system to keep functioning are acquired through conquest, systems of debt, as well as children of slaves. However, in most cases human reproduction plays some role, especially in those where tribe or gens plays a fundamental role in the relations of production. The reproduction of large families, often polygamous, is crucial for the mode of production to sustain itself. So it is with this story, although with a few twists.

First, there is the curious pattern of reproduction that seems to follow another rhythm from that of sex itself. In order for Hannah to conceive, she first goes to Shiloh, prays at the shrine, receives a blessing from Eli, is remembered (1 Sam. 1.19) or visited (2 Sam. 2.21) by God and then has sex with Elkanah. It seems as though she needs three men for the whole process to work (1 Sam. 1.20; 2 Sam. 2.21). As far as the rhythm of the story is concerned, it is only after the annual sacrifice and vow that the correct combination comes together for conception. This odd pattern is reinforced by the obverse, when she does not go (1 Sam. 1.22), promising to do so when she has weaned the child. Then, when Hannah brings Samuel to dedicate him at the shrine, there is no pregnancy either, for there is no blessing, visitation or sex in the story at that moment either.

It seems that the story has the making of a sacred commerce, a divine economy in which the system requires the activity of God to keep it running. But there is another feature that at first seems to undermine all this: is the dedication of Samuel as a Nazirite, to live and work at the temple, not an undermining of the need for labour power in the unit of the extended family? Would it not fit the logic of the system better if he were to grow up in the family and take his share of the workload? In the end, I would suggest, Hannah has the system at heart, for in dedicating the child to Yahweh at the shrine she ensures that the sacred commerce will continue. Not only does she fulfil her vow (1 Sam. 1.11)—necessary to avoid a divine curse—but she ensures that the role of the shrine and its priesthood in the production of sacred space is maintained. This is the reason, in a spatial analysis, why the sons of Eli, as well as Eli himself, must appear worthless and corrupt in the story (2 Sam. 2.12-17, 22-36). Their sin is so great for it is a sin against God rather than other people (2 Sam. 2.25). Samuel, therefore, is their designated replacement, and

Hannah thereby performs a crucial function for the maintenance of this particular production of space and its mode of production (the Asiatic mode of production). Her boy, the product of her womb, must go to the shrine in order to underwrite its continuance at the hub of the spokes. Hannah is crucial to the story, as Meyers among others argues on the basis of the frequency of her name, her role in naming Samuel and her use of dialogue (Meyers 1994: 96-100), but this is only because she is central to the ideological economy of the narrative.

Do even the spaces of representation fall victim to the spatial practice of a particular mode of production? Does Hannah's womb also, despite the utopian glimpse it provides, reinforce the system as a whole? It would seem so, except for one detail: it all takes place at Shiloh, not Jerusalem. Here I make a dialectical move, characteristic of Lefebvre and other Marxists indebted to him, such as Fredric Jameson, taking the whole discussion to another level and widening out the problem in a whole new way. What difference does Shiloh make? A whole lot, it seems to me.

The story is curious in the context of the larger scale into which it falls, especially if we keep Noth's construction of a 'Deuteronomistic history' in mind.[2] I want to pick up but one piece of this proposal, namely, the centrality of the construction of the first temple by Solomon in the structure of the work. One of Noth's arguments was that the work exhibited an overriding structure into which the ethereal author, creatively named the 'Deuteronomistic historian', fitted the bits and pieces cobbled together for the history itself. At the centre of this planned work, and at the middle point of the chronology, Solomon begins building the temple (see 1 Kgs 6.1). But not only is the temple central in a chronological sense; it also functions as the only place for legitimate worship of Yahweh. The other places, especially the high places, but also the other shrines and minor places for worship are therefore illegal, not to be tolerated. And this applies even to those with some apparent pedigree, such as Bethel, Dan, and of course Shiloh. So, a continual pattern becomes apparent in the 'Deuteronomistic history', in which worship must be carried out in Jerusalem, at the temple, and nowhere else, and yet alternative worship continues. The various shrines and high places become contested zones,

---

2.　I write 'construction' advisedly, for, as I argue in *Novel Histories*, the 'Deuteronomistic History' is produced in the space between the biblical text and Noth's critical work. He read Deuteronomy–Kings as though it were the 'Deuteronomistic history', and in order to construct it as such he saw it as an historical novel. See Boer 1997, especially pp. 13-14, 77-103.

the subject of polemic and theological condemnation.[3]

Spatially, such a conflict is crucial on a number of levels. The split between Rehoboam and Jeroboam is read in terms of the legitimacy or otherwise of the sanctuaries *to which people travel for sacrifice and worship*. Jeroboam, in order to stop the people going to Jerusalem, sets up worship in Bethel and Dan so that the people may go there, so that the hubs are now located within the territory of Israel and not Judah (1 Kgs 12.25-33). This becomes a leitmotif for the rest of Kings, any condemnation now connected with the proverbial sins of Jeroboam. The contest closes with Josiah's destruction of the sanctuary at Bethel (2 Kgs 23.15-20). Indeed, Josiah's reform, with its long list of items destroyed, abolished, annihilated and ground into dust, embodies such a spatial contest in intricate detail, for the danger exhibited there is that if such a pattern of religious observance were allowed to go unchecked, it would infect the temple in Jerusalem as well.

Finally, there is not unexpectedly a theological glue to all of this that runs through from beginning to end. The basic theological bifurcation of this 'history' is between obedience and disobedience: following the laws and wishes of Yahweh will lead to blessings, understood in terms of land, long life, wealth and offspring; falling away, worshipping other gods, and thereby disobeying Yahweh's commandments, which appear strategically at the beginning in Deuteronomy, will mean early death, misfortune, and ultimately, the spatial punishment of dispossession from the land, which is of course the punishment, according to this story, for continued apostasy.

So, in the broader context there is a spatial dynamic at work that lifts the whole consideration of Shiloh to a new dialectical level. If Shiloh falls into the category of one of these shrines, a hub of sacred space outside Jerusalem, then it is, as a whole, part of the spaces of representation. If sacred space seeks to control worship and economics in the central city and temple—and for Lefebvre sacred space relies not so much on the shrine alone as on the sacred city—then Shiloh is in another place, namely, that of suppressed spaces, of the elements of an older spatial organization that has now succumbed to the new order. Along with the various high places, grottoes, trees and so on, it is now a space of representation, on par with domestic patterns and bodies themselves. What this means is that whereas in the story of 1 Sam. 1–2 Hannah's womb, the major space of repre-

---

3. This is where I disagree with Fokkelman's suggestion that Gibeah, Shiloh, Bethel and Bethlehem are all part of the same central zone around Jerusalem (1993: 1-2). Rather, they form the outposts of Jerusalem itself.

sentation in the text of 1 Sam. 1–2, acts as one pole over against the
sanctuary of Shiloh, in the larger context, her womb and the sanctuary
fold into one space. The spatial logic of this is that the very possibility
of a story about her womb can only take place in a narratively marginal,
suppressed space, such as that of Shiloh. Were it set in the Jerusalem of
Solomon's temple, then it would have faced a narrative fate comparable to
the suggestion of Solomon that the baby fought over by the two sex
workers in 1 Kgs 3.16-28 be cut in two.

Also, the sheer absence of descriptions, plans and designs of the shrine
at Shiloh marks it off as less a representation of space than as a space of
representation. All I was able to glean from the text was the centrality of
Shiloh for the annual journey of the family to worship. By contrast, the
issue of plans, building programmes, sources of finance, interior design
and so on is inseparable from the consideration of the temple in Jerusalem.
Thus, 1 Kgs 5.15 (ET 5.1)–7.38, is concerned with various facets of the
building of the temple, roughly a third of the total textual space given over
to Solomon's reign (1 Kgs 3–11), let alone the dedication in the long ch. 8.
Chronicles pumps this up even further, with 2 Chron. 1.18 (ET 2.1)–4.22
devoted to temple construction, and then a further slab of text, three
chapters (2 Chron. 5–7), given over to the dedication of the temple. This is
not all, for further temple plans appear in Ezek. 40–48, and a good section
of Ezra and Nehemiah is given over to the story of the rebuilding of the
temple and then the city of Jerusalem itself. Various prophets (Haggai,
Isaiah, Jeremiah, Ezekiel) agonize over the temple, Psalms sings its praises
and hopes for the future rest there (the Maccabees). Finally, the only other
stretch of text with as much detail about the construction of a sanctuary is
of course that of the tabernacle. The detailed instructions of Yahweh,
down to the fineries of interior design, curtain material and clothes for the
priests, are passed on to Moses over 40 days and nights on Mt. Sinai itself
(Exod. 25–30), and then replicated in the description of its construction
(Exod. 35–40). This is no less a representation of space than the temple in
Jerusalem, and the two are linked through the wayward track of the ark of
the covenant, which makes its way finally into the temple in Jerusalem.

The fleeting description of Shiloh pales by comparison to the inordinate
attention given to temple and tabernacle. Boring stretches of text to be
sure, but interesting precisely because of their boredom and tedium,
particularly in terms of space. Let me return, however, to the tension I
noted earlier between the central sacred space of Jerusalem and its temple
that is so characteristic of the Asiatic mode of production. In the same way

that worshippers and their acts of worship flow to the temple, so also their tribute flows into the city and the ruling class that feeds on the surplus product extracted from the peasants. Should we read the narrative presence of alternative, submerged and repressed spaces as sites of resistance, as places where older types of space remain and also from where new possibilities might arise, especially if they are connected with patterns of bodies that we find there as well? On one level it seems as though this is indeed possible, but I want to make another point here: it is not so much that we should side with one or the other as a better space, but that the contradiction between the two is part of the very production of space for such a socio-economic system. That is, the centripetal site for sacred observance, with its temple and palace, the site for political and economic power that is simultaneously religious, cannot exist without the centrifugal spaces of alternative sites for worship, and so also political and economic activity. Jerusalem cannot exist without Shiloh, and vice versa, for this is the dialectical logic of such a production of space. It is therefore a mistake to argue for either the correctness of the henotheistic/monotheistic ideology of certain dimensions of the text or for the viability of wide-spread polytheism. Both exist within this particular mode of production as necessary counterparts to each other.

Thus far I have read 1 Sam. 1–2 at two levels—the immediate one of the story centred on Shiloh and then a larger one of the relation between Shiloh and comparable places with Jerusalem. But there is another, wider, level that reinforces my argument (but which cannot be argued at length here), for if we look at the larger context we find that for most of its existence Jerusalem found itself in tension with stronger imperial centres, whether of the Egyptians, Babylonians, Assyrians, Persians, Greeks or Romans. On this level, Jerusalem becomes an outside rim on a much vaster wheel, perpetually oscillating between subservience to larger imperial centres and limited independence. On this level too, then, the fundamental contradiction of the Asiatic mode of production cannot be avoided, namely, the centrifugal force of the periphery and the centripetal force of the centre. Such a pattern perpetually replicates itself on a range of scales.

Chapter 5

GEORG LUKÁCS: THE CONTRADICTORY WORLD OF KINGS

Apart from Ernst Bloch, and even he was undecided, Georg Lukács is the only Marxist who lived and worked for the bulk of his life (1885–1971) in places where the communist revolution had some permanence. He spent a good deal of his time, when not writing, either in revolutionary activity or cautiously resisting the damping of the revolutionary fire under Stalin. But it is his literary work that interests me most, and in what follows I will consider a specific contribution to genre in literary theory. A necessary selection for the work I want to do with Kings, it leaves out a whole delectable range in Lukács's thought—the interplay between analysis and evaluation, text and social situation, the commitment to historicism, the insistence on key historical moments for marking transitions, the focus on the traces of a socio-economic period emerging in the form of the literature it produced, as well as the function of an all-pervasive reification and class consciousness on literature and philosophy under capitalism.

As with many of the most influential thinkers of the era, he came from an upwardly mobile middle-class Jewish family that had assimilated into the high culture of central Europe, specifically Magyar Hungary. The contradiction of such a situation is that while it provided the socio-economic conditions that gave the opportunity for an extraordinary education and precocious children (mostly sons), it was precisely this socio-economic condition against which the offspring revolted. So it was that Lukács found his family's status intolerable from a very early age. This is not to say that Lukács did not make the most of the opportunity as a young man, travelling widely in Europe for cultural and literary reasons (to meet his hero, Henrik Ibsen, for instance). Prolific from adolescence, he continued to write through some of the most tumultuous times in Europe. Through the First World War, the revolutionary unrest throughout Europe in its aftermath, the Second World War, the Hungarian Revolution, communist activism, exile in Germany and then in Russia under Stalin's 'iron broom' years, Lukács trod a thin line between conformity to Stalinist orthodoxy and an uncompromising critical independence of thought.

Although highly critical of the middle-class culture of turn of the century and early twentieth century Europe, Lukács did not begin as a communist. His early leanings were to romanticism and the Enlightenment traditions of high liberalism, although he saw his own time as intolerably second rate. For a time, in his late teens and early twenties, he fancied himself a playwright, helped found the influential Thalia Theatre, but later, in characteristic fashion, he burned his plays. Even the celebrated *Theory of the Novel* (1971) was not Marxist, arguing for the basic urge of the novel as the desire to find home. Once he had made the decision to become Marxist, it was not one he went back on, and so he remained faithful to the cause for the rest of his life. Lukács's move to communism, as with any political or religious conversion, contains within it elements from his personal life and social and historical context in which he happened to exist and operate. Yet, in Lukács's case the decision was very much one made after careful reflection, a rational choice after all of the available options had been considered. Any of his moves after such a decision flowed logically from the initial move, for Lukács was not given to hypocrisy or double-thinking. In this respect he is a profoundly appealing figure.

As with my use of the other Marxist critics in this book, my interest in Lukács is quite specific, focusing on his discussion of genre in *The Historical Novel* (1983) and *Theory of the Novel*. In these works he offers a highly dialectical argument: the form of the novel, as an abstract effort at totality in the context of a world in which integration and totality had gone (abandonment by God), is both only possible in such a context and shows the tensions of such a situation in the very form of the work itself. That is, genre is not merely a conflation of genres, but the effort to resolve certain historical, social and economic tensions that enable it. Similarly with the historical novel, the genre itself arose at a determinate historical moment, before the revolutions of 1848, when the genre itself provided the means of a distinct historical consciousness, a necessary connection with the past, as a way of understanding the present. The historical novel lost its way when the bourgeoisie began to forget its origins and the relationship to the past became arbitrary.

Subsequently, I will offer a reading of the tension between prophetic and royal narratives in 1 and 2 Kings. The analysis begins with Lukács' dialectical theory of genre, tracing the tensions in these narratives between the prophetic material that dominates in 1 Kgs 17–2 Kgs 9.10 and the narratives about kings that dominate the remaining material. For the books of Kings sit uneasily between being 'historical books' in critical scholarship, or as part of the 'prophets' in the Jewish canon. In doing so I will be on the lookout for what Lukács calls the 'historico-philosophical' feature or moment, the determinate ideological element that is peculiar to this genre. My concern in this essay is deductive rather than inductive, that is to say, I am concerned with the whole of the book of Kings rather than a particular text that acts a microcosm of the book as a whole.

Let me begin with the earlier work, *Theory of the Novel* (Lukács 1971). The primary tension, here identified in cultural terms, of the novel, is 'of a world that has been abandoned by God' (1971: 88). Of all the other passings and losses the novel laments—youth, an 'inner voice', home— the loss of faith or abandonment by God is the one that binds the others together. The natural response, for Lukács, is the deep desire to find home, or, as he puts it, the longing of the soul for home. Yet in The *Theory of the Novel* this is a belated point, coming a little after half-way in the book.

But what does it mean for apostasy to provide the conditions of the novel? Is it apostasy—the turning away from God, a loss of faith—or God's abandonment? Lukács speaks of both. On the one hand, the novel signals a loss of the voice 'that will clearly tell us our way and determine our goal' (1971: 86). The heroes of youth, the gods, have gone. Lukács uses the trope of adult life, with all the melancholy of passing youth and maturity, to speak of the context of the novel.

Already in this supposedly pre-Marxist study, he makes the characteristic dialectical move of his later work in comparing different genres in order to bring out the features of the item under discussion. While in *The Historical Novel* the comparison will be between the historical novel and historical drama, in *Theory of the Novel* it is between tragedy, epic and the novel. Further, he seeks the 'historico-philosophical moment at which great novels become possible' (1971: 88) in a way that is similar to the social and historical conditions, now with a distinctly Marxist angle, for the rise, moment of greatness and decline of the historical novel. In both cases, the conditions provide both the limits and possibilities.

As far as the novel is concerned, the abandonment by God in the world that provides the possibility of the novel shows through in the novel itself; there is also discreteness and the separation between interiority and adventure. The passage from tragedy to the novel is also the passage from destiny to adventure, from exteriority (soul and world are one) to interiority (soul and world are antagonistic). The epic also does not know of adventure: the hero knows he will pass through the tests put in his way. In his attempt to provide a typology of the novel, Lukács traces two types of the incommensurability that God's abandonment produces, between soul and work and between interiority and adventure: the soul of the hero can be narrower or smaller than the outside world that is its scene of action (his example is Don Quixote); or it is wider and larger than what life can offer (the romanticism of disillusionment of Flaubert's *L'education sentimentale* or Balzac's *Comedie humaine*).

Interiority, adventure and discreteness—these items appear along with divine abandonment as necessary features of the novel. Along with these items is a particular psychological makeup of the hero that Lukács characterizes as demonic, the mark of God's absence:

> Biological and sociological life has a profound tendency to remain within its own immanence; men want only to live, structures want to remain intact; and because of the remoteness, the absence of an effective God, the indolent self-complacency of this quietly decaying life would be the only power in the world if men did not sometimes fall prey to the power of the demon and overreach themselves in ways that have no reason and cannot be explained by reason, challenging all the psychological or sociological foundations of their existence (1971: 90).

At this point, the world's God-forsakenness becomes insubstantial and the world crumbles away to show 'a glass wall against which men beat in vain, like bees against a window, incapable of breaking through, incapable of understanding that the way is barred' (1971: 90).

All of which results in irony, the refusal to depict anything more than the way the 'demons' operate in the novel. Yet irony is also a result of abandonment by God: by means of the very avoidance of knowledge or its desire one can in fact glimpse the God who no longer exists. For Lukács, irony is the mark of the novelist's freedom 'in his relationship to God' (1971: 92). In contrast to the mystic, whose freedom is predicated on complete dissolution into God, the novel's hero finds freedom in a world 'whose ruler he has become because of his fall' (1971: 91). The paradox here is that precisely in the historico-philosophical context of God's abandonment of the world, the hero's actions and ethics assume God's existence and redemption. It is only through irony that such a paradox can be resolved, only when the novel achieves a perfect form, since only in such a form 'God himself becomes the substratum of form-giving, homogeneous with and equivalent to all the other normatively given elements of form, and is completely embraced by its categories' (1971: 91). Thus, precisely when the historico-philosophical context witnesses God's departure does it become possible to subsume God into the 'material authenticity' of a form, and this is what the novel achieves. Or, in philosophical terms, this technical immanence in the form of the novel is only possible in a proper relationship with transcendence; conversely, the transcendental possibility of the novel's form can only happen through the immanence of the novel itself.

So it is only irony, the mark of a novel at the height of its aesthetic possibilities, that can achieve this dialectic of transcendence and immanence: 'irony, with intuitive double vision, can see where God is to be found in a world abandoned by God' (1971: 92). A series of contradictory possibilities flow from this: the glimpse of home and the realization of its subjective and psychological conditioning; itself demonic, irony perceives the demon within; it seeks a world within only never to find it; and irony expresses both God's disdain for weak human rebellion and the suffering of God's inability to redeem the world. In the end, irony is

> not only the sole possible a priori condition for a true, totality-creating objectivity but also why it makes that totality—the novel—the representative art-form of our age: because the structural categories of the novel constitutively coincide with the world as it is today (1971: 93).

All of these tensions and the effort of the novel to overcome them appear not merely in its relation to the world, but also in its inner form. The traces of the attempted resolution that continually abolishes itself appear in the attempt to provide a distinct unity or totality in the context of a world that is no longer integrated. And yet such a totality can only be abstract, a system that resists aesthetic form-giving:

> Thus the elements of the novel are, in the Hegelian sense, entirely abstract; abstract, the nostalgia of the characters for utopian perfection, a nostalgia that feels itself and its desires to be the only true reality; abstract, the experience of social structures based only upon their factual presence and their sheer ability to continue; abstract, finally, the form-giving intention which, instead of surmounting the distance between these two abstract groups of elements, allows it to subsist, which does not even attempt to surmount it but renders it sensuous as the lived experience of the novel's characters, uses it as a means of connecting the two groups and so turns it into an instrument of composition (1971: 70-71).

This means that the novel's content, the focus on a biographical individual, becomes the means of attempting the abstract totality. Lukács is here already operating with dialectical categories, for it is only in the context of a disintegrated world, one in which totality is no longer possible, that the novel can attempt such a thing; and yet it is doomed to do so only in abstract form precisely because of this context. And it is this effort, the effort to resolve a contradiction, that gives rise to irony.

This particular argument, which is part of his effort to understand the form of the novel in what he calls its historico-philosophical context, is the conclusion to a much longer discussion that I do not want to spend too much time over. The sweeping question he seeks to address is the contrast between integrated and problematic civilizations and the resultant forms of literature. It turns out that his discussion of ancient Greece, so vastly different from 'our' world in its integration between world and soul, is but a way of characterizing through contrast the context of the novel itself. The polemic here is against the Greeks as the fount of Western society and culture, precursors to modern concerns and preoccupations. Lukács plays heavily on the sheer difference of the Greeks. From this context emerges epic and tragic literature, which become the subject of detailed comparisons with the novel: tragedy survives, but the epic had to give way to the novel in a different historico-philosophical context, the one thinking in terms of totality in an age where totality had become a problem, the other in a world where it was no longer possible to think in terms of totality at all.

If the Greek world collapsed, then Christianity was able to provide an alternative integrated civilization more complete than the one it surpassed:

> the world became round once more, a totality capable of being taken in at a glance; the chasm lost the threat inherent in its actual depth; its whole darkness, without forfeiting any of its sombrely gleaming power, became pure surface and could thus be fitted easily into a closed unity of colours; the cry for redemption became a dissonance in the perfect rhythmic system of the world and thereby rendered possible a new equilibrium no less perfect than that of the Greeks (1971: 37-38).

But this for Lukács is also the last unity; once it was gone, only a disintegrated world would be possible. It is from here that he describes the context of the novel as a world forsaken by God.

Lukács would later, in the preface to a reprint of *Theory of the Novel*, criticize the lack of historical specificity, particularly in Marxist terms, of his argument. Yet his method of literary criticism, however refined, retained its concern with form, particularly that of genre, and the historical and philosophical tensions that gave rise to the particular form in question.

In many respects *The Historical Novel* (Lukács 1983) is the Marxist answer to the still idealistically tainted approach of the earlier work. And the value of that Marxism is that it enables Lukács to connect literature with its social and historical ground in a systematic and sophisticated fashion.

The form of the historical novel marks, for Lukács, a new consciousness of history: '[W]hat I had in mind was a theoretical examination of the interaction between the historical spirit and the great genres of literature which portray the totality of history...' (1983: 13), or, as Elisabeth Wesseling puts it, the historical novel 'strategically combined novelistic means with historical materials in order to do something for the disclosure of the past which the historian could not do' (Wesseling 1991: 32). Lukács's great model was Walter Scott's first *Waverley* novel, whose major features he identified as follows. First, the colourful and varied yet artistically faithful and specific description of the historical period in question, often placed in the mouths of characters, so that readers were put in touch with the 'inner life of an age' (Lukács 1983: 50) not possible in other forms of literature.

Secondly, the depiction of character in relation to its social ground, especially the 'mediocre' hero—the most well-known item of Lukács analysis. In one respect there is a follow-on from *Theory of the Novel*, where the problematic individual, drawn from everyday life, is the element that gives the novel a false sense of cohesion in a disintegrating world. For Lukács the main characters of the historical novel were 'mediocre', 'passive', or 'wavering', who became unwittingly involved in political events beyond their comprehension. The strength of Scott's characters lay in their populist and collective nature, appealing to readers who could more easily identify with such heroes than 'great men' themselves. The mediocre hero, by maintaining contact between the common people and the 'great men', who appear only obliquely, allows Scott to portray the reactions of people in different classes to the major events of history that form the historical context of the novel. The characterization of Scott's historical novels provides for Lukács a signal of the treatment of history itself. The ability of the mediocre hero to pass back and forth between 'history' and everyday life indicates a shift in the experience of history, and thus of the rise of historical consciousness. History becomes, as a result of the great upheavals in Europe from 1789 (French Revolution) to 1814, 'a mass experience and moreover on a European scale' (1983: 23)— marked by the new citizen and mass army that generates feelings of national identity in its own people.

Yet each item on its own—realistic historical context and mediocre hero—does not comprise a historical novel, for it was their combination that constitutes the new genre: 'What is lacking in the so-called historical novel before Sir Walter Scott is precisely the specifically historical, that is, derivation of the individuality of characters from the historical peculiarity of their age' (1983: 19). Closely related to these combined elements is Lukács's argument that historical novels were able to depict social collisions and raise issues about periods of revolutionary upheaval, such as the French Revolution, the Jacobin rebellion in Scotland (*Waverley*) and the conflict between Normans and Saxons (*Ivanhoe*). The key issue here is that the form and the content of the historical novel respond to and represent the profound tensions of the revolutions of the late eighteenth and nineteenth centuries, revolutions that were themselves a mark of the transition from feudalism to capitalism. Lukács sees the depiction of this gradual and painful transition in Scott's work.

I will tarry a little with the question of social conflict, for it is to this situation that the genre itself functions as a response. For Lukács, Scott's genius is not that he describes the 'great monumental dramas of world history', but that, following a 'law of literary portrayal which first appears paradoxical' (1983: 42), it is the small everyday events and interactions that register the larger historical and political events far more effectively, even if they are never mentioned directly. A second dialectical feature of Scott's work is that his conservative politics, like Balzac, enabled him to perceive and represent, however unwittingly, the vast transformations at all levels of society in the slow change of mode of production from feudalism to capitalism. Critical of capitalism, he sympathized with those who took on the brunt of the changes, although in the end he sought a middling solution that sought to reconcile warring opposites. There is, thirdly, the dialectic of what Lukács calls 'historicism' or 'historical fidelity':

> the writer's historical fidelity consists in the faithful artistic reproduction of the great collisions, the great crises and turning-points of history. To express this *historical* conception in an adequate artistic form the writer may treat individual facts with as much licence as he likes, for mere fidelity to the individual facts of history without this connection is utterly valueless (1983: 166).

Finally, there is what he calls the non-simultaneity of the simultaneous (*die Ungleichzeitigkeit des Gleichzeitigen*), the bringing together of incompatible social and economic formations in a 'dramatic concentration and intensification of events' (1983: 41). Scott and other practitioners of the historical novel after him bring together and concentrate in their novels conflicts that took place over a greater period of time, intensifying those conflicts themselves. This is a distinctly Marxist element of his work, for the transformation of society through the clash of economic systems is a fundamental motif of the best of Marxist literary analysis. For Lukács of course this was the painful process of the transition from a declining feudal order and an emergent capitalist one. For my reading of Kings, the dialectical features of Lukács's understanding of Scott's treatment of history are crucial. In the text of Kings it is virtually impossible to make any statements about the historical background with any certainty. However, the whole question of social collisions and their function in Scott's work indicates that any adequate concern with history must trace the development, changes and shifts in modes of production. This, it seems to me, is far more workable notion of history than that which still prevails in biblical studies—concern with the particular items of history, such as the dates of documents or rulers, the establishment of time lines and so on.

In the end, Lukács's argument is similar to that of *Theory of the Novel*, except that now the historico-philosophical feature of the historical novel is not the God-forsakenness of the world but the development of historical consciousness. For Lukács the historical novel is possible only with the rise of the consciousness of a new perception of the relation between human beings and historical time. In contrast to antiquarianism, as well as the historiographical forms of the chronicle and the annal, Scott expresses the difference between the new perceptions of time and history compared to those perceptions that had gone before; the difference lay in the awareness of a vast gulf between the society of nineteenth-century Europe and those that preceded it. But Lukács is a Marxist, and so he identifies the cause of that change in the bourgeois revolution, a mixture of sudden events (1789 in France) and gradual change, as in England, with its smaller breaks and ceaseless class struggle. It was the constant presence of that process of change that produced a distinct historical consciousness.

Lukács is also interested in the historical development of a genre itself, and so he traces the decline of the historical novel in terms of a loss of the specific necessity of the historical period it treats to the present. The historical periods reconstructed in historical novels were not mere backgrounds or settings for dealings with current issues; they were intrinsic to the genre itself: 'the past portrayed is clearly recognized and experienced by contemporary writers as the *necessary prehistory* of the present' (1983: 61). There is what he calls a 'necessary anachronism', a process of simultaneously enhancing and clarifying aspects of the historical recon-struction and the characters' responses. However, with the decline of the historical novel, this necessary anachronism fades away and the historical reconstructions become mere backgrounds for contemporary questions. This is what he calls a process of archaeologizing and modernizing: a greater concern with the details of history produces a setting for thoroughly modern characters and their problems. The historical novel becomes a 'parable of the present' (1983: 338).

The reason for such a decline comes from the shift from feudalism to capitalism: by the revolutions of 1848 a significant shift took place—the new bourgeoisie became the dominant social formation, crushing the new class that emerged from capitalism as well, the working class—that affected the historical sense of bourgeoisie's own emergence. In an effort to gain ideological dominance over the working classes, with whom they were in armed conflict for the first time, the bourgeoisie began to forget its own historical emergence. Thus the claims began that the central bour-geois principles—private property, the private individual, the profit motive, competition—are part of human nature, that they existed since the first human beings. In other words, bourgeois capitalism must be the final realization of the most fundamental of human desires and characteristics. The emergence of the bourgeoisie becomes one grand myth based on class amnesia. Thus, after 1848 the specificity of the historical period recreated in the historical novel ceases to be an issue, since the pressing need to focus on one period over against another has dissipated. History becomes an elaborate decoration for eternal human problems and concerns.

Despite the distinction Lukács himself liked to make between the pre-Marxist *Theory of the Novel* and his Marxist *The Historical Novel*, the continuities are significant. Their basic argument is that genre functions as a specific ideological response to a historical situation in all sorts of contradictory and complex ways. What, then, can I draw from Lukács in my reading of Kings? The most obvious point is a dialectical concern with genre, in terms of the complex ways in which genre functions in relation to other genres and to its historical context. However, I will not be able to apply Lukács's method directly, for the historical context remains opaque at the more detailed level at which he works. What I will do, initially here and then more fully in the conclusion to this book, is focus on his interest in the larger question of mode of production, for my discussion of Kings may be regarded as one item in tracing out the ideological features of the cultural dominant of the mode of production in question. The whole notion of mode of production involves a complex and overlapping periodization of political economic eras, but the distinct value of such a concern in literary and cultural studies is that it avoids the tendency to treat questions of genre, along with other literary questions, purely in terms of themselves and their own literary history in isolation from the political economic context without which they cannot be understood. 'In such an inquiry it is obvious that even the inner, most theoretical, most abstract dialectic of the problem will have an historical character' (Jameson 1983: 13). Or, in Lukács words, 'This work is intended to show how the historical novel in its origin, development, rise and decline follows inevitably upon the great social transformations of modern times...' (1983: 17).

I will therefore need to give detailed attention to the features that are characteristic of the genre of Kings. The problem with the study of genre in the Bible is that so often the pool of examples is painfully small, so that it becomes difficult to speak of genre. In the case of Kings, there are a couple of other texts that fall into a similar genre, namely, Chronicles, Ezra–Nehemiah, Samuel and possibly Joshua and Judges. For the sake of my discussion, I will take these as sufficient to form a small collection that enables a genre identification to take place. What interests me with Kings is the way it enacts its own transformations of the genres in question.

Generic Tension

In the same way that Lukács focuses on particular aspects of the novel—biographical form, characterization of the hero, means of representation, irony, intention, the demonic, totality and contingency—or the historical novel—mode of historical representation, character, social conflict and its decline in archaeologizing and modernizing—so also I will give attention to the specific features of Kings in order to ask about what Lukács calls its historico-philosophical context.

The notable feature of Kings is the conflation of prophetic cycles and royal narratives, or even chronicles. In this respect it intersects not only with other works, such as Chronicles and Samuel, but also the prophetic works of Isaiah, Jeremiah, Ezekial and the Book of the Twelve. Thus, the designation 'history' (Long 1984: 7-8) hardly does justice to the presence of the generic connections with the prophetic books. In a broader perspective, 1 Kgs 1–16 and 2 Kgs 10–25 are primarily narratives concerning kings, whereas 1 Kgs 17–2 Kgs 9 focuses on prophets, specifically Elijah and Elisha. At the level of content, the arbitrary division between Samuel and Kings conceals the fact that royal narratives have been part of the books of Samuel since at least the appearance of David in 1 Samuel 16, if not Saul in 1 Sam. 9 and the request by the people for a king in 1 Samuel 15. Further, the splicing of prophets and kings runs throughout Kings itself, although not in the vast servings that I noted above. In the main royal narratives, prophetic stories appear at 1 Kgs 1.8, 10-14, 22-27, 32-40, 44 (Nathan); 11.29-39 (Ahijah the Shilonite); 13.1-34 (the man of God and the old prophet of Bethel); 14.1-16 (Ahijah the prophet); 2 Kgs 19.1-7, 19-34; 20.1-11, 14-19 (Isaiah the son of Amoz); 21.10-15 (Yahweh's servants the prophets); 22.14-20 (Huldah the prophetess); 23.15-18 (the man of God from Judah). Apart from 1 Kgs 13 and 2 Kgs 23.15-18, which I have suggested elsewhere functions as a 'national allegory' (Boer 1996), each of these appearances of the prophets is for the purpose of delivering an oracle concerning a king; that is, the focus is on a particular king or kings.

Whereas in the prophetic cycles—and I am using source critical terminology quite deliberately—the oracles at times concern kings, especially Ahaz (Elijah), and Amaziah, Jehoshaphat, Jehoram, Jehu and Ahaziah (Elisha), by and large the stories concern the prophets themselves in a range of activities in which kings are often absent. By 2 Kgs 10 the royal narratives return, although Elisha has one last gasp in 2 Kgs 13.14-21. The prophetic and royal narratives, then, are spliced closely together in Kings, so much so that the precise generic identification of this text remains problematic: for the Jewish canon it is part of the 'former prophets', whereas in critical Christian scholarship it is one of the 'historical books'.

Until now I have remained at the level of content, a curious way to proceed in the question of genre, whose primary determinant is always form. The distinct formal feature of what I have called the royal narratives is the regular pattern for both the kings of Israel and Judah, especially with the divided kingdoms, of longer or shorter accounts of the reigns of various kings encased by the regular rhythm of formulae that mark the beginning and end of each reign. There is often a tension between these chronicle-like formulae and the stories they contain, as well as variations in the formulae themselves that I have dealt with in detail in my *Jameson and Jeroboam* (1996), but I want to stress that this regular pattern of regnal formulae and narratives is the major formal feature of 1 Kgs 1–16 and 2 Kgs 10–25.

The first of the formulae appear not with Saul but David (1 Kgs 2.10-12)—a marker of Kings as a text distinct from Samuel—and the last of the formulae for Mattaniah/Zedekiah in 2 Kgs 24.18-20, even though he was appointed by the Babylonian king. Gedaliah the governor is no king at this formal level, for he has no standard formula and flees to Egypt (2 Kgs 25.22-26). He disappears from the narrative, whereas Jehoiachin, who begins his reign with a formula (2 Kgs 24.8-9), has no closing formula, the book ending with his release from prison, in Babylon, a food allowance and status above the other exiled kings in Babylon.

This formal feature—of formula and royal story—also creeps into the prophetic cycles of Elijah and Elisha. Thus, the long narrative of Ahab is encased by formulae in 1 Kgs 16.29-34 (a much lengthier version that presages the narrative stretch to come) and 22.37-40. A cluster of formulae appear for Jehoshaphat (Judah) and Ahaziah (Israel) in 1 Kgs 22.41-46 and vv. 51-3. A few more follow: 2 Kgs 2.17-18 (Ahaziah and Jehoram); 2 Kgs 3.1-3 (Jehoram of Israel); 2 Kgs 8.16-19 (Jehoram of Judah), 8.25-27 and 9.29 (Ahaziah of Judah). At this level, it may indeed be argued that the prophetic narratives are stretched-out versions of the stories encased by the formulae elsewhere in Kings, and in the prophetic cycles we do indeed find another level of complex splicing. However, although at times the distance between formulae rivals that of Solomon (1 Kgs 2.10-12–11.42-43), particularly with Ahab (1 Kgs 16.29-34–22.37-40) and Jehoram of Israel (2 Kgs 3.1-3–8.25), there are some notable differences.

First, the various stories over the long run of Ahab's reign contain accounts in which Ahab disappears entirely from the scene and Elijah himself comes to the fore, such as the widow of Zarephath (1 Kgs 17.8-24), the contest on Carmel (ch. 18), the retreat to the wilderness (ch. 19) and so on. In the second section during Jehoram's reign the stories again, now with Elisha as subject, spin away from Jehoram to include material like the Shunnamite woman (2 Kgs 4) and Naaman the Syrian (1 Kgs 5).

Further, even the regnal formulae buckle under the pressure of the string of prophetic tales, so much so that they descend into virtual nonsense by 2 Kgs 8.16-19, where Jehoram morphs into Joram, and Jehoshaphat, at least in the MT, becomes king all over again with a second formula to kick off a reign that had already been well under way by 1 Kgs 22.41-44.

Finally, the prophetic stories have a curious knack of bringing the kings of Israel and Judah together. Jehoshaphat and the 'king of Israel', belatedly identified as Ahab only in the closing formula of his reign in 1 Kgs 22.39, come together against the Syrians in 1 Kgs 22.1-26. Jehoshaphat and Jehoram fight together against the Moabites in 2 Kgs 3.1-27, and the distinction between Jehoram/Joram, son of Ahab and king of Israel and

Jehoram/Joram, king of Judah, blurs (2 Kgs 8.16-29)—hence the old theories of a united kingdom under one king.

I have spent some time on the various features of the regnal and prophetic sections of Kings, since it seems to me that, following the emphasis of Lukács's own analyses of genre, we have in Kings a generic item that can only exist in a profound dialectic tension between the two genres of what might tentatively be termed historical narrative and prophetic texts. However, instead of Lukács's characteristic move of comparing the genre in question with another—tragedy and epic in *Theory of the Novel* and historical drama in *The Historical Novel*—we have in Kings a generic tension within the text itself. One way of proceeding would be to compare Kings with either the prophetic texts of Jeremiah, Isaiah, Ezekiel and the Twelve on the one hand, or with the contradictory theocratic 'history' of Chronicles on the other. However, I want to focus on the tension within Kings, drawing out the features of the tension in an effort to outline what this curious text that is Kings might be. And the features that point towards the ideological function of Kings include: narrative rhythm or time, the question of life and death, the function of Yahweh and of character as such, and the 'historico-philosophical' moment of Kings.

By narrative rhythm or time I refer to an aspect I have already noted: the stretching effect that the appearances of Elijah and Elisha have on the reigns of the kings in question. Both Ahab and Jehoram, kings of Israel of the same house, have reigns that are Solomonic in textual space. It is as though their reigns are suspended, thinned out while six chapters pass, for each of them, chapters crammed with one magical story after another concerning these two synonymous prophets. It is almost as though the regnal material, particularly the formulae, falls over itself to catch up when the time for Elisha to succeed Elijah draws near, a staccato of formulae at the close of 1 Kings.

Yet this is precisely the contrast, for the kings of Israel and Judah before and after this middle slab of prophetic text follow each other in condemned succession at a regular beat. At times cryptic, at others less so, but without fail one dies and another follows. Only Solomon has a comparable, if not longer, suspension of the death notice—one argument perhaps for a narrative break at the beginning of the divided kingdoms (see Jobling, forthcoming). Solomon's story reads like a temporal pause before the beat of the text falls into its regnal rhythm.

The dialectical point here is not merely that the length of the prophetic narratives, that is, those concerning individual prophets, shows up the brevity of those of the kings: rather, a deeper ideological tension lurks in the text. The houses of Israel and Judah, or at least that of Judah, for all the condemnation that everyone apart from Hezekiah and Josiah receive, are ones that are supposed to be eternal. The promise to David is that there will never be a king lacking from the throne, that the throne of his kingdom will be established forever (2 Sam. 7.13-15). The well-known tension between this and the so-called conditional covenant that Solomon receives (1 Kgs 9.4-8) manifests itself, I would suggest, in the rapid turnover of damned kings. The rhythmic rapidity with which the kings keel over in disgrace puts immense pressure on the promise of perpetuity. Further, one function of Elijah and Elisha in the structure of the text is to provide examples of that which the kings should have been but are not. The two prophets are, in other words, the true successors of Solomon purely in terms of the temporal pattern and narrative content, highlighting the tension between the promise of eternity and the rapidity with which the individual kings fall short.

I have disciplined myself to what I have called narrative rhythm, a musical allusion that draws attention to what might otherwise be called textual fill, or the physical arrangement of the text that determines how long it takes a reader to cover certain sections of the text. A second feature of Kings, closely related to this first one, is the issue of life and death—precisely the sort of item on which Lukács focuses. When we peer more attentively at the prophetic cycles of 1 Kgs 17–2 Kgs 9, accustomed to the regular pattern by which kings come to the throne and then die, what stands out is that the prophets themselves do not die.

Thus, in the drawn-out process of the succession of Elisha from Elijah it turns out that Elijah does not die. As the narrative pushes towards the isolation and difficulty of Elijah's death, it is overloaded with signals that negate death. Elisha says, after Elijah's third effort to leave him behind, 'As Yahweh lives [חי] and as you yourself [נפש] live [חי], I will not leave you' (2 Kgs 2.6). In the oath formula, Elisha swears he will stay, but it is the elision of Yahweh's 'living' and that of Elijah's *nephesh* that hints at what will happen to Elijah. And the threefold 'tarry here' that leads up to this declaration, when Elijah attempts to drop Elisha off on the way, has the undercurrent of a refusal of death: just as Elisha refuses to 'tarry' (שב), so also Elijah himself will not remain in death. (The more obvious meaning here is that Elisha should stay behind, in this life, with the prophets, and not follow him in his own path.) The heavy symbolism of the parting of the water of the Jordan with Elijah's mantle, with all of its Mosiac

echoes, links birth and death, amniotic fluid and the male act of pene-
tration. Then the mythical language of vv. 11-12 signals Elijah's transport
beyond death. Not only does he move on rather than die, but he lives on in
Elisha, who now takes his mantle and repeats the water trick to return
from the liminal space of death. And Elijah returns for Elisha in the image
of the horses and chariots of fire that defeat the Syrians (2 Kgs 6.15-19).

But then Elijah's sidestepping of death is well known, along with that of
Enoch and Moses. I will consider in a moment other aspects of the prophetic cycles that point away from death, but less observed is the way
Elisha also avoids death. Well after the end of the narrative concerning
Elisha himself at the close of 2 Kgs 9 comes the afterthought of the
narrative of his death (2 Kgs 13.14-21). It begins with the notice, 'And
Elisha was ill with the illness with which he was to die' (2 Kgs 13.14). It
goes on to speak of Joash's lament that echoes with its 'chariots of Israel
and its horsemen' both Elijah's step beyond death (2 Kgs 2.12) and the
continued presence of Elijah with Elisha (2 Kgs 6.17). Is Elisha to repeat
Elijah's death-defying stunt? Not quite. Rather, this death too is not to be
of the usual sort. In his apparent death he offers Joash a prophecy of
partial victory over Syria, but the sign itself is mixed. The arrow shot out
the window signals Joash's victory, but his striking of the ground only
three times with the arrows (the ones remaining?) points to a limited victory. Yet there is also another arrow that Joash shoots out of the window to
the east. Is this also a reference to Joash's victory (Syria lies to the north),
or perhaps the direction of Elisha's own death. For in the following verses,
we have the curious account of his burial. In the context of bands of
Moabites entering the land in the comng of the year an unidentified man is
also buried:

> And it happened that they were burying a man, and behold, they saw the
> band and they cast the man into the grave of Elisha. And the man went and
> touched the bones of Elisha and he came to life and stood upon his feet
> (2 Kgs 13.20-1, my translation).

Apart from the dark comical image of a burial being interrupted mid-
stride, the pall-bearers unceremoniously dumping the body in the nearest
grave in order to race off and stop these damned Moabites, I want to know
why Elisha's grave is still open. Is this event meant to take place at the
moment of Elisha's burial? The waw consecutive form 'and they buried
him' (2 Kgs 13.20) for Elisha's burial suggests not, for Elisha is well and
truly buried before this indeterminate little account. Who is the unidentified man (שׁיא)? Elisha? The narrative distinguishes between them but then

hints otherwise. And it does so through the ambiguity of the subject of the verbs, 'and he came to life and stood on his feet' (2 Kgs 12.21). It is unclear whether the subject is 'the man' who appears twice as subject of earlier verbs, or Elisha, whose name comes immediately before 'and he came to life and stood upon his feet'. We do not need to decide either way, for both possibilities point towards Elisha's continued existence in weaker and stronger forms: his bones have revivifying or even resurrecting power *and* it is Elisha himself who stands on his own feet, alive again.

So, neither Elijah nor Elisha die in these stories, at least in the sense of the kings who die all too regularly and are buried, mostly, with their fathers. Yet the story of Elisha's continued power and life is not the only occurrence of revivification. Both Elijah and Elisha in closely parallelled stories bring a woman's son back to life (1 Kgs 17.8-24; 2 Kgs 4.11-37), apart from a whole series of comparable accounts: rain on a dry earth (1 Kgs 18.45); fire from stone (1 Kgs 18.38); turning bad water into good (2 Kgs 2.19-22); the continuous flow of oil from the widow's jars (2 Kgs 4.1-7); the bad pottage (2 Kgs 4.38-41); the endless barley (2 Kgs 4.42-44); and the raised axe-head (2 Kgs 6.1-7). All of this suggests that the stories of Elijah and Elisha may be read as one continuous narrative concerning the same prophet, for Elisha bears Elijah's mantle and his *nephesh* that lives like Yahweh.

However, while the prophets never keel over themselves, and while they are busy bringing all sorts of things to life, they also deal in death. By now their targets should not be hard to guess: the kings. They prophesy and bring about death in all manner of gory variations, especially with Ahab and Jezebel, Ahaziah and Jehu, who wipes out the house of Ahab at prophetic command over two blood-stained chapters.

Alongside narrative rhythm and the question of life and death, a third, typically Lukácsian, concern is that of character, although with a distinctly Hegelian–Marxist dialectical turn. In both *Theory of the Novel* and *The Historical Novel* Lukács identifies the middling or average hero over against the world-historical individual. In the former work such a hero provides the cohesion for a disintegrating world, whereas in the latter text this middling hero provides the mediation between the great events, everyday life and the readers. It is hardly possible to apply this directly to Kings, for in this text the major character types are all the male kings and the prophets, whose dominance in the text is enhanced by the troubling presence of Jezebel, Athaliah, Huldah, Rehoboam's wife, the widow of Zarephath, the Shunammite woman and others. But there is a third dominant character central to the whole text, namely, Yahweh.

However, I have already written of character—at least a particular aspect of it—in my discussion of life and death. The tensions I noted there carry through to the wider questions of character. Over against the magical and all-powerful prophets Elijah and Elisha, whose feats range from raising the dead to life and calling down bears on little boys, from standing up to kings on pain of death to raising axe-heads, come the relatively ordinary and flawed kings who are rarely able to do a thing right. In respect of this contrast, I want to pick up a general theme of Kings concerning which I have written before (Boer 1996: 155-58): the tension that Yairah Amit has described as a 'dual causality', divided between divine and human characters (Amit 1987), such as are found in the stories of Joseph in Genesis, Ehud in Judges and Solomon's succession in Kings. In my earlier analysis I argued that 1 Kgs 12 operates with such a dual scheme. The narrative of the break-up of the kingdom by Rehoboam and Jeroboam proceeds according to the closed world of human interaction. Thus, the request of the people for an alleviation of Solomon's burdensome requirements meets with a declaration of even harsher measures by Rehoboam. In reply the people, under the leadership of Jeroboam, declare their independence from Rehoboam. But just when the story builds up a picture of human interaction and causality—king, people, older and younger advisers—the text slips in the deflating phrase 'for it was a turn of affairs brought about by Yahweh' (1 Kgs 12.15). The introspective section that follows (1 Kgs 12.25-33) works on a similar tack, focusing on the introspective Jeroboam and his decision to set up golden calves for worship at Bethel and Dan, only to become the key narrative of the 'sins of Jeroboam' (see 1 Kgs 12.30). In what I termed with a deliberate anachronism the 'historical determinism' of Kings, I argued that the at times covert and at others more overt control of events by Yahweh generates a distinct ideological contradiction in Kings.

David Jobling's point—that this in fact describes a good deal of the Hebrew Bible, over against Amit's pseudo-historical effort to argue for an increased 'secularization' and its effects on Israelite literature (see Jobling 1989)—assists my argument. For if we focus on the question of character, the tension between divine and human 'causality' applies to the regnal narratives throughout the book of Kings, most clearly in the tension between the regnal formulae where Yahweh's approval and disapproval is more overt and the narratives encased by the formulae. By contrast, the prophets face none of this tension, being in constant communication with a Yahweh who spends little time behind the scenes. In fact, it precisely the prophets who bring the element of divine 'causality' squarely into the world of the kings.

The tension between human initiative and control by Yahweh is the constitutive factor in the characterization of the kings, for it renders them desultory and error-ridden, given to actions that attract Yahweh's condemnation, even though Yahweh apparently controls all narrative events, including the kings' actions that bring about Yahweh's disapproval. The contrast between these characters and the prophets couldn't be sharper: there is none of the tension that comes through with the kings. The prophets are completely under Yahweh's direction, so much so that they manifest a curious array of divine powers, ranging from major collective events with profound religious import to ridiculous and trivial magical tricks. If Yahweh is more surreptitious in regard to the kings, then he swamps the narratives of the prophets. They become superhuman beings, at odds with the characters they encounter, especially the kings, but even with the cluster of 'sons of the prophets' that is omnipresent in the prophetic cycles. But this is a feature of the characterization of the prophets in the books of Isaiah, Jeremiah, Ezekiel and the Twelve, for their prime conversation partner is Yahweh. More often they function as his assorted mouthpieces, spouting forth his words but also following his directives. Despite the protestations of the commissioning narratives, the prophets are without sin. In the prophetic books and in Kings they are not condemned for disobedience to Yahweh. The so-called 'false prophets' provide the counter-point that reinforces the sinlessness of the sanctioned prophets. The false prophets, such as those in 1 Kgs 22.1-28, are those 'other' prophets against whom the prophets themselves rail but who also provide the foil for their own sinless piety.

This feature of prophetic characterization—found also in the prophetic books—is so distinct from the kings who are full of sin and waywardness that it becomes one of the deepest contrasts in characterization in the text of Kings, which is starting to look more and more like a generic mix. But there is another character—Yahweh—who constitutes the major effort to resolve this contradiction at the same time that his own character bears all the marks of the contradiction itself. Yahweh is a unique character: there is only one of him and he dominates the others, retiring during the regnal formulae only to emerge at various points to guide events or pass judgement, either in the mouths of the prophets or in the narrator's own voice, particularly in the formulae. And he is all over the place in the prophetic cycles, speaking directly with the prophets and directing their every movement.

I am not so much interested in the way the narrator's voice and those of the prophets merge with Yahweh, or indeed how narrator and prophets merge into one, but rather how the interaction of Yahweh with the other characters has a profound effect on their characterization. Yahweh ensures a hierarchization of characters, with primacy given, after himself, to the prophets, then to the select kings Solomon, Hezekiah and Josiah, and then the sinful rabble of remaining kings. In other words, the first level of the effort to deal with the contradictions between the prophets and kings is by means of this hierarchy of characters in terms of who has access to Yahweh and who meets his requirements. Yet the contradiction within this mode of characterization is that Yahweh is the character who enables the characterization of kings and prophets in the first place. That is, the tensions I have traced thus far are contained within the figure of Yahweh, a vicious cycle within the text.

At a second level the interaction between the major character types in Kings touches on a much wider theological problem in the Hebrew Bible: the tension between divine control and human initiative. It is banal to read this in terms of the contradictory experience of 'God' that we find recorded in so many different ways in the Bible, or theologically as the contradictions of the human condition, for the initial form of the problem comes from texts like these. Rather, it indicates the workings of a particular ideological system, a cultural template that I will explore in the conclusion to this book. As far as this particular problem is concerned, the characters end up being either superhuman magical figures who sin not and are Yahweh's instruments, or they turn out to be characters who are so far from Yahweh that they can only be condemned. It seems to me that this is one of the key determining devices of characterization in Kings, that which produces the contradictory characters of kings and prophets. Both become explorations in the two character types possible within this particular logic.

It always strikes me that the world of the book of Kings is exceedingly strange, so far removed from the ideological and cultural systems under which we live in capitalism that it is a foreign text, far removed from any perceptible world of which we can make sense. If anything, it resembles the books and computer games known as *Myst*, peopled with magicians, hidden lore, wayward kings and evil characters, quests and the excruciating presence of an arbitrary and unknowable occult dimension. The problem with Kings, and other biblical books like it, is that it is part of our familiar literature and so its oddness escapes us, squashed out in perpetual rereadings. What Lukács allows me to do, through his literary analysis, is point out the extraordinary otherness of a text such as this. But I am drawing near to that elusive notion of 'historico-philosophical' consciousness with which I want to close this chapter.

Now I want to make a move that follows the logic of Lukács's analysis but goes beyond what he would do himself. Thus far I have written of characters that fall within a system of which Yahweh is less the result than the cause. Yet each of the figures in the hierarchy of characters is within the system and is perfectly understandable in its terms. Such a system, however, inevitably relies upon exclusions that must remain outside so that the whole ideological structure does not collapse, and for Kings these are the women. In most cases they fit within the larger system, subservient to the men: the two prostitutes for whom Solomon passes judgment, Bathsheba in the succession from David to Solomon, Abishag as David's hot-water bottle, Solomon's wives, the Queen of Sheba, Jeroboam's wife, the widow of Zarephath, the Shunammite woman and the cannibal mothers. But there are three who create distinct problems: Jezebel, Athaliah and Huldah, one the dominant wife of a petulant king, another a queen mother and 'king', and the third a prophetess. In other words, they seem to be part of the main character divide between kings and prophets, but they hardly fit within the schema of characterization.

In terms of content—the condemnation of Judah and the sparing of Josiah from punishment due to his obedience to Yahweh—and in function—as mouthpiece of Yahweh—Huldah is like any of the other prophets in Kings. But she delivers the last prophetic word in the book (2 Kgs 22.14-20) before the long-awaited destruction of Judah and exile of the royal house. Why does a woman deliver the death knell, the final prophetic word in a long run of prophets who are all men? I would suggest that Huldah is necessary for the ultimate word of destruction in a text that constructs a world of men that then generates its own ideological problem. As far as the text is concerned, only a woman can bring about that destruction, for the male prophets are unable to do so, constantly repeating the threat of destruction without actually bringing it about. They cannot, in other words, destroy the world that brings them to life as characters in the first place. Huldah is, therefore, both the means for the end of the strange world of Kings and its prophets and also the culmination of the character-type of the prophet. She provides the unravelling of both, precisely as the mouth-piece of Yahweh.

What of Athaliah? In many respects she is the extreme logic to which Jezebel points. In a perverted echo of Yahweh's own control of the characters in Kings, the domineering Jezebel controls the actions of one of the most condemned kings, Ahab, so much so that a gore-fest is the only way to rid the world of Kings from her influence. After this massacre enacted by Jehu (2 Kgs 9–10), at the behest of Elisha as his final act, in which the extermination of the house of Ahab extends to Ahaziah, king of Judah, Athaliah the mother of Ahaziah turns up. If Jezebel was bad for Israel, then Athaliah is much worse for Judah. But the problem here is, as with the drawn-out succession of Elijah and Elisha (the ideal model of succession for the kings?), the succession of the kings themselves. The solution that Athaliah represents in this situation—the king's mother as ruler—presents a serious problem that must be eliminated.

In dealing with that problem, Athaliah shows up the anomalies of the whole character type of the king. She rules for six years (2 Kgs 11.3) but for her there are no regnal formulae. In their place we find: 'Now when Athaliah the mother of Ahaziah saw that her son was dead, she arose and destroyed all the royal family' (2 Kgs 11.1) and 'So all the people of the land rejoiced; and the city was quiet after Athaliah had been slain with the sword at the king's house' (2 Kgs 11.20). There is no burial or notice of succession, even though Joash, who has been protected from her and rules after her, is her grandson. This is precisely where a succession notice would be most expected. But it cannot be in a text for which the succession must be from king to son. Nor is any theological judgment passed on her reign: she is, in other words, one of the 'kings' and yet not, outside the system and within, the one who must be eliminated to make the system work. In Kings she fulfils a similar function to Huldah, being the anomaly that is the logical extreme of the character type of the king, so thoroughly sinful that one can only rejoice at her execution.

Like Huldah, she brings destruction, but it is not merely destruction of the royal house, the 'seed of the kingdom' (Athaliah), nor even of the whole of Judah (Huldah), but of the narrative itself. The collision course of the two major character types, who themselves comprise the working out of the ideological problem that Yahweh constitutes, is in the end enacted by women. Or at least the threat of the collision and destruction of the narrative and ideological problem it represents must be transferred to the women, who become the extreme types of both prophets and kings and can therefore function as the scapegoats through which the narrative may cohere.

I have followed Lukács's lead in many respects, focusing on the dialectical tensions of the text, particularly in terms of the features that constitute genre: narrative rhythm, life and death, character and ideology. And
yet there remains Lukács's concern with the historical location of such
generic features. The problem with a text like Kings is that a foray into
history remains exceedingly hypothetical, and so I want to focus on
Lukács's notion of the historico-philosophical moment.

Lukács's habit was to identify such a moment in terms of crisis: the
disintegration of the world that he later identified in terms of capitalism in
Theory of the Novel or the new historical consciousness of *The Historical
Novel* that faced its own crisis is part of the story of the bourgeoisie facing
the new proletariat in the 1848 revolutions. And the temptation to do the
same with Kings, itself caught in a generic tension between so-called
historical narrative and prophetic books, is strong as well. Most famously
there is Noth's argument that the whole of his proposed Deuteronomistic
history was an attempt to deal with the crisis of the destruction of Israel
and Judah, and any number of variations thereafter. However, what I want
to suggest is that the historico-philosophical moment of Kings is one of
stasis, not crisis, and that that stasis is exceeding strange. The contradictions I have traced, in narrative time, life and death, and character,
constitute the ideological working out of a stable system that I have earlier
described as the Asiatic mode of production. In other words, the profound
contradictions form one part of that larger system in its normal working
order. And the concern of Kings is with the cultural dominant of the
sacred (by 'cultural dominant' I refer to the overriding way in which the
varied aspects of human existence are understood, that 'language' in
which life is rendered manageable and meaningful), the overriding ideological system of what I will for the time being call the Asiatic mode of
production. But the result is a very weird world indeed, one that we
assume follows the ideological patterns to which we are accustomed at our
interpretative peril. That such a system in stasis faced almost impossible
contradictions is based on Marx's insight that any mode of production
works on the basis of, not despite, contradictions that eventually see it
collapse. The continuous efforts to keep it operating, to ensure its survival,
is the task of ideological texts like Kings, where the effort becomes one of
exploring the contradictions in order to undertake vital ideological repair
work. The historico-philosophical moment, then, is the normal workings
of Yahwism, itself a distinct ideological option within the broader terms of
the sacred under the Asiatic mode of production.

Chapter 6

ERNST BLOCH: ANTI-YAHWISM IN EZEKIEL

Ernst Bloch, straddling what was once the Berlin Wall, not sure about
leaping one way or the other, presents almost too much for the biblical
critic. A Marxist writer who read not only the Bible avidly, but kept
himself up to date with biblical criticism, who reflected deeply on the
Bible in his major works and drew much of his vocabulary and concepts
from it, who argued for the importance of the Bible in any politics of
revolutionary liberation and socialist construction, and who wrote a book
on the Bible itself. In one respect we might feel that he is too close to
biblical criticism to be of much use, too open to the internal debates of the
discipline and thereby vulnerable to its critiques. In other respects,
however, his knowledge and work on the Bible seem to make the initial
task of searching his work for relevant ideas less daunting, for he gives
plenty of help on the way.

   In fact, the inseparability of Bloch from the Bible means that I can add
another category to my discussion—the major elements of Bloch's biblical
hermeneutics—alongside the more usual treatment of major ideas and
methods and their relevance for the Bible. After this, I consider his philosophical hermeneutics of utopia, his own strategy of biblical interpretation
drawn from the more general programme, and then the deeper question of
religious commitment and the study of sacred texts.

   The way Bloch becomes interesting for biblical studies is in the notion
of a logic of anti-Yahwism in the texts and their study. Texts like Ezek. 16
and 23 have featured in the recent debate over 'pornoprophetics', although
the usual way of dealing with such texts is that such a representation of
Yahweh is problematic and therefore should be discarded. Yet there is a
noticeable move in these studies that develops an implicit protest against
Yahweh. That is, there is a logic of atheism itself within the study of such
texts as Ezek. 16 and 23. In order to see whether that protest operates
within the texts themselves, I consider Ezek. 20.1-38, where the impossible words of Yahweh emerge from Ezekiel's mouth.

Whose Bible? Bloch's Use of the Bible

Bloch's engagement with the Bible operated at four levels, ranging from sustained exegesis of biblical texts to the pervasive presence of biblical vocabulary and phrases in his writing, often not acknowledged explicitly. A glance at the index of *The Principle of Hope* (Bloch 1995), for instance, will show how often and for how long Bloch sustains his biblical analyses, reminding one a little of comparable moments in Barth's *Church Dogmatics*. In these stretches key issues include the role of Paradise, of Eden, Exodus, promised land, Moses and Jesus, the resurrection, Judgement Day and the new Jerusalem. Bloch's exegesis often has a distinct turn, to which I return a little later. His second usage of the Bible involves continual references to ideas, texts and biblical figures in the context of other, longer, arguments. A text may appear as an example, as evidence for certain beliefs and practices, as a crucial piece of something completely different, such as the utopian function of music where a biblical text may play a key role. Thirdly, there are whole series of allusions and passing references. For instance, the very language of speaking about the road to utopia, which for Bloch is a code word for socialism, is permeated with both the Bible and Goethe's *Faust*, the two great inspirations for *The Principle of Hope*. More often than not the biblical and Faustian allusions are unmarked by Bloch, and it is here where the language of the Bible becomes part of the regular vocabulary of Bloch's sentences that the Bible blends into the conceptual structure of his work.

And this leads to the final category of Bloch's use of the Bible, where the linguistic capillaries of his texts open out to the fundamental themes on which he builds his work. I have argued elsewhere (Boer, forthcoming) that some of the deepest currents in Bloch's work—most obviously the utopian—could not have been thought in the first place without the Bible. Where the language slips into the sentences without the signal of biblical references or even the mention of the Bible, I think we get closest to the function of the Bible in the conceptual structure of Bloch's work. A minimal version of this argument is that the specific shape of Utopian longing and reflection has been affected profoundly by the Bible, by the figures of Moses and Jesus, and by the themes of Exodus and the Kingdom of God (e.g. Bloch 1995: 496-515) particularly in light of the Bible's foundational role in the fabric of mediaeval culture and society in Europe. Yet I prefer the stronger version of this argument, that it is the Bible itself that generates the category of Utopia.

Bloch's use of the Bible in his work, particularly the way it provides a constant source of reflection and ideas, along with Goethe's *Faust*, raises a curious question about his potential value for biblical studies. That is, if he draws from the Bible so extensively, does it not seem odd to read his work for its contribution to biblical studies? It seems to me that Bloch embodies a paradox, not only about Marxist theory, but about all such efforts to draw insights from outside biblical studies. For in all sorts of hidden ways a discipline like literary criticism succeeds in covering its tracks, and if we were to find the spoor, through all its double backs, crossings and forks, we would find that the emergence and possibility of literary criticism, let alone Marxist literary criticism, lies in pre-modern biblical studies. Even those elements that seem to come from ancient Greece and Rome have been mediated through the long tradition of mediaeval biblical exegesis. And yet the discipline of literary criticism, in all the directions it has run, into various groupings and subgroupings that have taken on a life of their own (cultural studies, linguistics, postcolonial criticism, English, German and so on), now have little of the content of biblical studies left in them, except perhaps at an odd moment or two. It is perhaps the forms that still retain the mark of biblical criticism, through such basic concerns as meaning, levels of interpretation, intentionality or its lack, social context, the value of texts and the canon. In this light, it only seems appropriate that these new methods that have developed far beyond their ancestral moment in biblical criticism should now return in order to be used for interpreting the Bible.

I have made this argument at greater length elsewhere (Boer 1999), but it is what I see happening with Bloch's sustained interest in the Bible, but now from a thoroughly 'secular', communist and atheistic position. But what I find intriguing in such moves as Bloch's, by people who are trained in a range of disciplines other than biblical criticism, are the possibilities they raise for interpreting the Bible itself.

Utopian Hermeneutics

Compared to Benjamin or Adorno, or even Deleuze or Eagleton or Gramsci, Bloch has not fared so well in recent criticism, except for the occasional enthusiast like Jack Zipes. But his argument for a hermeneutics of hope has entered into the fabric of critical discourse, marked now as the hermeneutics of recovery, of reconstitution, first posited by Paul Ricoeur along with the hermeneutics of suspicion and then taken up by Fredric Jameson and others.

Bloch's lifelong—and it was indeed a long life—project was the recovery of the very idea of Utopia, drawn from the Bible itself, particularly
when it had been successfully relegated to the realm of the dreamy and
impractical. It is not only Fredric Jameson, after all, who has been
responsible for the return of Utopia (capital 'U') to the agenda of any
respectable political, literary or cultural criticism. For Jameson himself,
along with Jack Zipes and the group around the journal *Utopian Studies*,
have indicated their profound respect for Bloch and his perpetual search or
the utopian.

Through many detours and byways, both physical and mental, Bloch
winds his tortuous way around the question of what it means to have hope.
In all its multifarious forms, this is the thread that runs through the whole
corpus, a hermeneutics that searches everywhere—in literature, folklore,
myth, architecture, nursery rhymes, popular culture, music, of all ages and
places—for the hope of a better world. Indeed, for him it is less a particular doctrine of thought than a hermeneutical strategy in itself, a frame
of reading, viewing, analysing. Utopia becomes a philosophical principle
that Bloch was able to lift off from the literary text and cast over any
object, cultural, political, sacred or economic. Apart from the fact that
hermeneutics, as the demarcated question and discipline of interpretation,
derives from the whole issue of how biblical texts might be read, nego-
tiated and appropriated (and I will of course return to this)—apart from
this fact, Bloch's continual and irrepressible desire was to read all he came
upon as in some way marked by a utopian desire, a repressed wish for
another, better world. Even if he thought he was tracing a new dimension
of the psyche as momentous as Freud's more pessimistic discoveries, there
have been fewer taken with this line of his thought than the hermeneutics
he pursued relentlessly. One of the differences is that between clinical
practice and the reading of texts—although Freud did plenty of that too—
and this means that Bloch is less a navigator of the psyche than a ponderer
of texts. I for one, despite all my liking for Freud and Lacan and Žižek, am
happy that Bloch is in the end a reader of texts, for that is what I am too,
especially of philosophical and sacred texts, like Bloch.

To Bloch may be credited the lifting of 'Utopia' beyond its status as a
literary category, for which Thomas More's work remains the founding
moment, into a philosophical and hermeneutical category. In doing so,
Bloch sought to answer the tendency for utopias to regress, to long for a
lost golden age. In these regressive utopias there is contradictory process
of forgetting and remembering: the past becomes the basis for Utopia by
means of denying the role of the past in determining the present system

against which the Utopia is posited. In other words, the future is but a return to pristine origins, bypassing the undesirable present. When utopia and restoration become identical with one another, then one has the hallmarks of regressive and reactionary utopias, or dystopias. Over against the longing for a restored past, Bloch argued for a basic orientation to the future as characteristic of utopian thought. If there is a utopian moment in what is felt to be the past—Eden or Paradise, the secret guild of masons who look back to Solomon's temple as the ideal model, the Island of the Blessed, Atlantis, and so on—then their energy derives not from the past, according to Bloch, but from the utopian vision of the future. He sought a discovery of the future in the past, understood in the sense that what may have begun in the past requires the future for its completion. The central philosophical category in Bloch's system is therefore the future, the Novum, a radical openness to a future that cannot as yet be imagined, formulated or even spoken about rather than tinkering with the present in order to make it slightly better.

Alongside the philosophical category of the future, where one can debate the relative truth claims of different utopias, there is also the hermeneutical category. Compared to the philosophical, a utopian hermeneutics seeks the various and unexpected utopian fragments and glimpses in the ruins of the present, even in the worst ideological and cultural products available. In such a dialectical reading strategy many negative and unredeemable items turn out to be concealing a positive and utopian moment. In other words, the negative is crucial for the positive to be there: only by means of an oppressive moment can the positive emerge. Yet even the moments that presage a utopian future do so not through their immediate content but through their finite nature; even hope itself is driven forward not by what is hoped for but by 'a dissatisfaction at the very core of hope' (Jameson 1971: 138). It is therefore possible for the most reactionary and violent political programme to function as a figure for a utopian community: in this way one may make an ethical assessment while not giving up on utopia itself (apart from being able to account for the continued presence of the negative). The world may be understood in the light of such a hermeneutics as a vast thesaurus of traces or figures of utopia, particularly in the commonplace human experiences of everyday life.

Dialectics

Like Adorno and Benjamin, Bloch was a dialectical thinker, an ability at once maligned (German obscurity) and envied among writers of English sentences. Whereas the English sentence urges conciseness, brevity, a point made, German can evolve a sentence or paragraph, holding off ever so long the close with the verb. But it is not just sentences that give over to dialectical or analytical thought, nor is it merely a search for the utopian moment of any particular item, a scanning of the horizon of available items in order to locate the telltale blips. Some of his work did involve this, but Bloch's was more of a dialectical operation, and his utopian hermeneutics is unthinkable without dialectics. Rather than read utopian elements off in a direct fashion, Bloch was also interested in dystopia, in the trajectories that produced images and hints of oppression and exploitation, of fascism, empire and domination.

Yet this is not quite dialectical enough, for it assumes that utopian and dystopian elements are clearly marked, that they have a clearly visible identity tags on them. In some situations this may be the case, but Bloch gives the whole approach a further twist, for the overtly utopian texts may have a distinctly dystopian outcome. For instance, the image of the promised land, intrinsic to the story of the Exodus in the Bible—a text central to Bloch's own work—bears within it a mandate for dispossession and destruction of the people in the land. Inversely, I have argued in other places (Boer 1997) that Chronicles may be read as utopian (or rather, 'uchronian') politics, that its agenda is one of rereading the story of Israel in order to cast it and the future that arises from it in utopian terms. Yet the result is a thoroughly dystopian text, one that is exclusive of women and the maternal body, that is extremely hierarchical and painfully pious, and one that has in its theocracy of immediate divine retribution an absolutely repressive state apparatus. This is where the hermeneutics of suspicion begins to function properly, to watch more carefully for the negative within what appears to be utopian. The obverse, however, is also the case, since it becomes possible to locate a distinctly utopian moment in the most debased and degraded items, in clearly dystopian texts and products. As with the deceptively utopian material, one needs to look for signals other than the overt content for such utopian hints in the midst of dystopia. If I return to my example of Chronicles, it is not so much the content itself and the mechanisms of producing it that are important, but in the very act of thinking and writing about a collective possibility in the first place, radically distinct from the surrounding political and economic situation. One may, then, find within an unredeemably dystopian text a formal or perhaps gestural hint of utopia itself, without valorizing the content in any way.

In its full, original, Blochian sense we have here the utopian hermeneutics of suspicion and recovery. These terms will in fact be somewhat familiar to those who work in certain types of biblical studies and theology: reformist feminisms, postcolonial studies, but also a whole series of strands of liberationist theological and biblical studies for whom the agenda remains that of a recovery of the text, a way of holding onto its ultimate value for religious communities, whether synagogue or church in whatever shape. The problem here is that the language of 'suspicion' and 'recovery' is drawn primarily from Paul Ricoeur, in whose work the 'masters of suspicion'—Marx, Freud and Nietzsche—become the source of Ricoeur's own hermeneutics of suspicion, which must afterwards have a theological moment, the hermeneutics of recovery, of something that is finally beneficial, useable, for building up religious and political commitment. However, Ricoeur derives his method not so much from Bloch as from Freud, for he seeks to discover the repressed fantasy fulfilment of desire from beneath the surface. The hermeneutics of suspicion becomes the moment when the repressive is unmasked, shown up for what it is, whereas the moment of recovery is when the fantasy satisfaction is released. But Freud is one of three who have sealed the end of 'innocent' interpretation, and with Marx Ricoeur attempts a more political edge in his hermeneutics. In the end, however, it remains resolutely individualist— the marks of his Freudian beginnings—and inherently theological. Yet the unacknowledged debt to Bloch runs deeper, for Ricoeur argues that the hermeneutics of recovery does not seek to bypass or overturn the obstacle to recovery as find what is positive in the moment of obstruction, of negativity, in order to complete the process of interpretation (see Ricoeur 1970; 1986). And yet the shift from Bloch is not only the individualist focus but also the sidelining of Marx in favour of what might be called the 'ultimately determining instance' of theology. What is required, it seems to me, is a discovery of Bloch (it is not even a rediscovery), in order to gain a deeper sense of how such a utopian hermeneutics operates out of a properly Marxist theoretical framework.

Detective Work

Thus far I have spoken about the implications for biblical studies of various aspects of Bloch's method. However, he also has a distinct practice of biblical interpretation of his own, and in this respect he is unique among the collection of Marxists in this book. Some may draw upon elements of the tradition of biblical studies, others from theology in developing their methods, but no one has a specific biblical hermeneutics. Then again, none of them has written a monograph on the Bible like Bloch, the extra-ordinary *Atheism in Christianity* (1972).

Part of Bloch's agenda is to make an apology for the Bible over against the Marxist rejection of it along with theistic belief. An Enlightenment that rejected the Bible was more often a pseudo-enlightenment—the path of such a rejection led as easily to bourgeois rationalism as it did to Nazi neo-paganism and socio-biologism. For Marxists, Bloch argues, the Bible is a document that should not readily be discarded, for it is the book of the peasants and workers with and for whom the communists worked. Not only that, it is also a book with a revolutionary force.

The key feature Bloch wishes to introduce into biblical criticism—this in the 1950s and 60s—is the category of class, since the Bible, he suggests, is very much a text of both those who labour and those who live off that surplus labour and do none themselves. In all its variety and contradictions, there are stories in the Bible that have become homely in the smallest of peasant households, but also those used by the overlords and religious professionals. And it is not just that such class differences indicate a different reading strategy, different assumptions about the various narratives, poetry and statements: the texts themselves tend in either direction, their content and form speaking with a double voice, one that is and is not folly for the rich and powerful. The Bible is then a text riven with class conflict: not a conflict that may be read in terms of bour-geoisie and proletariat alone but in terms of the basic Marxist category of the class difference, however that may be articulated historically, between oppressors and oppressed, rulers and ruled.

The litmus for such a method of reading—which is very much part of Bloch's famous utopian hermeneutics—is the conflict between the re-former Luther and the peasant leader Thomas Muntzer. While the former could invoke Paul and the cross of Christ as the lot of all, the latter called upon the Exodus and the Bible's anger 'against the Ahabs and Nimrods' (Bloch 1972: 23). But the deepest affinity of the Bible, despite its 'adapt-ability to select master-ideologies' (1972: 24), is to ordinary, uneducated people, who took the stories as their stories, something the clergy and rulers could not do.

For what Bloch seeks to do in *Atheism in Christianity* is to uncover both the way in which ruling class ideologies have been imposed on the text, and to examine the patterns and strategies of subversive slave talk. The interlacings, overlays and myriad complexities of such materials require readings that are attentive to the subtle shifts and changes that have taken place. Thus, Bloch is not interested in submissive varieties of slave talk (and so the Psalms do not appear), but rather subversive texts that have been altered by later authorities and that may be recovered, as well as texts that have been rendered subversive through later usage. The one that survives is the masked text 'it wears its mask, rather, from below, and wears it freely, as a first form of alienation, a characteristic change of ground' (Bloch 1972: 14). Such texts have a double function, a 'sly irony', appearing to appease the rulers while openly criticizing and lampooning them. 'Men often spoke in parables, saying one thing and meaning another; praising the prince and praising the gallows to prove it' (1972: 15).

As an example of the complexity of such readings, Bloch offers an interpretation of Korah's rebellion in Numbers 16, a text that as it is now speaks of a priestly rebellion, centring on the issue of ritual and incense, which is crushed through divine intervention. As the story stands, it is an account of a 'premature palace revolution' (1972: 80) within the priestly upper class, but what catches Bloch's attention is the way the revolt is dealt with: God opens the ground which swallows them up as an example to any one else who would rebel, who would burn incense before the Lord. This is not a God of war, waging a fight for survival, but a God of 'white-guard terror' (Bloch 1972: 80), one who emerges from the redactor's pen. For Bloch, an echo of political rebellion reverberates through the text. Not only does the punishment itself signal this, but the perpetual recurrence of the Israelites' grumbling throughout the chapter indicates for Bloch a subversive, rebellious, anti-Yahweh voice that has been turned into something else—the sign of disobedience and recalcitrance on the part of the people themselves.

It is this kind of reading that Bloch undertakes again and again, sifting through the text, with the assumptions and strategies of biblical historical criticism (his biblical criticism as a whole assumes the viability of such an approach)[1] at hand along with the hermeneutics of class. And it leads him to argue that there are two concepts of God, one 'which has the *Futurum* as its mode-of-being' and the other that 'has been institutionalized down from above' (Bloch 1972: 81). The latter, with its radical transcendence, patterns of submission and atonement, is the one against which the rebellions of the text are directed.

Throughout the rest of *Atheism in Christianity* Bloch pursues such a

---

1. For a fuller criticism of Bloch's engagement with historical criticism, see my *Criticism of Earth* (forthcoming).

bifurcation along class lines. He identifies two contrary principles: 'murmuring', in contrast to tail-wagging, is the leitmotiv for the textual and
political strain that Bloch will seek in all its different forms throughout the
Bible and its associated literature, the pseudepigrapha and apocrypha. One
of the criticisms levelled at Bloch is the difficulty of finding a continuous
line like this throughout the disparate literature of the Bible. In the end I
am not sure that this quite identifies the more important questions that may
be asked of Bloch, such as the implications of such a strong valorization of
religious discourse for a Marxist agenda.

Yet in his hands such detective work becomes a political tool, the
various traditions and layers of the Bible full of politics and economics.
Although he finds major elements at the ideological centre of the Bible,
especially the Exodus and the Apocalypse, he assumes that by and large
the dominant textual traditions are those of official power, priestly establishment and institutions—the ones who write, copy and preserve texts,
but also the ones who impose ideas, political and economic domination,
and negative representations of the people. It is here that Bloch locates the
alternatives, the possibility of opposing the hierocratic system of control
and oppression. So he focuses on the murmuring of the people against
Moses, the trenchant prophetic critique of political economics, the early
forms of Christianity rejected and persecuted by the early Church, such as
gnostics, Ophites and so on, who championed the serpent in the Garden,
saw the God of the Hebrew Bible as an evil power, a demiurge who sought
to ensnare human beings within this world. These things indicate for
Bloch a healthy revolutionary force or tradition in the Bible. All of which
leads Bloch to posit a distinct, although highly diverse, thread, potentially
revolutionary, anti-ruling class, anti-powerful, anti-wealth, that appears in
many different guises throughout the Bible. And this stands over against
the texts of the oppressor, in which Baal and Yahweh become one, where
the literary elites work tirelessly as ideologues for the ruling class.

What Bloch calls the hermeneutical principle of Creation versus Exodus/
Apocalypse is a curious one, for it emerges as much from the Bible as
from Bloch's philosophical and hermeneutical imperative to read for
Utopia. *The Principle of Hope* manifests this principle even more clearly.
In 'the Bible and the kingdom of neighbourly love' (Bloch 1995: 496-515)
Bloch pays out a line, responsible for the earliest form of social utopia,
from the Bedouin nomadic communism of the desert, through the prophets
and Jesus to the early Christian communism (and then on into the work of
Augustine and Joachim of Fiore). The sharp distinction between such a

line and its opposite—Canaanite hierarchies, wealth and poverty, the church of Baal that runs through to the Christian Church, the 'ideologically profitable insurance company' (Bloch 1970: 89)—is both illuminating and problematic, not least because the initial distinction of nomadic/ settled, Israelite/Canaanite can no longer be held. Yet this is an important distinction for Bloch, providing a basic structural element for his reading of the Bible in all his exegeses. At many particular points Bloch does identify something central, but, as Geoghegan points out (1994: 99), the attempt to trace a structural dialectic continuously throughout the Bible strains the text. Bloch is well aware of the complexities, layers, varying voices to be found in the Bible, and I would agree that a dialectical reading is able to deal with such contradictory complexity better than any other approach. However, what is needed is an even more sophisticated dialectical reading that accounts even better for the twists, foldbacks, curious alliances and changing oppositions of the text, one that reads back and forth between the ideological, social and economic contradictions that are inevitably found there.

Atheism and Biblical Criticism

Yet there is a distinct teleology to Bloch's own argument, let alone the stream he follows in the Bible. He has an unflagging zeal for anything that serves to raise and value human beings, and it begins with the interpretative rule: '…only critical attention to the *veiled* (and, in Exodus, *ineradicable*) *subversion* can bring to light the organon of the non-theocratic axis in the Bible' (Bloch 1972: 82). All that rails against theocracy and its attendant hierocracy, against transcendence and obedience, and against the diminution of human beings has a distinct logic that sends it in a path beyond the Bible. He wants to bring the *homo absconditus* out of hiding and he does so through a number of strategies. One is a dialectical inversion of key theological categories: the *Deus absconditus* is in fact a cipher for the human being who remains hidden under the dominant religious systems of the Bible. Uncovering the suppressed rebellions of the Bible will bring him forth. Another is the argument that the God-hypostasis needs to be placed on its feet, in the same way that Marx performed a podiatric move on Hegel's idealist dialectic: 'God' is merely a hypostasis of what human beings can and will be, the utopian possibility of a transformed human nature. This is a temporal, horizontal transcendence. A third way, and this is the burden of *Atheism in Christianity*, is to argue that the various protests against Yahweh or Elohim in the Bible have inherent within them what may be called protest atheism. Impossible within the various interlaced logics of the biblical text, such atheism can only emerge later, after that world has closed down. For the protest against God carries with it the assumption that human beings can only emerge in their full potential when everything that draws away from this potential and makes human beings subservient to something or someone else has been dispensed with. Thus, a religion that raises human beings up from submission to powerful overlords, as Bloch finds in various parts of the Bible, is one that will wither away like a vanishing mediator once the lords of this and any other world have gone. It is precisely this type of promise and hope that he finds in the Bible and in no other religious literature.

One of the advantages of biblical study is that its practitioners can distance themselves from theology and religious commitment, even though the Church and Synagogue have assumed that the Bible is their text and that any other claim is false. Apart from the obvious point that the Bible is first a literary and cultural document, and that the methods most appropriate to its interpretation are those of literary and cultural studies (however much they may owe their enabling possibilities to biblical studies itself), Bloch himself provides an indication of how the Bible is itself a document appropriated by religious institutions. For he debunks the assumption of religious institutions that this is their own text. It is not, for Bloch, a document of religious communities by default. Less an effort to wrest the Bible away from its 'natural' home—church, synagogue or mosque—his argument assumes that such institutions have in fact appropriated and colonized the Bible. The marks of such a troubled appropriation, of a text ill at ease in these contexts, are precisely those elements that Bloch seeks to uncover, those that run against and subvert the institutions in question.

Was Bloch himself a believer? Negative. So, what are we to make of one who seems so amenable to biblical studies, yet remains outside the assumed fold of shared religious commitment? Do we count him in, or not? But then who is this 'we'? For not all biblical critics would stand on the confessional side of biblical criticism; in fact an increasing number identify themselves as at least agnostic if not atheistic. Apart from reflecting on this curious development in biblical studies, Bloch provides me with a distinct opportunity not only to draw from an extremely rich tradition of Marxist criticism for biblical studies, but also, in a moment where I can look awry in order to see more clearly, to face the question of atheism and biblical criticism.

But let me draw near to this question from a different side. In my preceding discussion of Bloch's biblical hermeneutics I noted a theme that came out of gnostic thought, namely, the evil demiurge of the Hebrew Bible who must be opposed and overcome. A mere creator, he seeks to trap souls in the evil matter of the world, from which they then struggle to escape. Bloch does not follow through the whole gnostic position, inimical as it finally is for Marxism. But what the gnostics abhor, the God of the Hebrew Bible, interests Bloch immensely, for it is this God that is the target of so much opposition within the Bible—something the gnostics were not the first to notice. And so it is that time and again human beings find themselves at the harsh end of a punishment—death by fire, disease, snake bite, opening of the ground, the odd child of sinners destroyed here and there—at the hand of Yahweh. The rebellions of the people are repressed by Yahweh: but the point of all this is to show that invariably this God is a key element, a central symbol, of the ruling class action, both physical and ideological, against opposition, a dimension of ruling class hegemony, to borrow a phrase from Gramsci.

If God, or at least certain representations of God, is inseparable from such an ideological system, itself crucial for the particular socio-economic system in place, then opposition to God is opposition to the system; conversely resisting the rulers is a challenge to God. The logic of this brings us to Bloch's central theological argument, derived very much from the Bible: if human beings are to realize their full potential, bring about a fundamental change in human nature, both collectively and individually, to end exploitation, then that involves not so much removing the ruling class while replacing it with another, but rejecting the gods who form part of the ideological structure. Atheism is then the outcome of this internal biblical process; or, the religious logic of the Bible, namely a utopian longing for human transcendence, is towards atheism. So, Bloch's argument comes to the dialectical conclusion that atheism is the fulfilment of the religion of the Bible, and so of Judaism and Christianity.

In another place I explore the strengths and weaknesses of this argument, but it is intriguing. Bloch's polemic may be understood as an attack on transcendence, by which I mean the continual exclusion of God as a narrative or poetic character. In other words, in much biblical criticism 'God' remains outside the text, beyond the distinctly human world of the text, especially in those forms of criticism that use the Bible as a source for historical data. By indicating that the kind of material in the Bible that has God as a key player is of no use for history, critics conveniently sideline the questions that this character raises. At another, more explicitly theological, level the text is seen to refer beyond itself, to make some types of referential statements about 'God' that one must then weigh up in theological fashion. That is, the particular character 'God'—although in fact there are a number of characters with names like El, Elohim, Yahweh, theos—also seems to have a referential function beyond the text. Bloch's reponse to such assumptions—the historical and the theological—is more subtle than, say, the assertion that 'God' is a mere character, or that the texts are worthless precisely because they talk about 'God'. Rather, both assumptions take a significant twist: the character in these stories must be dealt with directly, in all his (or their) multiple and contradictory ways; and the referential assumption also needs close attention. For if there is a protest, a rebellion, within the text against this character, does not the logic of the theological readings also require that this becomes a rebellion against the 'God' to whom these texts would seem to refer.

There is a curious correlation between Bloch's arguments and biblical studies. For a growing number of biblical critics count themselves as atheists. Some of these have moved from a default position of religious commitment to some form of agnosticism or atheism through biblical studies, others have come to biblical studies in a stage of post commitment, while others again are attracted to biblical studies without any prior religious baggage, confirmed atheists who find it strange indeed that anyone would believe this material. Perhaps it is a mark of biblical studies in this era, but an increasing number of scholars profess allegiance to no church or faith. I remember when I first began biblical studies, opting for the more critical approaches taught at Sydney University, the Calvinists in my immediate circle, including relatives, warned me that the outcome of such study was atheism. And when I taught at a hellhole of a theological college I used to joke that once students entered its shabby precincts one of the demons inhabiting the roofs would possess them before they knew it (the consensus at this place of profound illumination is that the demons left when I did).[2]

---

2.   I remember another situation at the aforesaid college, where, in response to my own work, the college reworded part of its job description in relation to research. To the phrase 'the lecturer will undertake research' was added 'of benefit to the church'. To my mind this was remarkably astute, for it recognized a certain trajectory of biblical studies that would carry the Bible's diligent and careful readers in the other direction, that biblical studies could best be done without the dead and hampering weight of religious and ecclesiastical commitment. They were also wise enough to curtail such research as much as possible, in terms of time, money, opportunity and exclusion from the wider circles of scholarship.

Yet might it not be the case that there is an inherent logic in the Bible and biblical studies, as Bloch argues. Is there not a lurking atheism within that text, one that might best be read, in line with Marx, as a protest atheism?

Anti-Yahwism in Ezekiel

I want to keep together in my discussion of Ezekiel two elements of Bloch's work: the dialectics of utopia and the implicit protest atheism of the Bible. In other words, I ask, what is utopian about Ezekiel, especially such offensive texts as Ezek. 16, 23 and 20? In doing so, I take up Bloch's insistence on a theological dimension to biblical criticism, a moment of theological suspicion that must be part of any interpretation.

Ezekiel 16 and 23 have been part of an intense discussion of what Athalya Brenner has dubbed 'pornoprophetics' (Brenner 1995), defined as the degrading representations of women in prophetic texts that legitimate male power. Other texts included in this debate are Isa. 40–55 (Baumann 2001; Magdalene 1995), Jer. 2 (Brenner 1995), and 3 (Shields 2001a), Jer. 13 (Magdalene 1995), Zech. 5.5-11 (Sals 2001) and 14.2 (Magdalene 1995), Nahum (Gruber 2001), Malachi (O'Brien 2001), as well as a concentration on Hos. 1–3.

I do not want to quibble with the definition of pornography (the objectification and degradation of women based on unequal power that encourages abuse of women and renders female sexuality as one of servitude), although it is restricted to heterosexual pornography, includes an instrumentalist understanding of graphic and written texts and does not consider the range of debate. What interests me here is the way Yahweh becomes an abusive character, particularly through the use of the marriage metaphor for the relationship between Yahweh and Israel. Not only does a question hang over those responsible for such representations in authoritative sacred texts, but the question is also directed at Yahweh himself, at, as Bloch points out, the 'God' to whom Yahweh points.

Thus, F. Rachel Magdalene writes:

> Within these verses, God, characterized as male, is regularly threatening, in judgement, to rape, or otherwise sexually abuse, the cities of Israel, Judah and their neighbours, all characterized as female... God is an active perpetrator of such sexual violence against women in the Hebrew Bible (Magdalene 1995: 327).

In the end, however, these are 'patriarchal views of God' (1995: 352) that need to be opposed. Gerlinde Baumann concludes that 'in the entire book of Ezekiel, however, YHWH as husband does not deviate from his role of imposing (and carrying out) the death penalty on his wife' (2001: 97). For Mary Shields the body, rhetoric and gender characterization mask Yahweh completely in Ezek. 16.1-43: '...this chapter represents a portrayal of God's character, which is, to say the least, difficult to reconcile with the picture of God's abundant love and mercy which many commentators would read into the text' (2001b: 137). A major dimension of Shields's essay is to show how 'both the woman and Yahweh are characterized in terms of gender' (2001b: 139). As the first person subject of the passage, the woman is constituted as a subject only in Yahweh's speech, which simultaneously enables his elision from view. The difficulty with such an I-you structure, argues Shields, is that it prevents any distance that allows one to question God (hence most critiques have focused on the meta-phorization of women). And the reason for such an absence of question-ing, structured by a text that obscures God, is that 'if we dare to look at his character, we will be repelled by what we see' (2001b: 150). Following Renita Weems's *Battered Love* (1995), Shields faces the problematic nature of God's character, although unlike Weems she finds no redeeming features. God is 'abusive, wounding and cruel' (2001b: 152). But even Shields refuses the conclusion to which her argument moves, suggesting that texts like Ezek. 16 need to be deconstructed so that they can no longer be used to justify religious points of view that sanction male violence and abuse. Such a deconstruction leads to the conclusion that Yahweh does not have absolute power, for he becomes the female figure—an argument fully developed in her study of Ezek. 23 (Shields 2001c).

In the end, Shields does not want to take Bloch's step, preferring to hang on to God and seek 'constructive theologies which are non-violent and non-abusive' (2001b: 155). Without such an explicit theological agenda, Erin Runions uses René Girard's material on mimetic desire to reread the metaphorical language of Ezekiel 16 so that it 'can no longer be used as normative for violent gender relations by those who read the Bible as instructive' (2001: 157). Runions does so by recasting Yahweh as a parent (man or woman) with sexual preferences for men and by interpret-ing the woman as a surrogate victim in an economy of desire and violence, all through a sophisticated analysis of the interplay between the literal and the metaphoric. For Runions Yahweh becomes both a male homosexual figure with desire for the nations and a feminine heterosexual parent of the child, especially in Ezek. 16.1-13. The deity's violence towards a woman who is no longer the sexual object of male desire is the result of the deity's inability to deal with mimetic desire. The woman herself is not a wife of a jealous husband but a prostitute who becomes a surrogate victim, a scapegoat, a quasi-sacred figure who can be sacrificed for the community. This is the character Runions wishes to reclaim from a jealous and violent God, but she focuses her liberative reading on the woman without asking what it means for the character of Yahweh in Ezekiel.

There is, as S. Tamar Kamionkowski points out (2001), little sympathy for Yahweh in many feminist readings of Ezekiel—and, I would add, others like David J. Halperin's (1993)[3]—in contrast to the sympathy of traditional theological scholarship. And yet her argument, that the chaos of gender relations, identity and power is resolved at the close of Ezekiel 16, does not deal with the implications for Yahweh himself.

Although I now have plenty of material from which to begin a reading of Ezek. 20 via Ernst Bloch, Nancy Bowen's 'Can God Be Trusted?' (1995) draws a little nearer to my own interest. She argues that the deceptive God of Ezek. 14.1-11 may be a liberating figure, for 'she' is one who brings about the collapse of the old order for the sake of a new one. The feminine pronoun would be subject to Bloch's theological suspicion, but the dialectical notion of deception, of a sly text, is one that I want to pick up. For there is a direction to the studies I have glossed that is time and again refused for theological reasons. They require, in other words, the theological suspicion that is so characteristic of Bloch's work.

In order to indicate how this suspicion works I turn to Ezek. 20, which is not usually listed in the 'pornoprophetics' debate. It does not use the marriage metaphor, nor are women used as metaphors for land, city or people. However, it does push the logic of Ezekiel to its extreme. But this logic is, I want to suggest, the same logic that the critics of Ezekiel show in their work, particularly those who question the portrayal of women and Yahweh in the book. For, in a way that I have noted earlier, the biblical texts themselves have an uncanny knack of anticipating the critical positions taken in biblical scholarship. I also argue that there is a utopian

---

3.   Halperin's argument (1993), that the arbitrary and cruel God of Ezekiel is the result of the prophet's sexual pathology (a terror of female sexuality), is interesting because it questions God directly. However, the effort to psychoanalyze a supposed 'historical' person on the basis of ancient texts in order to find a mode of healing from such pathologies is open to all sorts of problems. Psychoanalytic readings of texts hardly need to anchor themselves in a hypothetical individual.

drive in Ezekiel, especially ch. 20, but that this utopian element is hardly what we would expect.

Through Ezek. 20's narration of Yahweh's dealings with Israel the various episodes pile on top of one another in a rising crescendo that ends with the enforced return and faithfulness of Israel. A rapid read through suggests that the emphasis is on Yahweh's patience and Israel's wilful disobedience and sin, so that Yahweh must reluctantly punish Israel only to restore the people from their punishment. And indeed, one refrain (Ezek. 20.9, 14, 22) stresses the perpetual delay in punishment, but the content of that refrain suggests a curious motivation. It is not that Yahweh is patient or kind or loving, or even full of mercy: 'But I acted for the sake of my name, that it should not be profaned in the sight of the nations among whom they dwelt, in whose sight I made myself known to them in trying to bring them out of the land of Egypt' (Ezek. 20.9; see vv. 14 and 22). What sort of motivation is this? Ego-centred and vain? The key Ezekelian themes of Yahweh's name and avoiding embarrassment among the nations appears here in full force.

But if we look at the text more patiently, a fourfold pattern emerges only to break down with the forced redemption. The first four episodes, beginning with 'Thus says Yahweh' (Ezek. 20.5) and 'Then I thought' (Ezek. 20.8b, 13b, 21b) mention a specific act of Yahweh and the sinful disobedience of the Israelites in response. The first (Ezek. 20.5-8a) speaks of Yahweh choosing Israel, the house of Jacob, and of the promise to bring them out of Egypt to a 'land flowing with milk and honey'. Three times Yahweh swears to Israel, once to make himself known, another to swear 'I am Yahweh' and a third to bring them out of Egypt. The content concerns the primary 'making known' of Yahweh and the promise. But it also contains the command, 'Each one of you cast away the detestable things [שִׁקּוּצֵי] of your eyes, and do not defile yourselves with the idols of Egypt' (Ezek. 20.7). Self-revelation, promise and command are followed by the adversive waw and the response of the people: they rebelled and refused to listen, worshipping precisely those things forbidden by Yahweh (Ezek. 20.8). The pattern here is one of Yahweh's act and command, followed by the disobedience and response of Israel.

This is a standard and by now somewhat tedious pattern that reverberates throughout the Hebrew Bible. Yahweh or El lays down the law, elects Israel and occasionally performs some mighty deed, the people rebel and punishment looms. It seems to me no accident that this chapter of Ezekiel sets out to re-enact the sequence that is found in so many other places, especially the Pentateuch and the so-called Deuteronomistic History. Except that now, in the second cycle (Ezek. 20.8b-13a), it becomes clear that Ezekiel has pushed back the disobedience of the first cycle to a moment in Egypt before the Exodus (Ezek. 20.8b). In the second cycle itself there are both acts and commands from Yahweh—leading them out of Egypt along with 'statutes' (חקות) and 'ordinances' (משפטים) (Ezek. 20.10)—to which are now added the 'sabbaths' in order to make the people holy (Ezek. 20.12). In other words, Yahweh has increased the pressure with even more rules and regulations and the people respond in like manner with an even more wilful disobedience. In a specific terminological reiteration, they reject statutes, ordinances and sabbaths (Ezek. 20.13)

The third and fourth episodes or cycles (Ezek. 20.13b-21a, 21b-26) follow the same pattern, although the people are now locked in the wilderness (Ezek. 20.10, 13, 15, 17, 21, 23) with only a hint of the 'most glorious of all lands' (Ezek. 20.15). The intensification starts to lag, with the statutes, ordinances and sabbaths appearing in a pattern that suggests Yahweh is condemned to repeat himself (Ezek. 20.16, 18, 21, 24), except that now the specific sin of the first cycle is added to the list. These detestable things now become the 'idols of their fathers' (גלולי אבותם, Ezek. 20.24; see vv. 16 and 18). With this addition, vv. 16 and 24 repeat the condemnation of v. 13 that they did not follow Yahweh's statutes and ordinances, profaned the sabbaths, and now worshipped the idols of their fathers.

By this time the pattern starts to break down, for there are no further acts of self-revelation or deliverance—the suggestion of land is cast in a negative promise (Ezek. 20.15)—and Yahweh merely repeats the condemnation ad nauseam. The only positive words, namely, the command to walk in his statutes and observe his ordinances, follow the warnings not to follow the ordinances, statutes and idols of their fathers. The repetition becomes wearying (as does writing 'statutes, ordinances and idols' once again), but by the fourth cycle the text strains to a breaking point, dropping off bits and pieces, losing speed rapidly as it grinds to a halt. The key lies in vv. 15 and 23. Both begin with 'moreover I stretched out my hand to them in the wilderness' only to move from 'that I would not bring them into the land' in v. 15 to the threat of v. 23 'to scatter them among the nations'. The latter stands in tension with the phrase of sparing in Ezek. 20.21b-22 that echoes those that appear earlier (20.8b-9, 13b-14). In other words, by v. 23 Yahweh spares them merely to destroy them. However, already in 20.13b-14 Yahweh appears to spare the people not for another act of deliverance as in 20.10 but for a more exquisite punishment—denial of entry into the land. A dangling promise that is drawn away, with pleasure, at the least provocation! By Ezek. 20.23 there is no longer any promise removed: Yahweh spares the people for the sake of pure punishment. The bent, twisted and strained logic comes to a complete collapse by vv. 25 and 26:

> Moreover I gave them statutes that were not good [חקים לא טובים] and ordinances by which there was no life [ומשפטים לא יחיו בהם]; and I defiled them [ואטמא אותם] in their gifts by making them offer by fire every first born so that I might horrify them, so that they would know that I am Yahweh (Ezek. 20.25-26).

It is a logic of taking the people's sins to their extreme—a little like smoking to excess in order to give up—but in doing so the text shears off and shatters. The people are trapped: until now they had ordinances and statutes from Yahweh against which they rebelled and for which they would be punished. But now Yahweh has spared them only to spring the theological trap. They can either follow the earlier statutes and ordinances and be condemned for not following the new ones, or they can obey the new ones only to be punished for not obeying the earlier ones. They are damned (somewhat literally) if they do and damned if they don't. The breathtaking theological leap—that the people so consistently disobey as if they follow an alternative law—collapses the whole structure of what has gone before. Yahweh has them surrounded, so that any leeway they might have had for their own initiative has been snatched away from them.

Had Ernst Bloch not been so enamoured with texts concerning the serpent in Eden, the Exodus, the various heterodox sects of Christianity, he would have seized on a text like this for what he dubbed the 'exodus out of Yahweh'. With this phrase he designates those texts whose dialectical path actually leads away from the conventional Yahweh of the Hebrew Bible, ones that protest against the god of overlords and rulers and in the process move out of Yahweh himself. But Ezek. 20 also shows the logic of the critical works on Ezekiel I discussed above, even though time and again they refused the conclusions for which they were reaching.

Before I track the directions of these conclusions more closely, I need to consider the remainder of Ezek. 20. This section of the chapter falls under the rubric of Yahweh's commandments that are 'not good'. So, the people arrive in the promised land, even though Yahweh said he would not bring them there (Ezek. 20.15), only to follow these new ordinances. In liturgical promiscuity they offer sacrifices and pleasant aromas and drink offerings on 'any high hill or any leafy tree' (Ezek. 20.28). They sacrifice their sons by fire and worship idols (Ezek. 20.31). After vv. 25 and 26 all of these acts are perfectly legitimate, and yet they lead to condemnation at the hands of a Yahweh in severe psychological distress.

The transition from ordinances that the people disobey to their own destruction to those they obey with the same result opens up the final stretch of text. It begins with a mitigated 'promise'—imperative would be a better word—in Ezek. 20.33-39 only to move into a full-blown enforced restoration in 20.39-44. The breakdown in theological logic, the unbearable paradox of vv. 25 and 26, is necessary for the final verses of the chapter. There are two possibilities that now present themselves. The first, in Ezek. 20.33-38, is the punishment of the people, the judgment of vv. 35 and 36. Here we find a contradiction with the earlier condemnation of the whole people as unfaithful and idolatrous: now it is just the 'rebels' who will be purged and prevented from entering the land of Israel. Exodus and Exile merge into one, but it turns out that only those who have transgressed will be punished, not the whole people. How are we to understand all that has gone before? Is the earlier narrative about these rebels alone, or of the whole people? Why then are they not all punished?

My suggestion is that this contradiction has been set up by the earlier one concerning the statutes that are 'no good'. But this suggestion looks rather flimsy until the final stretch (Ezek. 20.34-44). The impossible trap of good and bad commandments now closes on the people from both sides. Just as the people had no option but to offer their first-born, following Yahweh's command, they are equally without option regarding their restoration. Here is what might be termed a 'forced repatriation'. Yahweh no longer provides statutes that they can obey or disobey. He tells them what they will do: 'On my holy mountain…all the house of Israel, all of them, shall serve me in the land' (Ezek. 20.40). Yahweh will 'accept them', 'require contributions' (20.40), will 'bring you out from the peoples' and 'gather you out' (20.41). The people will 'know that I am Yahweh', 'remember' their ways, 'loathe themselves' (20.42; see v. 43). All of which will be done according to the curious logic of Yahweh's name.

Apart from the tension between all the house of Israel and the rebels who be punished by not returning to Israel (Ezek. 20.38), the possibility of such a forced return is set up by 20.25-26. Instead of punishment for sins committed against Yahweh's commandments, we have sins committed by following those commandments, which then leads to the inevitable punishment. But in this situation the restoration can no longer take place when the punishment is complete, a just reward for wilful disobedience, but it becomes something purely arbitrary, performed by Yahweh at his whim. The people had no option but to sin, now they have no option but to return, worship and serve Yahweh faithfully. Such logic would have made predestinarians like Calvin feel warm and fuzzy (except that I can hardly imagine Calvin feeling that way, however much I admire him): the beauty of the inscrutable modes of God's grace, except for those annoying vv. 25 and 26.

However, I am not following Calvin in my reading. Rather, Bloch's first question would be, What if the people don't want to? Here they are, dragged this way and that with no thought given to their own wishes and desires. Of course, punishment is rarely desired, except in a masochistic state, but a forced return? They have little option in a text like Ezek. 20. Is this perhaps a sly text? one of those that was written in apparently pious terms, but between the lines of which another, quietly derogatory and critical, tone emerges? I am not so taken with this aspect of Bloch's work, for it relies too much on historical critical notions of textual layers and editing, concerning which Bloch was fully conversant and somewhat en- amoured. Rather, I want to suggest that his dialectic of utopia and the implicit 'atheism', a protest atheism, is more persuasive.

Let me begin in reverse order, for Ezek. 20 brings out the conclusion that the studies I surveyed earlier refused to make. In Ezek. 20 Yahweh comes through as a complete bastard, to borrow Ed Conrad's phrase, one who must have the last word, be totally in control and anticipate any move the people might make. The radical move of vv. 25 and 26 makes Yahweh an impossible God to serve, one who forces people to 'sin', to do precisely what he has forbidden so that the whole notion of sin and rebellion no longer makes any sense. It is, to put it in Bloch's terms, the ultimate desire of the ruling classes, to co-opt and anticipate any move the people might make so that they are completely subservient. The extreme monotheism implicit in this chapter not only makes Yahweh responsible for good and evil commandments, but also entirely arbitrary. In doing so it shows the impossibility of such monotheism itself, at least in terms of any viable anthropology, of any notion that allows human beings to realize their utopian potential. The forced return of the last verses, where the people will simply do what Yahweh says—return, serve, worship, accept and know that he is Yahweh—makes a mockery of any sense of worship or serving in response to God.

Further, the repeated justification of Yahweh's actions—for his name and to avoid embarrassment among the nations—merely reinforces the breakdown of any viability that such a figure might have. No loving kindness (חסד) here; he is just a bad sport, a sore loser who asserts his superiority. The people of Israel will be his chosen people, entirely for selfish reasons on Yahweh's part, whether they like it or not.

The point I want to make is that in Ezekiel we have not an undesirable representation of God, one among many that falls short of his true nature. Rather, it is a text that shows the radical impossibility of a figure like this. In other words, by going to this extreme, it leads, as Bloch would argue, to what is later called 'atheism', if we allow the anachronism for a moment. I would prefer the term 'anti-Yahwism', however, since the hypothesis I want to put forward is that texts like Ezek. 20 give voice to a protest against the strictures of an ideological system that has Yahweh at its centre. In other words, given that the only way saying anything politically was in terms of the over-arching cultural dominant of the sacred, a political protest, an ideological critique, can only be put in terms of theological categories. To put it crudely, a protest against Yahweh is a protest against those for whom Yahweh is the ideological feature that holds a whole ruling class ideology together. However, in Ezek. 20 the possibility of such protest showing up relies on the contradictions of that ideology itself that emerge despite and through the text.

If my hypothesis that Ezek. 20 can be read in terms of an implicit protest that shows up through the breakdown of its own logic, then it may join the other texts that Bloch lines up in his search for the 'Exodus out of Yahweh', out of the god of the oppressors. These include the story of the serpent in Gen. 2–3, Cain and Abel in Gen. 4, Korah's rebellion in Num. 16, Balaam in Num. 22–24, the continual theme of the murmuring of the people, much of the prophetic material and so on. Bloch tends to argue that in the earliest layers of the text can we find this protest against the rulers and their God.

I am not sure, however, that this is the best line to take, for it is tied in too much to sources and intentions. I would like to emphasize the alternative psychological and philosophical dimensions of Bloch's work, the deep utopian impulse he felt he had identified in collective and individual human existence, over against both Freud and Jung. From this perspective, Ezek. 20—coming from those texts Bloch preferred as giving voice to the radical socio-theological critique of Yahwism—expresses less a conscious protest than an unconscious one. It contains an implicit 'protest atheism' that emerges by pushing the limits of Yahwism itself. In other words, it becomes part of Bloch's argument concerning the Bible in spite of itself, producing an intolerable depiction of Yahweh that becomes a criticism of Yahweh and all of his ruling class associations.

Is this not where the studies, mostly of Ezek. 16 and 23, lead? Magdalene, Shields, Runions, Kamionkowski, Bowen and Halperin all point out that Yahweh is a thoroughly despicable character in Ezekiel, yet their own conclusions vary from rejecting this specific patriarchal representation of Yahweh as flawed, deconstructing Yahweh's character so that the text loses its ideological power, seeking more constructive and liberating theologies, or suggesting that recognition of Ezekiel's pathology provides readers with the possibility of healing (so Halperin). Most would like to keep the God of the Bible in some fashion, although not necessarily the one of these texts.

Yet if my argument concerning the implicit rejection of Yahweh in Ezekiel is workable, then what these critics have done is precisely what the text itself does—find that Yahweh himself is objectionable and unbearable. My suggestion is that the proper conclusion to these studies is an atheistic one, for do not their works also function as a protest atheism, under the knowledge that no-one in their right, or even wrong, mind would believe in such a deity or the ideology of which it is a part?

There is one final aspect of Bloch's work that I have held until now— the question of utopia that I broached at the close of my chapter on Gramsci and Exodus. There I was less certain that Gramsci's reading of Machiavelli, or any reading of Exodus, could claim to be utopian. Bloch is a far greater theorist and interpreter of utopia and the utopian impulse, and with this in mind I want to argue that Ezek. 20, and possibly the whole book of Ezekiel, can be read as utopian.

But how in the world could such a misogynist and chauvinistic book with its thoroughly despicable deity be regarded as utopian? Let me begin with Bloch's observation that even in the depraved and degraded products of culture a utopian glimpse may be found. Here his dialectical analysis swings into consideration, for utopia may only emerge in these situations by means of a thorough suspicion of any ostensible utopian project. And it is not so much that the very effort to construct a utopia, even though it may turn out to be thoroughly dystopian, functions as a signal of the utopian imagination, that the effort to imagine another world, however bad it may be, is in itself utopian. No, the argument is more specific than that:

the utopian dimension of a religious text like the Bible lies primarily not in its images, dreams and hopes for a better world, nor even in the projection of such a world into the mythical past of paradise or Eden. It lies in the protest against the god or gods of the ruling class that we find everywhere in the Bible, in other words in protest atheism itself. Only then, from a theological perspective, does the possibility of utopia emerge.

Thus, I have argued for the implicit atheism of Ezek. 20 and those studies of Ezekiel 16 and 23, through the extreme portrayal of a deity who gives Israel statutes both good and evil, who forces them to return to the land and serve him, and who does so for the noble motives of his own name and reputation among the nations. And this implicit protest against Yahweh is also a utopian moment, a glimpse of a world without a god to which human beings are subjects. It is utopian because it is a protest against the political economic situation that produced such a figure and uses him as the linchpin of a ruling ideology. The rulers are under criticism as much as their God. As I pointed out earlier in this chapter, the notion of atheism is anachronistic, for the possibility of atheism arises only under capitalism. Under the political economic system of the Hebrew Bible, what I have tentatively termed the Asiatic mode of production until I can reflect on this question further in my conclusion, the dominant cultural mode of the sacred means that what we would now categorize as the psychological, social, sexual, gendered and cultural aspects of human life (the categorization is itself a signal of our own cultural dominant of reification) were articulated and understood in terms of the sacred. Thus, what I have described as an implicit atheism is more correctly a protest against this particular god, Yahweh, an anti-Yahwism that seeks an alternative within the cultural dominant of the sacred itself.

Chapter 7

THEODOR ADORNO: THE LOGIC OF DIVINE JUSTICE IN ISAIAH

Adorno may well be one of the most rigorously consistent practitioners of dialectical thinking in the whole Marxist tradition. For those weary of sloppy thinking and undemanding texts, Adorno's sustained intellectual discipline comes as something of a relief, a reminder that it is possible to keep to such a high standard. In part, this is precisely why Adorno is one of a constellation of major thinkers of the last century. For in the same way that his writing keeps to an unparalleled rigour, so also his ability to work through to new levels in Marxist thought have left their mark on contemporary thought.

For a relatively short-lived Marxist (1903–69), Adorno was extremely productive and influential, especially in the post-war reconstruction of Germany, where the left emerged, for a time at least, with the credentials of having opposed fascism from the first. The exiles returned from around the world, including the Frankfurt School of Social Research from its wartime domicile in New York, to take over the intellectual, moral and political leadership of a generation that had by and large been part of the Third Reich. As a German Jew, Adorno wasted no time in getting out soon after the Nazis came to power, but on his return to Germany, he was quite conscious of his influence in his home country and Europe.

Personally, I find Adorno, along with Lukács, the most attractive of the figures I deal with in this book. It is the sheer bloodymindedness, the rigour and discipline, the need to get on with the job without fuss, and the intellectual and practical commitment to Marxism as the best possible option in the current situation, both intellectually and politically, that attracts me. Of course, there is always the distinct appeal of asceticism, although in this case of the intellectual kind.

As with the other critics I deal with in this book, my use of Adorno is quite specific. In his *habilitationschrift* and first philosophical work, *Kierkegaard: Construction of the Aesthetic* (1989), Adorno argues that

Kierkegaard ends up with insuperable paradoxes in his effort to base a philosophy, ethics or aesthetics on theology. In a similar fashion, I argue, the common assumption that the divine justice found in the prophets, especially Isaiah, provides the basis for social justice faces comparable paradoxes that render any connection between divine and social justice highly problematic, if not impossible. The elements of Adorno's approach that I outline below before turning to Isaiah include his practice of immanent criticism, his distinct development of the dialectic that comes out of the Hegelian–Marxist tradition, and an attention to theology that often surprises Adorno scholars. As with my discussion of Bloch, I suggest that one of the benefits for biblical criticism of Adorno's work is the need for a thorough theological demystification.

Adorno's comments on his method of interpreting Kierkegaard are as good as any introduction to his practice of immanent criticism: 'There is no way to meet up with him in the fox kennel of infinitely reflected interiority than to take him at his word; he is to be caught in the traps set by his own hand' (Adorno 1989: 11). What are these traps in the fox kennel? They are nothing but theological, or, more specifically, biblical. Adorno will seek to use Kierkegaard's own method in order to read his work, which is theological exegesis.

> The impulse for the literal examination of Kierkegaard's language does not have to be imported psychoanalytically into his work, although there is more than enough occasion and temptation. It has its precedent in the work itself, in the theological Christian exegesis (*christlich-theologische Exegese*). Like the edifying writings, the pseudonymous *Training in Christianity* is exegetical; and all the pseudonymous writings are interwoven with exegetical sections. No meaningful exegesis can be conceived, however, that is not obligatorily bound to the vocabulary of the text. In Kierkegaard's work, the model of the exegesis is the canonical explication of the doctrine of the Parousia (Adorno 1989: 12).

Adorno follows Kierkegaard's method, an exegetical one that is based on the interpretation of biblical texts ('at every point Kierkegaard's statements refer to texts that he held to be holy' [Adorno 1989: 12]), but the upshot of this is that one of the sources for his notion of immanent criticism is biblical exegesis itself. The other source is Walter Benjamin. Like Benjamin, to whom the book on Kierkegaard is heavily indebted, only the complete immersion in the content and method of the text under question—an approach that I follow below with my reading of Isaiah—is able to identify the contradictions by which critique can move forward: 'every insight into Kierkegaard is to be wrung out of his own context'

(1989: 13). But this means that an immanent interpretation is also very much dialectical, for in Adorno's hands it becomes the means for pursuing the contradictions until they give out their 'truth-content', the historical materialist ultimately determining instant, for Adorno the 'concrete' without which thought is not possible.

As for dialectics, it seems to me that there is nothing quite like the relentless dialectical moves of Adorno, caught in both the content and structure of virtually every sentence he wrote. For Adorno, dialectical thinking is not merely the fruitful juxtaposition of two opposed or unrelated items—military and intelligence, for example—but the realisation of their fundamental unity when their differences are pushed to the extreme; or, the arrival at a sense of the profound dissonance between things that appeared unified and harmonious. For instance, at the earliest moment of talkies, of movies with speaking voices, he argued that the apparently natural combination of picture and sound led to a stilted effect, one that required the presence of music to cover over the resulting stiltedness, to distract our attention from it.

In other words, dialectical reading in Adorno's hands requires a notion of contradiction, seeks until it finds such contradictions in texts, culture, philosophy, music and so on (Jameson will make this a central aspect of his own work as well). Adorno's method properly begins when the crucial contradiction or contradictions have been identified: from this moment dialectical criticism can begin its complex and convoluted workings. Yet Adorno's dialectical criticism is not your shopping-mall-variety of dialectics. Marx's appropriation and development sought, in the famous phrase, to turn Hegel's idealism on its head, that is, to make the connections between thought and the realms of society, politics and economics. The advantage of dialectical criticism is that it can work such connections in a fashion that avoids direct links, reflective or homological patterns whereby the text represents its context. For a system like Marxism, the danger always lies with this tendency, a certain crude thinking or vulgar Marxism that seeks to explain elements of culture, philosophy, religion and so on by a direct correlation with political economics. Even though I am not averse to the distinct usefulness of such crude thinking on certain occasions, a dialectical approach like Adorno's prefers to avoid it in favour of a more demanding strategy: the relations between various elements run at cross-purposes to each other, aspects from culture (texts, thought, etc.) seeking to deal with problems in political economics, or moves in the social realm responding in various ways to culture itself.

At the risk of stating the obvious, the canonical form of Hegel's dialectic—thesis, antithesis, synthesis; or affirmation, negation, supersession—risks a profound misunderstanding. For Hegel's dialectic turns on mediation, being understood as a reconciliation of opposites, a compromise, something like a committee report or divorce settlement. Yet even this is not quite correct, for in Hegel it is *Aufhebung* that becomes the key: simultaneously an annulment or cancellation and a preservation, *Aufhebung* is a 'supersession' that shifts the whole problem onto a new plane where the original problem ceases to be what it was while new questions arise. For Adorno, however, the dialectic operates by pushing the oppositions, anomalies and contradictions to their extremes, and only when there seems to be nothing in common whatsoever does mediation occur. It is not about seeking common ground, but of removing any such ground that may have existed to begin with. In this way, a concept begins to show glimpses of its opposite, transformed in the process that identifies what has been excluded as the key to the concept itself.

The final advantage of Adorno's dialectics is its ability to be highly inclusive of what it considers. The very strategy of incorporating opposites, of moving an idea to its logical extreme, cannot but help open up further areas for consideration. The assimilationist danger of master narratives is always there, to be sure, but the perpetual workings of opposition, tension and contradiction allow the distinct place of a host of ideas and movements that would in other instances be excluded—often the fragments and pieces of philosophy and literary criticism, the progressive moments in a largely reactionary positions, or recent developments in feminism, deconstruction, psychoanalysis and so on.

Adorno's interpretative strategy may also be read in terms of demystification, something I have already broached on a number of occasions. In Adorno's hands, however, it is less of a direct hermeneutics of suspicion, where a first moment of unmasking leads one to identify the positive. By contrast, for Adorno a dialectical reading brings out what is normally hidden, cast in shadow by the reading process employed. Adorno does this with the role of the interpreter, but it also operates with some of the traditional concerns of Marxism, such as social relations, politics, economics and mode of production. What Adorno's reading enables us to do is to push the text, especially its interpretation, to yield up precisely these dimensions, which are always there but not recognized. For instance, in his brilliant engagement with Kierkegaard, Adorno argues not only that a philosophical system or an aesthetic cannot in the end be built successfully on a mythical or theological base, but also that if Kierkegaard's idealism is read dialectically it brings us to the social and economic conditions of its production. Thus, the inner flight, the leap of faith, the retreat into solitude before the unstoppable process of modernity and the reliance upon God alone—all of these speak of a man of independent means not merely evading the relatively new bourgeois world of the town, but expressing the deepest spiritual dimensions of precisely that bourgeois society. Or, in his famous debate with Walter Benjamin regarding his studies of Baudelaire, the 'Work of Art' essay and the Arcades project, Adorno is profoundly unsatisfied with Benjamin's efforts to integrate metaphysics and historical materialism. Rather than pursue such an unstable and ultimately futile aim, Adorno urged him to return to his theological approach, for if this were worked through dialectically, it would bring Benjamin to a Marxist analysis of far greater perceptiveness and analytic power. The directly materialist dimensions of Benjamin's work were less interesting than his mythological or theological moments, although for specifically dialectical reasons:

> If I were to close the circle of my critique with one bold grip, it would be bound to grasp the extremes. A restoration of theology, or better yet, a radicalization of the dialectic into the glowing centre of theology, would at the same time have to mean the utmost intensification of the social-dialectical, indeed economic, motifs (Adorno in Bloch *et al.* 1990: 114).[1]

The best thing to do would be to provide an example or two of Adorno's criticism in action, examples I have drawn from his study of Kierkegaard.

1.   In reponse to the Arcades project, of which the Baudelaire section was sent to the Institute, Adorno writes: 'This, I think, brings me to the centre of my criticism. The impression which your entire study conveys—and not only to me and my arcades orthodoxy—is that you have done violence to yourself. Your solidarity with the Institute, which pleases no one more than myself, has induced you to pay tributes to Marxism which are not really suited to Marxism or to yourself' (Adorno in Bloch *et al.* 1990: 130). Further: '...it would also be most helpful to the cause of dialectical materialism and the theoretical interests represented by the Institute, if you surrendered to your specific insights and conclusions without adding to them ingredients which you obviously find so distasteful to swallow that I cannot really regard them as beneficial. God knows, there is only one truth, and if your intelligence lays hold of this one truth in categories which on the basis of your idea of materialism seem apocryphal to you, you will capture more of this one truth than if you use intellectual tools whose movements your hand resists at every turn. After all, there is more about this truth in Nietzsche's *Genealogy of Morals* than in in Bukharin's *ABC of Communism*' (Adorno in Bloch *et al.* 1990: 131).

In this book he systematically demystifies the mythical appeal of Kier-kegaard's work and then reads it in a dialectical fashion to show how liberalism's valuation of the individual lies behind this aestheticization.

The dilemma for Adorno, of course, is that while European philosophy is inescapably tied to theology, he is profoundly suspicious of the value of a theological base for philosophy, and his argument will turn out to be that theology, in this case the theology of Kierkegaard, is saturated with mythology and paradoxes and therefore constitutes a shaky basis upon which to build a philosophical system. Adorno wishes to submit theology to the same dialectical moves that he applies to everything else, namely, that the 'truth-value' of theology must be sought in its dialectical other without which it cannot exist or operate. This will becomes the socio-economic logic of theology itself, but it can only be located through theology and not be imported from outside. This entails an intense immer-sion in theology—like his immersion in Kierkegaard's method and content—that locates its contradictions and then works through them.

There are three major arguments that Adorno makes against Kierke-gaard: that his retreat into objectless inwardness cannot avoid history; that Kierkegaard's theology slips into the myth it perpetually represses; and that the paradoxes of theology eventually break up the possibility of any system based on theological categories.

One of the major moves in Adorno's study of Kierkegaard was the argument that despite Kierkegaard's attack on idealism, his is itself an unavoidably idealist position. But the way Adorno is able to make such an argument is through the profound retreat that Kierkegaard makes to 'inwardness' (*Innerlichkeit*). Yet this is not a crass biographical move that seeks to unmask Kierkegaard by means of his own lived conditions—a reclusive writer living off an inheritance that he refused to invest—but rather a dialectical reading of the logic of Kierkegaard's own texts. After the preliminaries of the first chapter ('Exposition of the Aesthetic'), Adorno devotes two to the question of inwardness, veering closely to a critique of existentialism that became the subject of *The Jargon of Authenticity* (Adorno 1973).

What does Adorno do in the first lines of these chapters? Although one would expect a more direct move into the question of subject and object, the philosophical terms that form the default question for inwardness, instead he begins with Kierkegaard's complex and ultimately allegorical use of 'Scripture' (*Schrift*). In this crucial first step, that one is tempted to skip over in the search for the main direction of Adorno's argument, we

find that the Bible appears, although as 'Scripture' with all of its theological associations intact. The word 'Scripture'—burdened with an
institutional sacredness—is a mark of the contradiction of Kierkegaard's
philosophical aesthetics, although Adorno zeroes on the contradiction by
means of Kierkegaard's use of the Bible.

In characteristic fashion, Adorno weaves through a whole cluster or
constellation of problems in order to make his point. As far as Scripture is
concerned, Kierkegaard is caught between theological assumptions and the
historical particularity of this ancient text: while the Bible itself is subject
to historical contingency, to a 'historical deterioration' (*historische
Depravation*, Adorno 1989: 25), whereby its historical meaning has faded
and become difficult to decipher, Kierkegaard is committed to a theological assumption about the nature of this text. If God, the one ultimately
responsible for this text, is unchangeable and trustworthy, then the Bible
too must be unalterable and eternally true. But Kierkegaard is not a dog-
matic theologian, for whom the 'symbolic word' (*symbolischen Wort*)—
the christological allusion should not slip by here—unifies signifier and
signified. Instead the historical loss of meaning with the Bible must be
handled in other ways. In order to mediate such a contradiction,
Kierkegaard reads the text as cipher (*Chiffre*) and allegory: 'Implicit in
Kierkegaard's metaphor of scripture is: the unalterable givenness of the
text itself as well as its unreadableness as that of a "cryptogram" composed of "ciphers" whose origin is historical' (Adorno 1989: 25). Carrying
the theological logic through, the incomprehensibility of God renders the
Bible the same.

Before coming to Kierkegaard's attempted solution to the contradiction
of Scripture, I need to note Adorno's dependence on Benjamin here in the
function of the cipher. The Kierkegaard study relies heavily upon the
model of Benjamin's German Mourning Play book (Benjamin 1998), and
here Adorno invokes Benjamin on allegory—particularly the notion that
allegory is not merely a sign but expression—in order to show that *Chiffre*
is but one form of allegory. And in Kierkegaard's work, the cipher
operates by means of its 'affects' (Adorno 1989: 26). These affects are
none other than the existential categories, such as anxiety and despair,
marks of sin and damnation.

But what of the cipher, Scripture itself? Reading the affects is the first
step in dealing with the incomprehensibility of this cipher. As I indicated
above, the problem arises with history, which produces a 'fissure' between
the cipher and truth. This break then slides to the fissure between the

individual and the text, who begin to affect one another. That is, the meaning of the text, the cipher, itself begins to decay, so meaning 'separates from the cipher in the text' (Adorno 1989: 26). Yet it is through history that such a break appears, and history takes on the role of the Fall (rather than being a prehistorical 'event').

Kierkegaard's solution is not, however, an eschatological one that looks to the overthrow of capitalism, but a regressive one, saturated with the logic of capitalism itself. Kierkegaard resorts to the psychology of the individual in order to go back and recover, existentially, the lost meaning of the text, simultaneously hidden and glimpsed through its status as cipher. The catch, as we have already picked up a few sentences earlier, is that Kierkegaard's psychology is based not on phenomenology, nor even on traditional scientific psychology, but on theology. This is the impossible trap of a method based on theology, for it cannot escape the logic of the system: the effort to overcome a contradiction regarding the Bible that was generated out of theology itself (God's unchangeable word in history) can only produce a solution that is itself theological and thereby remains caught in the contradiction.

The implications of this critique from Adorno move beyond his own undermining of theology as a base for philosophy or a theory of aesthetics. If Kierkegaard has created his own problems through the particular theological assumptions with which he reads the Bible, then the options for getting out of his bind are either a different understanding of God (should he wish to hold onto God)—as arbitrary, untrustworthy and changeable—or the separation of the Bible and theology. In the latter option, the Bible is not Scripture, but a text that was written and compiled a very long time ago. Without the theological assumptions imported into the reading of the Bible, the contradiction fades away. In other words the theology that sees itself based upon the Bible is in fact a foreign body: this, it seems to me, is where Adorno's anti-theological approach leads. In fact, Adorno touches here on the possibility of a demystifying biblical criticism that points out to theology its status as unwelcome visitor.

As my second example of Adorno's criticism I move to the central chapters of the Kierkegaard study, where he makes a number of similar moves. After searching for the mythical underlay of Kierkegaard's theology—itself a complement of history, as Adorno's later writings will argue—he moves over to explore the various paradoxes that emerge from his analysis of Kierkegaard. Eventually these paradoxes, which Kierkegaard sets up in order to start his dialectical method, lead to impossible tensions that break up the system, of the very possibility of a system based on theology. Thus, Adorno piles one concise argument for the impossibility of Kierkegaard's theological philosophy on another: the inextricable link between paradox and sacrifice, the breakdown of the dialectic of historical specificity and eternal significance, and then between transcendence and immanence, the vicious circle of immanence itself that makes belief in God impossible, to the ultimate argument that he reiterates in *The Jargon of Authenticity*, the sacrifice of reason.

Let me focus on the question of sacrifice, for here Adorno returns to Kierkegaard's dependence on the theological primacy of paradox, since it is within sacrifice that the ultimate paradox of theology resides. Patiently, exploring, Adorno begins by reiterating the point that for theology, and so for Kierkegaard, paradox provides the answer and not the starting point for philosophical dialectics.

Initially, Adorno's identification of sacrifice with paradox seems odd, until Kierkegaard's effort at a dialectics is brought in, without explicit mention: 'The model of this sacrifice is paradoxy: a movement of thought, completed in our thought, and negated as totality in this movement of thought, in order, sacrificed, to draw toward itself the "strictly different", its absolute contrary' (Adorno 1989: 113). It is the model of Kierkegaard's thought itself. Adorno stays with theology for a few moments, moving through hereditary sin, Christology, belief, autonomy and determination until he notes that for Kierkegaard paradox is not restricted to the traditional theological forms. Thus, the paradoxes dear to Kierkegaard—revelation/mystery, happiness/suffering, certainty/uncertainty, ease/difficulty of religious truth/absurdity—arise from the fact that sacrifice is the basis of Kierkegaard's dialectics. Further, sacrifice and paradox are inseparable: 'every sacrifice is allotted paradoxy as the sign of its systematic seal of authenticity' (Adorno 1989: 115). Conversely, sacrifice is the 'essence of paradoxy' (1989: 116). The implications of this dialectical conjunction concern the remainder of Adorno's argument.

Since Adorno has already demystified the mythical status of sacrifice in an earlier part of the book, his interest now is the connection between sacrifice and paradox and the implications that this raises for the category of paradox itself: 'The paradox is Kierkegaard's fundamental, categorical form' (Adorno 1989: 115). But, as he has already argued, paradox is the source of the breakdown in Kierkegaard's dialectic, and so the yoking of sacrifice, itself the basis of Kierkegaard's dialectic, with paradox will have a disastrous effect on the possibility of that dialectic. That is to say, the relation between paradox, sacrifice and dialectics ensures a volatility Kierkegaard cannot contain.

Adorno's test case is Christology, particularly in terms of the tension between time and eternity. Nature, especially fallen nature, has for Kierkegaard no history: time is that which marks human existence as distinct from nature. The problem, according to Adorno, is that Kierkegaard attributes timelessness, a feature of nature, to Christ, in direct contradiction to Kierkgaard's insistence on the historicity of God's appearance in Christ. He picks up on Kierkegaard's phrase ' this *nota bene* on a page of universal history' to argue that this is precisely a mark of the lack of historical specificity in regard to Christ's incarnation: he might have appeared at any moment in time, interchangeable with any other.

Thus, rather than marking in a unique fashion the possibility of history itself, the central node of history as Karl Barth was to argue, the life of Christ becomes timeless, falling back into nature. And this nature is specifically 'fallen nature', the state of human beings in the world after the Fall. Timelessness, fallen nature and also abstractness form part of the trap in which Kierkegaard's Christology—and thereby his theory of the individual for which Christology provides the basis—is caught.

The choice of Christology to deal with the relation between paradox and sacrifice is not mere whim on the part of Adorno, for not only does Christian theology base its anthropology on Christology, but Christology itself is the locus for theological elaborations (Kierkegaard's included) of sacrifice. That this is also paradoxical is the edge of Adorno's argument, precisely on the tricky point of the history and the uniqueness of Christ.

Not only does the paradox of time undo Kierkegaard's Christology, but also his ontology, which itself cannot avoid the question of the two natures of Christ. Thus, the paradox of specificity and eternity—the one 'wiped out by sacrificial paradoxy' (Adorno 1989: 117), the other drifting away into abstractness—translates into the paradox of transcendence and immanence. On the one hand, the telos of the incarnation becomes absolute, incomparable and therefore indeterminate: it is beyond any compromise and thereby becomes an impossible category, a transcendence that disappears into space, with nothing to mark its passing. On the other hand, Christ's immanence is unacceptable and unbearable: having God at close quarters reveals him to be one with whom human beings cannot communicate (Adorno uses Kierkegaard's comments on Job, for here Kierkegaard says what he cannot say about Christ—that God's immediate presence is unbearable). But there is a further turn to Adorno's argument, for in the centrifugal force of Kierkegaard's paradoxes—historical specificity and eternity, transcendence and immanence—his argument, according to Adorno, becomes mythological, remaining in the realm of nature.

Given that the discussion of Christology is ultimately part of Kierkegaard's wider ponderings on the status of the individual, the result is that human consciousness becomes supreme. Reading between the lines: the paradoxical separation between the divine and human natures of Christ ends up being, in light of the inaccessibility of the transcendent, an option for the human, specifically human consciousness. And it is sacrifice that achieves this, now demonic: 'In the demonic sacrifice of consciousness, man is still the ruler of a sinful creation; through sacrifice he asserts his rule, and the name of the divinity succumbs to his demonic nature' (Adorno 1989: 117). The end run of this logic is that the sacrifice of Christ becomes the sacrifice of God, and Adorno argues that Kierkegaard's philosophy cannot help but make him an unbeliever. In fact this question—was Kierkgaard a believer?—cannot be answered adequately except through an absolutely relentless dialectic attention to Kierkegaard's philosophy.

Immanence may seem more friendly terrain on which to engage Kierkegaard. Yet Adorno shows how Kierkegaard's argument falls victim to a vicious circle. Drawing on a quotation from Kierkegaard on the ascension—in which the impossible necessity of the ascension of Christ arises from the need of his followers so that it becomes a certainty of faith—Adorno questions the ultimate pragmatism that vitiates the paradox of a faith where the sheer uncertainty itself is the basis for the truths of belief. It is precisely this pragmatism—the followers of Christ need the ascension for their own comfort—that indicates the closed immanence of the argument: 'In sacrifice immanence reaches out beyond itself only to plunge into the blind relentless context of nature in which the immanent follower is to procure assurance of the transcendent ascension, rather than the reverse' (Adorno 1989: 118).

Adorno's study of Kierkegaard, recognized as one of his most difficult works, is the model for my reading of Isa. 5. There too I will pursue an immanent dialectical interpretation that seeks the paradoxes of the text's own argument, an interpretation that does not seek to make sense of difficult material by importing suggestions from outside but rather works through such difficulties in order to locate the tensions and paradoxes within the text.

The Paradoxes of Divine Justice

In some respects Ezekiel, with whom I dealt in the previous chapter, is an easy target with its cruel and arbitrary deity. Isaiah, by contrast, is more on the level, focusing on Israel's disobedience in terms of both religious and social practice along with a large number of oracles of rescue and restoration. The centrality of this text in Christian thought has much to do with the extensive quotations found in the New Testament. But another reason is that Isaiah provides the foundations for the argument that social justice is based upon divine justice, and that any subsequent form of social justice, however secular, may be traced back to prophets like Isaiah, or Amos or Micah (see, for instance, Milbank 1992).

I argue that the connection between social and divine justice, made explicit in texts like Isaiah 5, faces a number of paradoxes comparable to those in Kiekegaard's work. This text is the well-known 'song of the vineyard', although it is more of an allegory *avant la lettre* with the interpretation of the various items in the allegory itself provided in Isa. 5.7. Nevertheless, I will begin in reverse with the 'woe' oracles that begin in v. 8. Here we have a distinctly socio-economic criticism of those with, or those who abuse (the distinction is important), wealth and power. In a term that Norman Gottwald has applied from Roman practices, the text speaks of *latifundia*, the use of debt burdens to appropriate land and houses at the expense of those in debt: 'Woe to those who join house to house and field to field until there is no more room' (Isa. 5.8). The economic and social effects follow: empty houses that have been appropriated and the inhabitants thrown out; a dramatic drop in production that sees vineyards and grain crops inadequately cultivated (Isa. 5.9). But lurking within this outcome is the judgment against the latifundiaries, for their own houses will lie desolate and their vineyards and grain crops will not produce what they expected. There is an economic logic to this, namely, that certain economic practices have disastrous outcomes within the political economic systems under which they are pursued. Yet this way of looking at the situation keeps God out of the argument, except as one who is part of the economic process itself. As far as Isaiah is concerned, the two can hardly be separated from one another, for the distinction between economic and divine cause would have been entirely foreign and anachronistic in a political economic system where the sacred provided the language by which the world and the place of human beings within it was understood. In this respect there is a seamless connection between divine and human justice, or rather between the sacred and the economic, so much so that economic depredation was a sacred or theological problem that required urgent divine attention. For this reason, the economic practice of *latifundia* brings a condemnation from Yahweh in the text itself.

The woe oracles that follow identify various social and economic ills, rather than the apostasy and worship of idols that we find in Jeremiah or Ezekiel, or elsewhere in Isaiah. So, there are criticisms of grog and partying that result in lack of knowledge (destruction of brain cells?), food and water (Isa. 5.11-12), criticisms of double-speak (Isa. 5.20) and the cultivation of falsehood and sin (Isa. 5.18-19), self-knowledge (5.21), drinking and legal corruption (Isa. 5.22). These woes begin slowly and with more detail (Isa. 5.8-17), only to tighten up in a series of brief condemnations (Isa. 5.18-22).

While these woes appear to be a series of moral denunciations, there is a distinct class element that points towards the first paradox of Isa. 5. Who are 'those who rise early in the morning that they may run after strong drink, who tarry late into the evening till wine inflames them' (Isa. 5.11)? Who are the party animals who do not 'regard the deeds of Yahweh or see the work of his hands' (Isa. 5.12)? Are they the latifundiaries of vv. 8-10? Only in v. 14 does the class identifier appear, namely, the 'nobility' (הדר). Along with this nobility are 'her multitude, 'her throng' and 'he who exults in her' (Isa. 5.14). The feminine third person possessive pronoun to all the nouns, including 'nobility' (הדרה), refers back to the earlier 'Sheol'. And so the latifundiaries are the 'nobility of Sheol'. The point here is a class critique: only those who do no work but rely on the work of others, that is, the owners of the means of production, have time to drink and party, and the dire socio-economic effects are the result of their exploitation. The 'nobility of Sheol' must therefore be read as a derogatory term for this class and all of the apparently moral denunciations become class specific: they carouse, steal land and houses, sin, abuse religious privilege, call evil good and vice versa, are wise in their own eyes and corrupt the legal system for their own benefit. They are 'haughty' (Isa. 5.15), heroes at drinking wine (Isa. 5.22), and guilty of wholesale corruption and injustice.

Herein lies the first paradox, for the entire prophetic denunciation is directed at one class. Now while this provides plenty of resources for those who wish to find social justice issues dealt with in the Bible, or even on a minimal level search for material that suggests between the lines social and economic formations for which class remains the best term (as I have been arguing here and in which I am engaging here), the paradox arises precisely when we turn to the allegory of the vineyard. The allegorical interpretation of Isa. 5.7 (a step up the narrative in my reverse reading) identifies the vineyard as the 'house of Israel', the vineyard itself as belonging to 'Yahweh Sabaoth' and the plantings of the vineyard as the 'man of Judah'. In v. 3 appear the 'inhabitant of Jerusalem' (יושב ירושלם) and again the 'man of Judah' (איש יהודה). The woes that follow immediately after v. 7 are therefore directed at these groups, which one initially might read as the whole people.

The problem begins with the tension between, on the one hand, the house of Israel, the vocative singulars, 'O inhabitant of Jerusalem' and 'O man of Judah' in vv. 3 and 7, and, on the other, the ruling class of vv. 8-23: the text seems to identify this class as the whole people, an ideological slip that implicitly recognizes the power of ruling class ideology. Thus far I have said nothing particularly new, as both Matthews (1999) and Chaney (1999), for instance, have argued in a similar fashion largely from social scientific and archaeological perspectives. Matthews uses evidence of viticultural practices in the ancient Near East to explain the effect of the allegory to its original audience, whereas Chaney brings together social scientific, comparison with other Isaiah oracles, genre and lexicographical analysis in order to argue for a consistent criticism of ruling class practices in Israel in Isaiah's time. The text is major source for Chaney of social justice issues. Apart from the positivist assumptions that we can actually speak of either an original audience or of Isaiah's time, let alone the traditional historical-critical Isaiah of the eighth century BCE, both studies operate on the unexamined assumption that the allegory must be consistent and must make sense. Thus Chaney, when faced with the problem of terminology I have noted, especially the 'man of Judah' and 'inhabitant of Jerusalem', wants to specify the terms to focus on the ruling elite: the former as a small body of large and powerful land-holders and the latter as ruler(s) of Jerusalem. Matthews engages in a massive effort of filling in what he feels to be the missing pieces in order to render the allegory consistent. My inquiry differs precisely on the question of consistency, for it seems to me that the tensions and paradoxes are the most interesting part of Isa. 5. And the paradox is between the ruling classes identified in the woes and the whole people of the terms 'O man of Judah', 'O inhabitant of Jerusalem' (in both cases the most common usage) and 'house of Israel'. The problem is that as far as the ruling classes are concerned, they are the whole people and their ideas are the ideas of the whole people, whom they epitomize, control and exploit.

This particular tension, between ruling and ruled classes where the former ideologically subsume the latter, means that the expectations of Yahweh in v. 7b are meant for the owners of the means of production, the latifundiaries and others who come in for such a hammering in Isa. 5.8-23. It is to these that Yahweh looked for 'justice' (מִשְׁפָּט) and for 'righteousness' (צְדָקָה), but ended up, in a word play, with 'bloodshed' (מִשְׂפָּח) and 'a cry' (צְעָקָה). Social justice, at least of the kind identified here, is something in which the rich and powerful engage, an economic and social agenda that is the responsibility of the ruling class. It is they who must show mercy to the widow, orphan and foreigner in the land, in much the same way that the kings must exercise justice.

An extraordinarily limited form of social justice, is it not? Trickle-down justice, to gloss a term from capitalist economics? It is an ethics of the rulers in which the marks of social cohesion and economic prosperity are fair practices by the rulers so that those at the bottom of the class system, and even those who do the bulk of the work, do not suffer unduly or beyond their capabilities. The issue for Isaiah 5 is adequate maintenance for those who work so that they will be in a fit state to do the work required of them. But the vision of social justice is an extremely limited one that implicitly supports the status quo—by seeking the best conditions for its continuity—rather than questioning and challenging that situation for its intrinsic exploitation and lack of social justice.

Isaiah's trenchant critique is a denunciation of a class that fails to ensure the workings of trickle-down social justice, for it is that system which will work to their best advantage. Paradoxically, the condemnation and judgment delivered to them leads to their restoration—if they heed the prophetic word—or to their destruction, and thereby of the socio-economic system itself, something they have in a glaring moment of stupidity brought upon themselves. Isaiah's text may be read as a direct ideological effort to deal with, as Marx would suggest, the inherent contradictions of an exploitative economic system.

Thus far I have skirted the explicit theological material in Isa. 5, focusing like Adorno in the first section of his Kierkegaard book on the social and economic paradoxes of the text's social and economic agenda. In the allegory of Isa. 5 the question of Yahweh's role becomes explicit. In my reverse reading, the identification of Yahweh as the creator of the vineyard (Isa. 5.7) throws all of what has gone before in a different light. (It seems to me artificial to separate allegory from its interpretation and allegorical key).

The allegory of vv. 1-6 concerns love and punishment, which must do duty for the question of righteousness and justice that underlies it. In tone, image and vocabulary the allegory would slip unnoticed into the Song of Songs. It is, after all, a 'love song' sung by an unidentified first person for 'my beloved' (Isa. 5.1), drawn from love poetry for an allegorical purpose.[2] It concerns 'his vineyard': the first person speaker and third person owner of the vineyard and subject of most of the verbs suggest that the first two verses are a foreign object, breaking the usual prophetic elision with the voice and perspective of Yahweh. Such elision will soon return to great effect in v. 3, but here the first person verbs and possessive pronouns become the word of the prophet and Yahweh becomes his 'beloved' or 'lover' about whom the prophet speaks. By v. 3 the arrangement shifts and the text calls on the inhabitants of Jerusalem and men of Judah to judge 'between me and my vineyard' (Isa. 5.3). From here the first and third persons, prophet and Yahweh crash together into a unified first person. The prophet becomes once again the speaking machine for Yahweh.

Although a rapid skim suggests that the whole allegory concerns Yahweh's love for his vineyard Israel—the aromas of love do tend to waft over into the later verses—the shift in pronouns and verbal subject breaks the connection. Verses 1 and 2 are about love, but the only love is that of the prophetic first person *for* Yahweh, 'my beloved', for whom he sings the love song. A second paradox emerges: the basis for social justice in the love of Yahweh, that one might assume in the connection between the earlier and later parts of the chapter, dissipates. Unwittingly, the text of Isa. 5 echoes Adorno's criticism of Kierkegaard, that divine love and ethics are incompatible, that one cannot base an ethics on a theological premise such as love.

Instead, once the distinction between the first and third person of vv. 1 and 2 closes, the allegory shifts from the theme of love to judgment. But with the unified first person that begins in v. 3 judgment formulae creep into the text, entirely severed from the words of love. Thus, Yahweh does not construct the vineyard out of a love that is then rejected by Israel, and Yahweh, like some disappointed lover, sadly punishes Israel. The only reason, as far as the text is concerned, why Israel should produce 'grapes'

---

2.   Gale Yee (1981), Adrian Graffy (1979) and John Willis (1977) argue that Isa. 5.1-7 is a juridical or self-condemnation parable, although they separate it from the woes of Isa. 5.8-23. If genre itself is understood as a dialectical category, bringing two or more genres together in tension, as I argued in my chapter on Kings, then its connections with love poetry become part of the juridical form.

rather than 'wild grapes' is that Yahweh has made the vineyard in the first place: 'What more was there to do for my vineyard that I have not done it?' (Isa. 5.4a).

Although there is a caesura between love (Isa. 5.1-2) and judgment (Isa. 5.3-4), so that the latter cannot follow from the former, what does carry through is the idea that Yahweh has made or created Israel. Thus, in v. 2 Yahweh digs and clears, plants with choice vines, constructs a watch tower and wine vat. This is what Yahweh does for the vineyard (Isa. 5.4), and the dismay of vv. 2b and 4b is based on the expectation that this work of construction should produce the expected yield: '…he looked for it to yield grapes, but it yielded wild grapes' (Isa. 5.2b); 'When I looked for it to yield grapes, why did it yield wild grapes?' (Isa. 5.4b). The echo here is backwards and forwards, back to the 'choice vines' of 5.2 and ahead to the 'pleasant planting' of 5.7. And the 'grapes' expected are 'justice' and 'righteousness' (Isa. 5.7), but all that came of it were the 'wild grapes', bloodshed and a cry. To complete the allegory the 'choice vines' of v. 2 are the 'men of Judah', the 'pleasant planting' of v. 7. So it is the men of Judah who are expected to yield the grapes of justice and righteousness, but they do not. Why should they produce such yield? The only reason is that Yahweh has made them the vineyard. Thus, purely from the fact that Yahweh has created Israel comes the assumption that they should exercise justice. There is no reference to commandments to be followed, divine directives that the people studiously avoid at their own risk and for which punishment is deserved.

All of which leads to the extraordinary third paradox: if Yahweh has constructed the vineyard in order to yield grapes, the only reason for the unaceptable yield is Yahweh himself. There is a flaw in the cultivation itself that leads not to cultivated grapes but to wild grapes. Without any commandments or directives that the people have an option to follow or not, the onus cannot be on the people themselves. And without the connection between the love of vv. 1 and 2 and the judgment in vv. 3 and 4, the reason for the wild grapes cannot be the rejection of Yahweh's love for Israel and Judah.

As with Adorno's criticism of Kierkegaard, the justification for an ethics of social justice begins to rattle to pieces: righteousness and justice must flow from the creation and cultivation of Israel and Judah, but if they, especially the ruling classes who come in for such a hammering, do not exercise such justice it is not because of their own sin—there is no room for that theme in the allegory—but because Yahweh has not cultivated them in a way that would result in righteousness and justice. Once again, the effort to base an ethics of social justice on theological premises faces a paradox.

In light of the two paradoxes of the allegory itself—the rift between love and judgment and the U-turn that places the reason for the absence of social justice on the vineyard cultivator himself—the third stanza (Isa. 5.5-6) floats free in the theological vacuum. These verses, again in the divine first person, outline the punishment that crashes down on the vineyard: Yahweh will remove its hedge, break down its wall, make it a waste, avoid pruning or hoeing, encourage briars and thorns to grow and order the clouds not to rain on it. The echo of Eden is strong, although the punishment does not follow from any human disobedience in Isa. 5.

Even though vv. 5 and 6 speak of the vineyard, there is a jarring mismatch between the various acts of cultivation in v. 2 and the promised destruction of vv. 5 and 6. Yahweh's ventriloquist does not threaten to undig it, scatter the stones, rip up the vines, knock down the watchtower and fill in the wine vat. Instead, none of these items from v. 2 are picked up in the punishment of vv. 5 and 6. On the one hand, this is a signal of the breakdown of the allegory's theological logic, the discontinuity between one part and another, here between vv. 2 and 5, that I traced earlier in the break between love and justice, but there is another motif that follows through. The first sign of this motif is the distinction between 'grapes' (עֲנָבִים) and 'wild grapes', or more specifically putrid or rotten things or berries (בְּאֻשִׁים from בָּאַשׁ, 'to stink') in vv. 2 and 4, between, in other words, cultivation and wildness, Culture and Nature. Yahweh seeks to cultivate a vineyard so that it will produce cultivated grapes, but only the putrid grapes of Nature result. The allegory thus falls into Lévi-Strauss's schema of civilization and its lack, the necessary elements that form a society of human beings and those that militate against such a society. For Lévi-Strauss, in his vast structuralist analysis of 187 South American myths, *The Raw and the Cooked* (1994), the passage through to social formation is marked in the myths by the passage from raw to cooked food, a process that counteracts the transition within Nature from fresh to rotten (the sense of בְּאֻשִׁים in Isa. 5.2, 4). Lévi-Strauss in his brilliant fashion, is able to read a whole variety of myths—concerning jaguars, crocodiles, lizards, birds and so on—in terms of this fundamental process.

A comparable process appears in the early verses of Isaiah 5 with their tension between cultivation and rottenness or wildness. Yahweh's dismay and anger result from the absence of a cultivated product, or rather, that rotten and putrid products emerge from his cultivated vineyard. The danger that must be avoided is, in other words, Nature itself, that stark Other to the cultivating desire of Yahweh. This tension between Nature and Culture carries through and makes sense of Isa. 5.5-6, for Yahweh promises to remove the boundary—the hedge and wall—between cultivation and wild Nature. The remaining acts in v. 6—to make the vineyard a waste, desist from pruning and hoeing, allow briars and thorns to grow and the withholding of rain—all seek to return the cultivated vineyard to the status of wild Nature, with its process from fresh to rotten, from which it has been wrested. After all, if grapes go rotten in the wild, then what point is there to all the cultivation if it produces rotten and putrid grapes? The appropriate raw materials produce an appropriate product! As if to say: these Israelites are obviously not cultured or civilized, then let them return to their pre-civilized, their wild, way of life. In this respect, the punishment is entirely deserved, except that it runs up against the previous paradox in which only Yahweh can be held responsible for the grapes produced by his construction and cultivation.

The whole question of cultivation and culture leads to a fourth paradox when Isa. 5.7 and the woes of Isa. 5.8-23 are brought into the equation, for the implication is that the cultivated 'grapes'—justice and righteousness—are elements of human civilization, that their absence is a sign of lack of cultivation, of the process of Nature itself towards putrefaction. On one level, the connection between civilization and justice is a profound insight, for how can human beings live together in society without social justice, without fair dealings between one human being and the other? All of the woes can then be seen as the causes and signs of the breakdown of human society.

The paradoxes, however, start mounting up. First, Isa. 5 presents justice as the result of cultivation, rather than as a necessary component, if not prerequisite, thereof. How can society function if justice is not there to begin with? Secondly, it restricts justice to the realm of human society, with all its borders that mark it off from barbarity and wild Nature, the realm where injustice rules. Yet elsewhere in Isaiah, such as Isa. 11.6-9, the region beyond the borders of human society is where peace and justice prevail. To be sure, what happens in the eschatological passage of Isaiah 11 is that the various features of civilization extend and dominate wild Nature itself. The eschaton becomes one vast civilized and cultured space. In such a space the possibility that Nature may have its own form of order outside human society is closed down. My point is not entirely fair, however, since it brings a criticism to a conceptual structure in which this possibility is not available. But it does run up against the Isaian theme that Yahweh is the creator of the whole of Nature. And therefore of injustice within wild Nature.

The restriction of social justice to human society, or the extension of human society into Nature, leads to the deepest paradox of Isa. 5. In tracing the first paradox I argued that the woes are targeted at a particular class, the rulers or owners of the means of production, for not exercising a trickle-down form of social justice, one which they dispense from a position of power and wealth. In their lack of social justice they therefore slip outside Yahweh's cultivation and back into wildness and barbarity. Human society breaks down when *this* class fails to act with justice and righteousness. Their injustices are the putrid grapes that appear in Yahweh's cultivated vineyard, and for this reason he returns it to the wild state of Nature.

The problem here is that Isaiah's assumed model of cultivated society is profoundly reactionary. The aim of the prophetic denunciations is to urge the ruling classes to act with justice and righteousness, that is, distribute favours so that society can function. But what sort of society? Is not the properly working society envisioned here profoundly unjust? A social and economic system that is structured in terms of those who control the means of production and extract the surplus labour from those who work for them is hardly a system overflowing with social justice. In fact, the opposite is the case, and a complete inversion of Isaiah's ideological schema is a about to take place.

If this society is functioning properly, at least for the text of Isaiah, then it is unjust and unfair. But the realm of injustice and barbarity is outside cultivated society, in the arena of wildness and Nature. Thus, Nature comes crashing through the boundaries to become the determining feature of Culture, whereas Culture leaps over the wall and hedge to take up its proper abode in Nature. Or, Culture itself, the cultivated society, is unjust and unrighteous, whereas Nature itself is where justice and righteousness may be found. The whole ideological structure of Isa. 5 collapses under its paradoxes.

In light of this breakdown, the refrain from Isa. 5.2b and 4 has its own peculiar logic. Of course the cultivated vineyard produces rotten grapes, that is, injustice and unrighteousness, because this is exactly how such a 'cultivated' society in Isaiah works. The return of Nature in the punishment of vv. 5 and 6 is an implicit recognition of the paradox that this cultivated society in fact operates according to the injustices of Nature. Except that Nature is now the place of justice...

There is one final paradox in the collapse of the effort to link social justice with Yahweh. The cultivator of the society gone awry is Yahweh himself, the great mechanism of social 'cohesion'. The ideological function of Yahweh is therefore as an engineer of a profoundly unjust society, for he is the one responsible, as I argued earlier, for the character of the vineyard itself. In contrast to this earlier paradox, in which Yahweh has created and cultivated the vineyard and is therefore the one who created it flawed, Yahweh now cultivates a society that is anything but just and righteous. Rather than a flawed production, he has succeeded only too well and the result is precisely what one would expect, given the reactionary ideological basis on which this vineyard, this Culture, has been constructed. His only problem is that he expected the wrong thing, cultivated grapes, since the only possible fruit that could possibly grow in his vineyard are the stinking and rotten grapes. But this faulty expectation is but a mark, a figure, of a text riven with paradoxes it cannot contain.

All of this means that the derivation of social justice, at least as far as Isaiah is concerned, is paradoxically impossible. Instead, Yahweh has become the source, creator and cultivator of injustice and unrighteousness. His only way out would be, in Isaiah's terms, that he is also the creator of Nature, where justice now abides, but that is outside the walls of the human society he seeks to cultivate. He is, as it were, trapped in his own paradox.

I close by returning to the woes with which I began in Isa. 5.8-23. In that earlier discussion I treated them as criticisms of the rulers of a social structure—albeit an oppressive one—that was not functioning properly, that is, in terms of a trickle-down notion of social justice in which the poor and needy must be grateful for what they get, a society of alms-giving and limited amelioration of the more atrocious extremes of unjust human society. However, in light of the subsequent run of paradoxes that I traced in Isa. 5 these woes now undergo their own inversion. They have become a perfectly good description of the cultivated vineyard of the earlier verses in Isa. 5. Is not this the way a cultivated vineyard, the realm of Culture and civilization as Isaiah views it, operates? And is this not precisely the vineyard of injustice that, after all the inversions and paradoxes of the text, Yahweh himself creates?

What I have argued with regard to Isa. 5, by means of Adorno's immanent method, becomes another element in the various ideological features I have been pursuing in the previous chapters. In this case Isaiah 5 becomes an excellent example of the paradoxes of a ruling ideology held together by the figure of Yahweh. Isaiah's text may then be read as effort to overcome these paradoxes, an effort that shows them up even more sharply in the attempt at resolution. I leave the question concerning the social and economic tensions that generate such paradoxes for a fuller consideration in the conclusion, although it seems to me that Isa. 5 is but another part of the dominant cultural form of the sacred, replete with its own problems.

Chapter 8

FREDRIC JAMESON:
THE CONTRADICTIONS OF FORM IN THE PSALMS

Jameson, one of the most well known and sophisticated critics writing today, is notable for introducing French and German Marxist theory to North America well before the translations were available. In a critical programme that has sought to engage with poststructuralism, deconstruction, linguistics, Russian formalism, psychoanalysis, film theory, architecture and cultural studies, Jameson has argued both for Marxism's viability in the current theoretical and literary scene and for its power as an interpretative method. His work is characterized by a commitment to the central questions of Marxism while arguing that they constitute problems and areas of debate rather than fixed ideas. My focus is on his more literary work, particularly the question of form and the way it operates within a complex dialectical method that works in the domains of politics, society and history. The key for Jameson is formal contradiction, which then allows one to move to content and history in a different fashion.

Jameson's influence has been enormous, having written—if one takes these things into account—at least two books that continue to be academic best-sellers (*The Political Unconscious* and *Postmodernism, or, the Cultural Logic of Late Capitalism*) and producing a number of developments in American academic culture that seem to bear out his own desire to work towards a Marxist culture in that most rarified of soils, the United States. Perhaps one sign of such an effect after almost 70 years (Jameson was born in 1934) is the Marxist Literary Group, first established by some of Jameson's graduate students and now a vibrant locus of left thought in the United States.

The epithet 'leading Marxist critic' so often attached even by people like Terry Eagleton (1996: 195) to Fredric Jameson is both a curse and a blessing. For many it would seem that leadership of what appears to be such a small group can hardly be a great achievement, especially in the

United States, the home of overdeveloped capitalism. Yet I want to suggest that with the death of the great generation of Marxist thinkers in Europe (many of whom appear in this book), there has been a continental shift in Marxist theory to North America, carried out by and large by the strength of Jameson's work.

Jameson, following in the footsteps of Adorno and Lukács, is a resolutely dialectical thinker. Thus, in taking on an item from the traditional superstructure—text, idea or other cultural product—he leads us eventually to the base, to economic, political and historical dimensions. Similarly, if we take up a particular item from the base—such as money, division of labour or surplus value—the end run is the realm of the superstructure. Let me take the example of the 'market', the autonomous self-regulating force of capitalism to which all seem subject from powerful states to powerless individuals. Yet the term itself is what might be described as a dead metaphor, for its basic meaning is a gathering of produce—fruit and vegetables, clothing, knick-knacks—in one space for barter, haggling and purchase. Yet this sense has been been extrapolated to the global workings of capitalism, which can only in an analogical sense be understood as a 'market'. All the same, this is only the first step, for not only is the market granted a peculiar status, imbued with the dynamics of human social relations (what Lukács called reification), it is also profoundly metaphorical. Only when it achieves, in the consciousness and imagination of its participants, a well-nigh divine, omnipotent and omniscient status, does the market function at full capacity. Yet, before we know it, we have been roaming about in what is properly the superstructure: the realm of ideas, belief, metaphor and analogy (see Jameson 1991: 260-78). The one realm cannot be thought without the other.

In the end, Jameson's whole programme may be said to be a massive expansion of Marx's analysis of capitalism, specifically in terms of its culture. And the key term in such a programme is the notion of 'mode of production', to which I will turn in detail in my conclusion. Against a sense that postmodernism denies history, Jameson insists on history as the final horizon, although it is highly abstract. Commonly understood to designate the base, Jameson takes it in a more inclusive sense, bringing the whole panoply of items of Marxist analysis—ideology, culture, law, philosophy, state, class, superstructure, base—into the vast epochal term of mode of production. These epochs are not static, but continually mutate in the process of time, bringing about different modes of production, such as feudalism, capitalism, or tribal organization, in which the nature and interrelation of the various categories changes. But the greatest immediate value of the idea of mode of production is that it functions to relativize the era in which we live—capitalism—as an era with an origin, history and passing away.

But my interest in Jameson on this occasion is what he now calls the somewhat archaic distinction between form and content, for his work in this area has been characterized by a campaign against the dominance of content—character, plot, image and metaphor—in literary criticism. This campaign is part of a much wider knack of always seeing things from another angle, of a different take on a problem that he draws from the Hegelian–Marxist tradition in which he works. My concern with form relates the stretch of Hebrew text I want to discuss, the Psalms. But my study involves an interaction between Psalms study and the text itself in a fashion often carried out by Jameson, which he has dubbed 'metacommentary'. Thus, the study of the Psalms operates in terms of content— historical location and usage, theological or devotional themes—and form—especially the form criticism that still lays the groundwork for so much work on the Psalms. Yet the text seems burdened with an earlier history of interpretation and organization, such as the five books, or as the psalms of David, Asaph, Solomon and so on, or by means of the 'musical' superscriptions, or by locating individual psalms in the life of David. The tension between form and content, I argue, relies on some more fundamental contradictions within the Psalms themselves, and I make use of Jameson's adaptation of Greimas's semiotic square to sort out the contradictions, both in the Psalms and in their interpretation.

For Jameson, the analysis of form in literary and cultural criticism operates in a number of ways, which I will designate as the imaginary resolution of real social contradictions and as the ideology of form. These are part of a much larger methodological project that winds its often covert way through his writings, themselves operating as ad hoc efforts constructed in terms of the object under analysis. In other words, those particular discussions explore a distinct moment of the larger method, developing its possibilities in ever new ways that are never locked into a template for interpretation. Marxism does not supply a set of eternal problems, but seeks to meet each situation on its own terms that raise questions for a particular problem within Marxism, such as class, ideology or mode of production.

As for that larger framework itself, which is an effort to deal with the variety of approaches within Marxism, Jameson speaks of three levels of interpretation, which I have in another place (Boer 1996: 30-42) traced through in terms of the four levels of mediaeval allegorical exegesis, Northrop Frye's transmutation of these levels and then Jameson's own reflections on Walter Benjamin. The first level begins with the individual text in question, focusing on formal contradictions that open out into ideology and the specific historical questions that are recognizable in terms of the biological individual—everyday events, the rise and fall of political regimes, major historical moments and so on. The second, in a Hegelian move, goes wider, situating the text as one player among a range of others in a contested ideological field. With the ideological focus, class conflict becomes important. The third, which operates with the widest notion of modes of production, seeks traces or figures of such modes in the text being interpreted. Significantly, Jameson's method connects the relation between base and superstructure (synchrony) with the history of modes of production (diachrony). In Jameson's critical practice, not all levels of the analysis work at the same time: often one will be sufficient, or he will explore a new area that does not necessarily fall within the schema.

But let me focus on the first of the two dimensions of form I noted above—imaginary resolution. The term itself has an increasingly widespread currency in literary criticism, largely due to Jameson's influence, but it is derived from his reliance on Althusser's definition of ideology that I discussed in detail in Chapter 1: ideology is the imaginary relationship of individuals to their real social conditions of existence. Jameson takes this a step further and argues that literary texts and cultural products more generally may be understood as imaginary resolutions to social and historical contradictions. And those resolutions take place primarily in terms of form. At the same time, an emphasis on form is able to show not only how the attempted resolution works, but also trace the marks of the social contradictions themselves. Jameson's great model is Lévi-Strauss's structuralist analysis of Caduveo women's face painting in *Tristes Tropiques*, where Lévi-Strauss argues that the tension between the symmetrical patterns of the face and the different axis of the facial art itself is a formal effort to resolve the contradictions between the social hierarchy of Caduveo society and the social relations produced by such a hierarchy. The analogy with literary texts is that they, like other cultural products, may be described as 'symbolic acts', as efforts to resolve on a formal and then ideological level the contradictions to which they function as a response.

Given that the resolution takes place in formal terms, textual analysis

must focus, at least at its first moment, on formal analysis in order to uncover the contradictions that leave their traces in the form of the text. But
what does Jameson mean by form? In his myriad texts, where definition
appears more as an assumption that then alters in the process of interpretation, form may include the particular structure of a literary product, such
as its organization into various stages or sequences (for instance Thomas
More's *Utopia*) or the arrangement of poetry, the tensions of genre that
constitute genre itself, the materiality of such cultural products as film and
television, and most consistently in language itself. On this last feature, he
often begins an interpretation with a discussion of 'sentence production',
the syntactical and grammatical features of a particular language, the use
of certain terms over against others, and the distinct practice of style. The
concern with sentence production also reflects Jameson's own work with
languages, variously professor of French and Romance languages, and one
whose ability with French and German is often remarked upon in more
informal discussions of his work. And yet the notion of 'language' in
Jameson's work often takes a wider sense, as in the understanding of
particular ideological and cultural ways of thinking, such as religion. Or
the use of the model of language to speak of his method, such as the
practice of transcoding, which itself operates with the assumptions that
language is about syntax rather than vocabulary, and the particular uses
of language and its variety rather the search for a genealogical origin or
Ur-language.

What of the ideology of form? An inextricable part of Jameson's formal
analysis, drawn from Adorno, is contradiction, for he seeks the tensions
and contradictions in form as a signal, of the contradictions of ideology
and ultimately social and economic conditions to which the text is a
response. In fact, the identification of a contradiction means that the
interpretation is going somewhere: a critic has not worked hard enough
until contradiction emerges. Time and again Jameson's various critical
gestures will work towards a contradiction or series of contradictions,
which then become the moment for moving onto another level of analysis.
That texts will have contradictions is an assumption drawn from the
Hegelian–Marxist tradition in which Jameson works, a dialectical
approach whose interpretative possibilities are enabled by contradictions.

In part, Jameson's fascination with formal contradiction is indebted to
the Russian formalists' notion of defamiliarization or Brecht's estrangement effect. For the formalists it took the form of an inversion of the
relationship between form and content, the latter becoming the mere

means of enabling the former—for instance, the details of plot and character have the primary purpose of realizing the form of the novel. In the case of Brecht, this involved a whole series of strategies—including stage directions in the performance of a play or the absolutely deadpan delivery of lines—in order to jolt the audience into a new way of perceiving the world, a political act that sought to break the stranglehold of capitalism on thought and life. The ultimate example of this estrangement effect is Jameson's use of it to read Brecht's own estrangement effect (see Jameson 1998).

Yet he is not, despite all the temptations of the 'frozen dialectic' of structuralist analyses, satisfied with the identification of contradictions per se, arguing for a deep structure of texts in terms of a fundamental contradictions. Rather, such contradictions are unstable, constantly shifting and criss-crossed with other contradictions, generating further contradictions with which texts work, all of which constitute a step towards seeking the real social contradictions that texts seek to resolve. A favoured strategy of Jameson is the use of Geimas's semiotic square (itself a development from Aristotle's logical square) in order to trace the further implications of the initial contradiction. Time and again the square appears in his work, although its use goes well beyond Greimas. For Jameson, the square with its relations of contradiction and contrariety enables him to map out the ideological structure of a text, the possibilities of such an ideological structure and its limits, the closing of other ideological possibilities. And it is these excluded items that then allow him to move onto another level for which the contradiction then becomes one between what is included and excluded (usually the historical, that is, political economic, features within which a text operates).

There are various ways in which Jameson will move when he begins with a formal analysis. Sometimes, he will seek specific historical moments to which a text's form can be connected. At others, it will be a move to questions of ideology and social class, ideology understood here as the opposed forms of class consciousness between those who own the means of production and those who do not. Often he moves to the broader category of mode of production, identifying the formal production as a specific feature of the complex and contradictory patterns of the culture and ideology of capitalism itself. Nearly all his work deals with literary and cultural products from the various permutations of capitalism, and so what any interpretation of a pre-capitalist text like the Bible requires is a consideration of the very different mode(s) of production that are in operation.

What interests me for my discussion of Psalms is the move from form to ideology, which constitutes a shift to a content that is always implicit in any formal analysis—the distinction itself is somewhat artificial, a strategic move that enables Jameson's interpretation to get under way. But that content or ideology functions as a crucial mediating step between the superstructure (the text itself) and the base (the social and economic conditions to which the text is a response). Formal contradictions in a text become ideological antinomies, a scandal of thought or conceptual paradox that resists resolution by means of thought itself. But that is to invert the relationship: a formally contradictory text functions as an effort to resolve an impossible antinomy at the level of ideology. But the ideological antinomy is itself the result of tensions in the base, in political economics, which any system attempts to resolve in order to avoid the possibility of chaos and collapse.

It is here, in the process of moving from form to ideology, that he makes use time and again of Greimas's semiotic square. I am going to spend a little more time on this, since it provides a range of examples of Jameson's criticism, as well as a means I will utilize in order to interpret the Psalms. Jameson's appropriation of Greimas's material, particularly the semiotic rectangle or square out of all the equations, schemata and non-verbal symbols, is one of his more fascinating raids into other methodological territory: it proves fruitful, in conjunction with Jakobsen's notion of axes or coordinates, to track down mechanisms of narrative closure (Jameson 1975a, 1983), or to explicate the crucial character systems of a particular story (1975a), or ideological systems in a novel corpus, such as that of Conrad (in Jameson 1981: 206-80), or a person's entire aesthetic framework, such as Adorno's (Jameson 1990b: 151-54).

The first formal treatment of Greimas appears in *The Prison-House of Language* (Jameson 1972) and from then on the square or rectangle makes regular appearances in subsequent analytic works. The most complete statement of how the 'interested outsider can navigate this conceptuality [of Greimas's semiotics] and occasionally beach and camp with profit and stimulation within it' (1987.vi) may be found in Jameson's foreword to the English translation of a number of key essays (1987).

In this foreword, the preliminary (but important) comments on meaning (the object of semiotics is the production of meaning that is the transformation of an already given meaning), give way to a discussion of the dialectical relation of narrative and cognition that comprise the two incompatible but dialectical forms of ideology, whose relationship the semiotic square then mediates (a narrative will be reduced to cognitive or ideological combinations, while a cognitive text will be rewritten as a narrative struggle between ideas and concepts). The visible and spatial capacity of the square is to present the logical outcome of that crucial initial binary opposition or contradiction: the initial term (s_1 in the canonical notation) and its hostile other (s_2) generate the simple negatives $-s_2$ and $-s_1$, which are at the same time enlargements of their pair in the upper register, yet like that pair always to be found at one another's throats.[1]

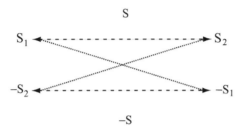

$$S$$

$$S_1 \longleftrightarrow S_2$$

$$-S_2 \longleftrightarrow -S_1$$

$$-S$$

Figure 1. *Greimas's semiotic square.*

Two further signs (compound terms) appear, S being the complex term in which the initial opposition is overcome, and −S being the location, as neutral term, of negation and privation. Along the sides run the lateral or deictic axes (s_1 and $-s_2$, s_2 and $-s_1$) with a different set of relationships in operation, while the whole diagram is shot through with the cross-connecting compound and the lateral terms, thus completing ten different possibilities that constitute the sum of possible ideological formations within the enclosure.

Jameson distinguishes both pedagogical and heuristic uses of the square, providing in the latter case a workshop stress test (Hayden White's cognitive *Metahistory*) in which the three crucial decisions involve: the identification of the primary opposition (on this decision rests the variety of ways in which the remainder will fall out); the necessarily polysemous nature of the four terms; and the motor force and/or unexpectedness of the elusive fourth term ($-s_2$). And it is this fourth term, at the lower left-hand corner of the diagram that often requires much patience, the blackening of many pages before the square works itself out.

In *The Political Unconscious* (1981) Jameson specifies that the location

---

1.   The terminology varies: in 1987 Jameson uses s_1, s_2 and their negatives, while elsewhere he uses S, −S, and their negatives.

of this major tool of narrative strategy is in the first horizon, where it functions to clarify the operation of binary oppositions or antinomies, to specify the ways in which ideological closure is achieved in narrative, the ideological boundaries beyond which the ideas and concepts within texts are unable to proceed (the next step is then to inquire about the historical circumstances of those limits, but also to rotate the terms themselves to indicate ways out of the closure [1987: xvii]). Its validity is local and incomplete, a beginning of the exploration rather than a conclusion that requires the shift to the social and historical dimension; a move that is intended to jolt the schema out of its static and ontological homologies into a more fluid and versatile tool (a potential located within the narrative of the discipline's development [1987: vii-viii]).

The regular appearances of the square within analyses—after the initial detention in *The Prison-House of Language* (1972: 162-68) and subsequent release—normally function in a capacity determined by the local text (where such analysis is demanded by the text); that is, the full range of possibilities is not always exploited. As the square is understood to mediate between narrative and concept, I will organize Jameson's uses of the square in terms of those that work from narrative to concept and then those that work the other way.

Thus, there are those that work from the side of narrative in producing conceptual arrangements: Greimas's own arrangements of Bernanos's novels (Jameson 1972: 165); the reading of Dickens's *Hard Times* (Jameson 1972: 167-68). Further, there is a more basic use of the diagram, cutting out at the complex and neutral terms, in order to explain the generation of utopian narrative by means of the neutral term (1988: II, 75-102). Jameson also analyzes the narrative system, which is in this case a libidinal apparatus, of Wyndham Lewis's *Tarr* (Jameson 1979: 99), where the characters appear as primary terms; the personality system of Wyndham Lewis as that appears in *The Human Age* (Jameson 1979: 120); the semiotic system of the body or sensorium in Rimbaud's poetry (Jameson 1984b: 80); and the complex ideological and narrative closure in Conrad's *Nostromo* (Jameson 1981: 276-77), which also opens up psychoanalytic possibilities regarding Conrad. Most recently, Jameson has made detailed use of the square in articulating the spatial systems in Hitchcock's *North by Northwest* (1992).

A major use of the square involves the analysis of character systems, whereby the arrangement of the characters of a work serves to indicate ideological options. Thus, one of the earlier and most extensive analysis of character systems appears in the study of P.K. Dick's *Dr. Bloodmoney* (Jameson 1975a): here the square is pushed to its extreme, unearthing the fundamental axiological paradox in the novel (and in Dick's corpus) which also provides an explanation of how Dick achieves closure (exchange of closure from one axis to the other).

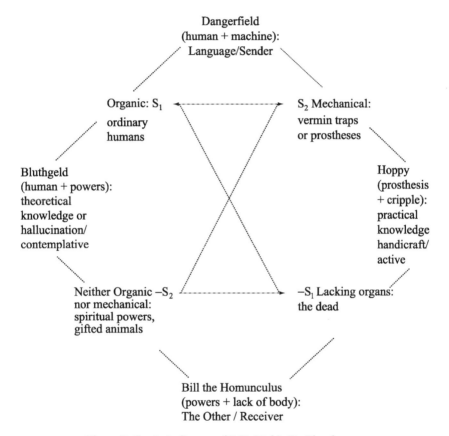

Figure 2. *Semiotic Square of P.K. Dick's Dr Bloodmoney*

Character analysis may also be found in the study of Balzac's *La Vielle Fille*, leading to a discussion of the meaning of 'character' (Jameson 1976b: 44; the rewrite for 1981 [167] omits the important second diagram); as part of the ideological closure with Conrad's *Lord Jim* (1981: 254-57); and once again in the film *Something Wild* (Jameson 1991: 293).

The second category are those studies that move from concept to narrative, transforming conceptual, often social, arrangements into potential or embryonic narratives: Greimas's own example of tribal marriage patterns

(Jameson 1972: 163-64); Lévi-Strauss's culinary triangle-become-rec-
tangle (1972: 166); the intricacies of Max Weber's thought, where his
sociology of religion generates the first example in Jameson's work of
character analysis where the compound and lateral terms designate figures
or characters in both story and theory, along with the only appearance of
extended concertina-type version (1988: II, 13-17, 33); the elaboration of
Lacan's signifying chain into a basic fourfold schema (1988: I, 111-14; the
diagrams do not appear in the original version [1977a]); the world-view or
understanding of history itself in Adorno (1990b: 113), along with his
aesthetic theory (1990b: 151-54); the formal and ideological combinations
available within the closure of contemporary culture, providing a schema
of cultural dominants themselves (realism, modernism, postmodernism)
(1990a: 161), a schema that then turns out, for the purpose of presentation,
to have an inner square articulating the dynamics of film production
(1990a: 198).

However, the square is not available for universal application, indicated
by Jameson's own selective use of it: it would seem that the texts provide
limits to such use, with reasonable evidence of a number of abandoned and
derelict squares in Jameson's work. The best exhibit is the removal of the
second and fuller square from the revision of the *La Vielle Fille* essay
(Jameson 1976b; 1981: 167); the obverse of this presence-absence pattern
is the absence of diagrams in the original Lacan article (1977a) and their
subsequent inclusion in the revision (1988: I, 111-14), including a basic
Greimasian square. A suggestive 'lopped' version, where the anticipated
fourth term never pretends to appear, is used in assessing the patterns, by
means of Niklas Luhmann, of signifieds and signs in Claude Simon's
nouveaux romans (1991: 141-42). At times it is resisted in places where
the work of identifying binary oppositions has been done but where the
square will not fulfil its proper function, as with the ecology, religion, sex
and war of Le Guin's utopias (1975b), or with the narrative closure of
Raymond Chandler's novels, where it probably should have appeared
(1983).

A related analytic tool comes from the replacement of the semiotic
square with the structural *combinatoire*, or 'structural permutation
scheme',[2] a set of parallel but intersecting oppositions laying out the logical possibilities and variables of a set of terms in which alteration of one
of the normally four constituents results in comparable changes in the

2. On one occasion Greimas's square is described similarly as a 'permutational
mechanism' (1988: II, 13).

others (and thus opens up the possibility of determining the changes in the others upon discovery of change in one), and in which it is possible to deal with conformity and variation at the same time (Jameson 1977b: 551). The ultimate purpose of such a structural approach, as with the closely related semiotic approach of Greimas, is to ensure that the analysis hits bottom; in other words, that it recovers the historical conditions of possibility and limitation of certain textual forms (see further 1981: 146-50).

Specific examples of the *combinatoire* or combination scheme include: the relationship between form and substance, content and expression in developing the structural dimension of genre (Jameson 1981: 146-47); the four possibilities regarding modernism and postmodernism depending on one's stand pro- or anti- (1991: 61); the traditional solutions to the problem of historicism, namely antiquarianism, existential historicism, structural typology and Nietzschean anti-historicism (1988: II, 152); and the four ways of looking at a fairy tale—surrealist, peasant or materialist, structuralist or protonarrative, and poststructuralist—although here the designation does not appear (1986); the permutations of film and novel, being novel into film, film into novel, novel and film composed simultaneously, and novel into film into novel (1980). The combination scheme would seem to be an alternative route for the arrangement of logical possibilities that does not require, or rather resists, the application of the semiotic square.

Yet there is some border crossing, or at least the exchanging of pleasantries, between the semiotic and the structural. First, what was initially described as a *combinatoire*—Hayden White's four-by-four table used to analyze the nineteenth-century narrative historians in *Metahistory* (Jameson 1988 [1976]: I, 157-58)—is transformed into a glorious square (1987: xvii-xxi), a transformation enabled by the crucial decision of the location of the initial contradiction with metaphor and synecdoche rather than White's own metaphor and metonymy). Secondly, the Weber paper noted above avails itself of a *combinatoire* in the midst of all its Greimasian construction in order to explicate—as part of the elaboration of the theory of the 'vanishing mediator' in Weber's work—the logical permutations (in the relationship between capitalism and Protestantism) between ends and means on the one hand and rational and religious stances on the other (1988: II, 23-24). Thirdly, there is the analysis on narrative closure in Raymond Chandler (1983), where a combination scheme turning around the presence and absence of offices and residences articulates the spatial configurations of the various social types. Closure does not, however, as would be expected in the structuralist aesthetic, take place when all the possibilities of the scheme are exhausted; rather, closure is enabled by the interaction or exchange between the axis of social typology and a second one identified as nature: the closure of the natural or geographical code is projected (by means of those passages in which the margins of the urban and the natural appear) onto that of the systematization of the social order. In this case, then, the closure generated by axiological contact that was achieved earlier by means of the semiotic square (on P.K. Dick, 1975a) is now brought about by means of the permutation scheme. Hypothetically both Greimas's semiotic square and the structural *combinatoire* might be used in every analysis, but their selective use in Jameson's own work suggests limits imposed by the texts and the need to follow one's hunches when interpreting texts, a little like the parable of Housman's flea in relation to textual criticism (the dog does not systematically search for fleas inch by inch, but follows an itch to pursue the flea).

My own specific use of Jameson's work for interpreting the Psalms is to focus on the question of form—precisely because that has been the major aspect of Psalms—in order to locate the formal contradiction(s). I then wheel in the semiotic square in order to say something further about formal contradiction, but also about the ideological system within which the Psalms operate. But the analysis will not be complete without some comment on mode of production.

The Inadequacy of Ideology in the Psalms

As I suggested earlier, the study of the Psalms falls within two broad categories, the study of their devotional, historical or thematic content, and the study of form. Indeed, form criticism, which initially persuaded biblical studies (see Gunkel 1967, 1968) as to its viability through Psalms study and that has set the agenda in so many ways since, attempted to cover both dimensions. The forms of the various psalms were first analyzed and then the famous *Sitz im Leben* of those forms—the desire for history interwoven with the still incomplete study of *Gattung*. Variations on these two great continents of psalms study, which I will divide roughly between form and content, still seem to be in operation.

I want to begin by taking a step back from psalms scholarship and look at what an earlier level or two of engagement with the psalms has done. Here I think of the various efforts to organize or fix them, all of which are curiously partial, running out of steam at a certain point in the process.

Apart from the organization into books, the five books that echo the Torah at least (although Goulder would have us believe otherwise): Psalms. 1–41 in book I, Pss. 42–72 in book II, Pss. 73–89 in book III, Pss. 90–106 in book IV, Pss. 107–150 in book V. The overwhelming weight of Psalms falls into two large groups, those with various half-known and guessed-at directions, possibly of a musical tone, with the dominant feature being the phrase 'to the choirmaster' (לַמְנַצֵּחַ) (these include 4–6, 8, 9, 11–14, 18–22, 31, 36, 39–42, 44–49, 51–62, 64–70, 75–77, 80, 81, 84, 85, 88, 109, 139, 140), and those ascribed to David, often overlapping the previous category (4–6, 8, 9, 11–17, 19–21, 22–29, 31, 32, 35–41, 53, 55, 61, 64, 65, 68–70, 86, 101, 103, 108–10, 122, 124, 132, 138–41, 143–45). Another group that seems to arise from those of David are the psalms identified with various moments in David's biography, in a pattern reminiscent of musicals: Pss. 3, 7, 18, 30, 34, 51, 52, 54, 56, 57, 59, 60, 63, 142. I want to take this as a distinct group, for they stand in contrast to the ones with the various musical notations, to which I would want to add the Songs of Ascents (120-29, 131-34). These psalms smell of liturgy, collective worship perhaps, but I am jumping the gun a little. What they do seem to do is provide a counterpoint to the very personal nature of the psalms ascribed to David at crucial moments of his 'life', even though this group of personal psalms at first appears closely related to the more general category of David's Psalms. By contrast, the Psalms of David are part of another group of superscripted authorship: the sons of Korah (42, 44–47, 49, 84, 85, 87, 88), Asaph (50, 73–83), Solomon (72, 127), Ethan the Ezrahite (89) and even Moses (90).

It seems to me that we have the raw material for an initial square, one that will turn out to be somewhat temporary yet useful in pointing the way forward:

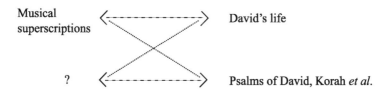

Figure 3. *Semiotic Square of Psalm Superscriptions*

The initial contradiction is that between the musical superscriptions and David's personal life, which stand at odds with one another in the traditional arrangement of the psalms. The former are obscure, half-understood, apparently in the context of worship and collective liturgy, whereas the latter is highly personal, the psalms in question being individual responses to significant moments in a life. The negative, in contrast to the initial opposition, to the musical notations, are the plethora of psalms ascribed to David, the sons of Korah, Asaph, Solomon, Ethan the Ezrahite and Moses, characterized by identification according to a distinct author over against the anonymous 'choirmaster' and other bits and pieces of information that float free. The two terms of David's life and the individual authors become part of the lateral axis that has as its feature the specificity of life and author, a way of fixing the psalms in a particular way. Yet all of these efforts end up being half-hearted and haphazard, the Psalms of David, for instance, being scattered all over the collection, as are those of David's life, or the authorship of the sons of Korah, and so on. In other words, the effort at ordering, of locating the psalms, runs aground at each turn. And so we find the elusive final term, the one I have identified with a question mark: the five books, an entirely arbitrary arrangement that rides roughshod over the others, disregarding what goes on in the other categories to achieve order at any price.

Yet, as I suggested earlier, this is only a preliminary square, one that indicates the initial efforts without facing the problem. And this problem shows up with the remaining psalms that are left free of any identifier, not located in any way until the arbitrary arrangement into five books. In other words, the question that the psalms raise is, What is to be done with this floating, disordered collection? For the feature of the psalms that emerges from reading them is that after a while one often seems to be very much like the other until they begin to blur and they feel like the same psalm repeated over and over again. They float or drift in an apparently timeless moment, unfixed by anything apart from the calls on Yahweh, the blessings and complaints, words of thanks, and on and on. And such a drifting sensation comes to the surface in the amorphousness of the collection in the Qumran texts, as well as the extra psalm in the Septuagint. Nor do the psalms remain within the MT collection of 150, for psalms appear in other contexts of the Hebrew Bible, such as those of Moses and Miriam in Exod. 15, Deborah and Barak in Judg. 5, Hannah's in 1 Sam. 2, David's in 2 Sam. 1.19-26 and 22.2–23.7. The spillage across the Hebrew Bible continues, for Pss. 105.1-15, 96.1-13 and 106.47-8 double up in 1 Chron. 16.8-36, a curious rearrangement that points to the interchangeability of bits and pieces of the psalms, the lack of fixation even in the demarcation, numbering and ordering of the existing psalms. This fluidity of verses and sections appears within the collection of psalms themselves, as with Ps. 108, a double over with Pss. 57.7-11 and 60.5-12. I want to draw on Robert Culley's argument—that the Psalms indicate a certain pool of images (the pit, sleeplessness, enemies, animals, temple and so on) that are quite limited in number but unlimited in usage—at this point, since it is precisely the interchangeability that is a characteristic of the psalms. But it also means, as he argues, that no one psalm can be interpreted in isolation. Thus, in his study of Ps. 88 (Culley 1988), one of the most gloomy and depressing in the collection, with no redemption or rescue, he argues that it must be understood within the context of the other complaint psalms, that its emphasis on abandonment by Yahweh becomes one part of a larger pattern in the complaint where a word of rescue appears at the end.

The initial problem, then, is one of floating, fluidity, interchangeability and lack of fixation. In this light, the various efforts I have discussed above—the musical superscriptions, the location in David's life, the ascription to Asaph, David, Moses and others, and the organization into five books can be understood as a response to the problem of flotation. In each case there is an effort to fix the psalms, to anchor them in some way that enables some sense to be made of the endless flow of emotion. So, the half-understood terms that seem to refer to music connect the written words with music, with singing and possibly liturgy itself. The long history of regarding the psalms as the core of Christian and Jewish sung worship carries on this attempt at locating the words in a collective sung moment, the materiality of voices and instruments tying them in. At this level, rather than opposing these musical associations, the identification of particular moments in the life of David, from caves (Pss. 57, 142) to madness before Abimelech (Ps. 34) become even stronger efforts to fix the psalms, creating a biography in song of David himself. The strength of this effort shows up not only in the long tradition that associated the psalms with David (texts like 1 Sam. 16.14-23 and 18.11 are part of this larger picture), but in the appeal of the individual biography itself, that item with which subsequent readers can identify most closely. Individual authorship follows a similar logic, the relative lack of fixation in comparison to the life of David compensated for by the sheer number of authors of psalms listed—81 psalms are attributed to David, the sons of Korah, Asaph, Solomon, Ethan the Ezrahite and Moses. But it is the organization into the five books that shows the tension between the fluidity of the psalms and the efforts to fix them in some way or another: the overarching ability to place the psalms in five books must sacrifice nearly all of the specificity that the other efforts achieve. And yet the efforts at greater specificity in their turn break down on the other side of the tension, for they can only cover some of the psalms, and the various attempts at fixation are both scattered and overlap with the others. The closest we come, after the five books, to a sustained organization is with the musical material, yet the anonymity and obscurity of these items gives ground on specificity for the sake of striking a little closer to complete organization.

The deeper tension with the psalms may be described as one between floating and fixation, between fluidity and the effort to cease the perpetual movement of the psalms into one another and across the Hebrew Bible.

Floating ⟵--⟶ Fixation

Figure 4. *Primary Contradiction of the Psalms*

There is, however, another feature of the psalms that this initial opposition does not face directly, and that is their number. Of course, there are 150 in the MT canon, but the sense of number is multiplied exponentially by the endless repetition of certain types of psalms, motifs, phrases, images and words themselves, so that the repetition gains the appearance of abundance and fullness. The effect of this endless runnning on is, paradoxically, an impression of completion, of absolute containment of all that there is to say about Yahweh and so on. If anything, the psalm of the law (Ps. 119) gives this sense in microcosm (and anyone who has been in a worship situation where the whole psalm was sung can attest to this), for its interminable repetition of a limited set of ideas—the notion that Yahweh's statutes are good, and that the wicked don't follow them while the 'I' of the psalm does—gives the impression of a much longer psalm. All that can be said, or sung, has certainly been said! I want to suggest, then, that the contrary term to flotation and interchangeability becomes fullness and completion, the sense that the psalms contain everything, so much so that they fall back into repeating the same thing time and again.

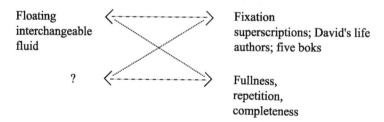

Figure 5. *Semiotic Square of the Psalms*

In what is becoming a common ascetic pattern I have restricted myself to a limited amount of material up until this point, focusing on the early efforts—at least those with some trace—at ordering, fixing and organizing the psalms. What I would like to do now is move on to consider the various critical approaches I outlined above, all the while leaving the crucial 'non-not' term, the one at the left-hand bottom corner—that which Jameson designates as the key term—until later.

The older concern with dating the psalms (see Briggs and Briggs 1914), has been revived in idiosyncratic form by Goulder (1983, 1990, 1997, 1998). The earliest critical efforts, those epitomized by the international critical commentary of Briggs and Briggs (1914), attempted a series of tasks, ranging through from identification of the author, dating the Psalms, trying to track the development of the collection itself by specifying when and where each psalm was composed and by whom, to detailed textual analysis. (The critical commentary is of course one of those extraordinary documents from the great flowering of biblical studies in the late nineteenth century). This critical text, published at the moment the First World War was engulfing Europe, embodies all that was best about biblical scholarship in the nineteenth century—a combination of what was then termed lower (textual) and higher (what we now term source) criticism. Its enterprise is one that falls within a certain logic, namely, that of treating the text as a layer, a Censor, which the critic must outflank in order to get behind it to the real concerns of biblical scholarship: the history of the text itself and the history from which it arose. Thus, in an effort that still remains unsurpassed for its thoroughness with the available sources as well as the linguistic skills of the authors, the commentary of Briggs and Briggs contains the most detailed textual analysis, including the use of the various versions (Greek, Latin and Syriac), in order to establish the earliest possible text behind the MT and the subsequent manuscript history of the text. At the same time that such a comprehensive task was undertaken, Briggs and Briggs attempted to determine the various ages of the psalms in place of the overweening desire to speculate on an author, although they do that too. In other words, while they denied the Davidic authorship, or even that of Asaph or Solomon or Moses, they sought to fix the psalms as far as possible in a temporal sequence. The concern with the impossible task of identifying an author still tempts some. For instance, for Kraus (1978) it was a private individual, for Mowinckel (1962) the temple staff were responsible, Goulder (1990) has it that Pss. 51–72 were composed by one of David's priests, whereas for Tournay (1991) the Levitical singers in the late period of the Chronicler, c. 300 BCE. My suggestion is, then, that commentaries like those of Briggs and Briggs, or the extraordinary and idiosyncratic revival of this older project in the effort to fix the psalms as completely as possible in Goulder's work (1983, 1990, 1997, 1998), along with the continued effort at constructing endless hypotheses regarding authorship, function as the lateral or deictic axis that links both fixation and completeness.

Another group of critics follow a similar logic, the effort to locate the historical context of the psalms, although with a very different focus from the now fossilized historical-critical efforts of Briggs and Briggs and the like. I think here of the social-scientific work of both Gottwald (1985) and Gerstenberger (1988). For Gottwald the psalms form part of a vast lumber room of bits and pieces that have their own socio-economic associations. And in the psalms Gottwald finds voices of protest against social, political and economic oppression, as expressions of oppression and poverty and the associated patterns of orientation, disorientation and reorientation, especially the laments and complaints. In Gottwald's terms, the royal psalms and some of the psalms of thanksgiving are more suspect, express-ing ruling class ideology against which the others protest. (But this carries on a debate begun with Gunkel, for whom the psalms expressed the emo-tions of the individual poor over against the rich.) Although this appears at first primarily like an alternative effort at fixing the psalms, it is also a comprehensive exercise, since Gottwald understands social-scientific approaches as the ultimate horizon of biblical interpretation. Now, at one level I agree with Gottwald, for his project comes very close to my own in terms of its Marxist agenda, but I am less certain about the large amount of historical-critical assumptions that inform his work. Gerstenberger also is interested in the social setting of the psalms, although in his commentary such an interest is more focused on the particular settings of the various types of psalms, whether individual moments of mourning, loss or socio-economic difficulty, or in collective rituals for different moments of com-munity life—harvest, defeat in warfare, victory and so on.

However, Gerstenberger's commentary is explicitly form critical, one point of the traditional tripod of historical criticism itself, and the over-whelming focus in various ways, whether as an explicit focus for dis-cussion or as the assumed background for further work, has been on the question of form. In this case, many carry on the task Gunkel set in speci-fying the various genres of the psalms—organized broadly into lament, complaint, thanksgiving, praise, royal, victory, Zion and Yahweh as king psalms on communal and individual levels—and their arrangement and interrelation (e.g. Kraus 1978; Westermann 1981; Gerstenberger 1988; Nasuti 1999). Others have pursued linguistic studies in order to make sense of the many hapax legomena and the sheer lack of sense that so many of the psalms seem to generate (e.g. Dahood 1966–70).

But it will be useful to go back and see what Gunkel does with the psalms. Gunkel's great effort was to bring together the concern with genre or Gattung and the *Sitz im Leben* of those genres. As is well known, he distingished between various types of psalms, such as lament, complaint, royal and thanksgiving psalms. With a background in German pietism, he tended to ascribe the Psalms to anonymous individuals, although in a collective context—his romantic image of the campfire around which the oral tradition was passed on—but what interests me here is less the fixation that the whole notion of Sitz im Leben implies as the alternative still highly promising notion of form or *Gattung*.

One direction of form-critical psalms study was to focus on the question of *Sitz im Leben*: over against Gunkel's individual readings and sought to specify and fix the psalms in the cult or liturgy. Thus, Mowinckel (1962) constructed the vast hypothesis, now fallen by the wayside, of an annual cultic ceremony, not referred to explicitly anywhere in the Hebrew Bible itself but appearing in other ancient Near Eastern societies. Mowinckel (1962) and Johnson (1951) built their interpretation around an annual enthronement festival for Yahweh, Eaton (1986), arguing that most are royal psalms, arranged nearly the whole lot in terms of ritual functions of the king focusing on a variety of royal festivals, whereas Weiser argued for an annual covenant festival and Kraus (1978) for one concerning royal Zion. More recently, Croft (1987) has revived the interest in the royal ritual, offering a new reconstruction on the basis of the 'I' psalms, and Goulder has constructed a whole world of Danite national liturgy (Goulder 1983), Solomon's coronation (Goulder 1990), Ezra's Passover and Tabernacle festival along with Nehemiah's Tabernacle festival (Goulder 1998) and the Bethel Autumn Festival (Goulder 1997).

However, it seems to me that the innovation that Gunkel brought about relates to the question of form, which may be read an alternative way of focusing on the problem that the psalms pose for interpretation, namely, the sensation of floating that one feels upon reading psalm after psalm, the feeling that one could start anywhere and yet end up with the same motifs, the same words and patterns. Psalm 108 is the example that explictly reveals such floatation, for its compilation of Pss. 57.8-12 (ET 7–11) and

60.7-14 (ET 5–12)—or is it that Pss. 57 and 60 provide the rough chunks that are then cut and pasted into Psalm 108?—brings to the surface a sense that has already been there for some time: the psalms float about all over the place, the one interchangeable with the other in a perpetual ebb and flow. Thus, even the transition between the two pieces is as smooth as that in Ps. 60: the 'so that' (לְמַעַן) of Ps. 108.7 follows on just as well from Ps. 108.6 as from Ps. 60.6.

> You have set up for those who fear you a banner
> to rally to it from the bow (Ps. 60.6).
>
> Be exalted, O god, upon the heavens
> And over all the earth your glory (Ps. 108.6).
>
> So that your beloved may be delivered
> Rescue with your right hand and answer me! (Pss. 60.7; 108.7).

It is not that Ps. 108 is the odd example in the collection, even in connection with the various pieces (Pss. 105.1-15; 96.1-13; 106.47-8) that make up 1 Chron. 16.8-36, but that it is the obvious example that characterizes the psalms as a whole, the moment when the tendency of the whole collection rises to the surface and becomes clear. What Gunkel attempted was not a fixation in time and place, but a way of making sense of the interchangeability of the psalms as a whole. With enough examples in the collection itself, Gunkel distinguished between lament and complaint, thanksgiving and praise, royal and victory, and Psalms of Zion and Yahweh as king. In one sense this is of course an alternative mode of fixing the psalms in a manner reminiscent of those that sought to order the psalms in terms of author, the biography of David or musical directions, but in the emphasis on oral material it differs qualitatively from these efforts, as well as the earlier historical-critical efforts at dating the literature and searching for the historical situation. To be sure, Gunkel was too much of a historical critic not to deal with these questions as well, but these interests must be seen as an effort to anchor the balloon of form itself, which has a tendency to float free from such fixation. Another way of putting it is that the potential of Gunkel's analysis of form has yet to be realized, as hinted by the scattered attempts at 'literary' readings, set free from the older concerns of historical criticsm itself (see, for instance, Hauge 1995). For was it not from form criticism that the first attempts at moving beyond historical criticism were made, marked now by Muilenberg's 1967 essay 'Beyond Form Criticism', itself an echo of Geoffrey Hartmann's 'Beyond Formalism' a year earlier.

What Gunkel achieved was less a fixation of the psalms into various forms as the recognition of the interchangeability and fluidity, since the various forms themselves serve to highlight precisely this feature of the psalms. What I mean is that what we now have—and psalms criticism cannot escape the delineation into various forms after Gunkel—are vast blocks of material within which the free flow of the psalms is enhanced. This is especially true of the larger groupings, such as lament, complaint and thanks, within which the flow of motifs and terminology is allowed to run without the effort at fixing them that has characterized so much criticism. In his studies of the complaints, Robert Culley has emphasized that no one complaint psalm can be read without the others in mind, or rather without the form of the complaint Psalms as a whole impinging on the particular psalm in question (Culley 1993). And yet psalms criticism gives in repeatedly to the temptation to take on a small idenitifiable chunk—the overwhelming focus is on individual psalms, or psalms of the sons of Korah, or most notably the royal psalms which are few in number. But even with the forms in place, the boundaries themselves remain fluid and debated, for not all of the psalms fit neatly into the various *Gattungen*. For instance, Pss. 57 and 60 are complaints with their characteristic pattern of complaint and rescue, but in their combination in Ps. 108 they become a psalm of praise. Although even here it is not a pure praise psalm, the echo of the complaint in the finale verses of Ps. 60 recurring at the close of 108.

Form criticism, then, and the possibilities that still remain to be realized, comprises the complex term of the semiotic square, the connection between interchangeability and fixation, not merely in terms of *Gattung* and *Sitz im Leben*, but also in the tension of the study of form itself, the incomplete delineation of various *Gattungen*, the focus on oral texts and the recognition of the fluidity of the psalms in the attempt to identity various forms.

What of the remaining lateral axis and the neutral term? I am going to suggest that the left-hand lateral axis is the realm of personal devotion and piety. So many studies of the psalms end up in here, arguing that the psalms themselves express either a personal devotion and were primarily for that use (Gunkel 1967) or a collective piety, a direct response of the heart to God. In fact, such devotional readings often form the other side of critical scholarship (Gunkel 1967, 1968; Kraus 1978; Anderson 1972; Broyles 1989; Cole 2000; Eaton 1995; Hauge 1995), the element of religious commitment that biblical critics time and again suspend in order to undertake their critical work. These readings may take the form of liturgical use of the psalms, and the long tradition of the central use of the psalms in both Jewish and Christian lectionaries, let alone their basis for singing, seeks to make use of them in a way that carries on their initial usage. Or they may be used in countless private devotional activities, biblical scholars lending their hands to devotional booklets produced by the various churches, collections of prayers and readings, or the occasional text that emphasizes their function in such a private realm.

The devotional use of the psalms gives free reign to the fluid and inter-changeable sense of the psalms, but what is the other term with which it connects? In order to get there I suggest that the neutral term of my dia-gram, the connection between the two categories at the bottom, is theology. Often tied up with devotional and pietistic moves, based on a notion that the psalms themselves give expression to such emotions, I want to separate the two, assuming the systematic nature of theology as a distinct enterprise from piety itself. In the work of Kraus and Anderson, for instance, or even Westermann, theological intepretations, however much they try to base their theological reflections on the purported original usage of the psalms, attempt to link theological categories with biblical material. The fiction that such categories actually arise from the Bible avoids the fact that theology and biblical studies are uneasy partners, a sign of the appropriation of the Bible by theology and the imposition of its categories on the unruly biblical texts. The relevance of this tension here is that theology seeks a certain completeness or fullness that is provided by the systematization that comes through the theological tradition. Through the foundational level of those categories—God, anthropology, harmatology, Christology, salvation, sanctification and eschatology—the master narrative of theology brings to bear a complete system on the material at hand.

A similar approach to the psalms, while apparently avoiding the sys-tematization of theology itself, seeks alternative theological systems, ones that seem to be suggested by the psalms themselves. I am thinking of the search for thematic consistency or developments also continues, often closely tied with theological readings. Gottwald (1985), for instance, argues that there is a movement from lament to praise, whereas Alter (1987) sees the themes of death and rebirth and the human–God relation-ship. The redactional concern with structure or themes dominates works that argue for an eschatological arrangement (Mitchell 1997), or with the move from questions about the loss of hope to God's answers and promised kingdom (Cole 2000), or the theme of refuge (Creach 1996), or that the Levitical singers attempted to fill the role of the classical prophets (Tournay 1991).

However, both devotional and theological interpretations indicate, through their focus and subject matter, a particular aspect of the psalms themselves that I have left until last, namely, their emptiness. For is not the focus of devotion and theology something that cannot be verified, a void in the structure that sustains the structure itself. This void is that which the psalms exhibit as well: the limited content, the emptiness of the language is both the opposition to the sense of fullness and interminable repetition of the same thing over and over again, as well as the negative of the drive to fix and locate the psalms in some way or another. Devotional interpretations then become the combination of both interchangeability and emptiness, while theology brings together the desire for a complete explanation and the empty and evasive focus of its work.

I can now complete my square as follows:

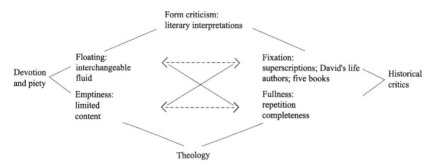

Figure 6. *Semiotic Square of Psalms Criticism*

The semiotic square, particularly in its ability to map the formal and ideological tensions of the psalms and their study, indicates that the problem of the psalms to which pre-modern and modern critics have responded in various ways is not mere their fluidity, but also their sheer emptiness. Not only is this a problem for the ideological system in which Yahweh is such a central feature—and I will return to this question in the conclusion—but I would like to put the question in a slightly different way: is the overwhelming concern with form in criticism of the psalms not a compensation for the content, that is, the overtly 'sacred' language that exhibits its shortcomings or lack most clearly in the empty language of worship and devotion?

Chapter 9

WALTER BENJAMIN:
THE IMPOSSIBLE APOCALYPTIC OF DANIEL

The enigmatic allegorical method of Walter Benjamin is one of the most intriguing of all the critics studied in this book. If the rapidly increasing secondary literature is anything to go by,[1] then people in a wide range of disciplines are drawn in by his work, which ranges over philosophy, literary criticism, aesthetics, art history, autobiography, translation theory, theology and biblical studies. Benjamin at first seems more amenable for biblical critics, given the way the Bible in many different modes runs through his work. And indeed some of the possibilities for biblical studies arise from this presence, yet Benjamin resists easy extraction, the lifting of a method or of categories from his work. Of course I will attempt to do this all the same, but the task is necessarily more fragmented than some of the other critics I consider. The great tension of Benjamin's work was between theology and Marxism, which was never quite resolved, the one side of his described Janus-face appearing alongside the other time and again. But, since my focus is Benjamin's promise for biblical studies, I am concerned with the questions of allegory and language.

The reason for my interest in these questions is that they provide me with an angle on some of the problems of Daniel 7–12. For in this text, which then becomes paradigmatic for similar apocalyptic material, there is a tension between the allusive and metaphorical language of the vision and a desire both by the text and subsequent scholars who have been lured by it to fix the references in this material to particular historical events and times. How is it that this apocalyptic language is both referential and anti-referential? But my work with this text throws a questions directly back at

1. In fact, scholarship on Benjamin far outruns all of the others in this book put together. At my last search on the MLA database alone, over 4,000 items on Benjamin are listed from 1979 and this does not include much of the German scholarship.

Benjamin, for whom allegory provided an alternative opening to the future, blocked by history.

In my discussion of Benjamin I am interested in the tension between the direct referential function of language, what became in his later work the urgent political use of language in Marxism, and the resistance of language itself to operate in this way. What he attempted to do was to overcome the former problem in light of latter. This tension forms the basis of my interpretation of Daniel, so I trace it through Benjamin's reflections of allegory and language.

The most consistent feature of Benjamin's work is allegory, a way of reading as much indebted to contemporary debates over allegory in German criticism as to the longer tradition of biblical interpretation that was pinned to allegorical modes of reading the Bible. Benjamin seeks both to provide a comprehensive analysis of the history and practice of allegory and to incorporate it into the capillaries of his own texts. First worked out at length in *The Origin of German Tragic Drama* (Benjamin 1998), the study of a Baroque dramatic form that influenced Adorno's method, Benjamin brought his allegorical method to an extraordinary (in)completion with the Arcades project (Benjamin 1999), whose allegorical method, with its double register of theology and historical materialism, is particularly pertinent for a text like Daniel. Allegory also provides Benjamin with a means to deal with the problem of the future in Marxism, a strategy somewhat like looking awry in order to see the way more clearly. Often apocalyptic in tone—the context of Weimar and then Nazi Germany cannot be forgotten—Benjamin's text seems to face the same problems as Daniel, so much so that they appear in many respects to belong to a far-flung coterie.

Allegory has a tradition in biblical criticism that runs back to the earliest interpretation of the Bible, used by Origen, for instance, who himself adapted a strategy used by the rationalist Hellenists, who found the myths of ancient Greece a little too crude for comfort and so interpreted them allegorically—as emotions, or the faculties of human activity, or as the forces of nature, and so on. Yet the paradox of allegory is that although it formed the basis of biblical interpretation for something like a millennium and a half, it is still in some disrepute in biblical studies, having to carry on a half-life in its various offspring, such as literary theory and cultural studies. The problem for biblical studies is that allegory is part of that whole world of interpretation dispensed with in the rise of 'modern' methods of interpretation that stressed the scientific and rational dimensions of the history of the Bible's emergence and of its literature.

But let me follow Benjamin's own explication of allegory. Unlike symbol, allegory operates by the non-expression of the object to which it relates. That is, allegorical language speaks of something that remains hidden, just below the horizon as it were, but nevertheless present. It is also a signal of the ruined and fragmented nature of history and human living, and for Benjamin the hidden 'truth' concealed in such ruins could only be opened with an allegorical method. The Christian origins and continued validity of allegory lies for Benjamin in the contest between the gods: officially banished as demons and idols before the orthodox doctrine of Christianity, allegory allows those divinities to live on in another form. Thus, allegory takes flight from the ruins of an older religious system, whether that of ancient Greece or Canaan, or that of mediaeval Europe. Ultimately, Benjamin has a theological agenda in such reading, and here he is close to the biblical allegorists, for the purpose of allegorical reading is to locate moments of 'redemption' in the detritus and disaster of human history and its artistic and literary products.

The task of allegorical reading becomes one of attempting to locate the allegorical referent that cannot but be absent and concealed in the very language used. If Adorno turned philosophical concepts over in order to speak the unspeakable, then Benjamin resorted to allegorical figures themselves, enigmatic items—forgotten plays, children's books, arcades or shopping malls—that foreground the allegorical process in the very act of interpreting allegorically. This is an extraordinary move, for it constitutes a thorough reworking of the Hegelian dialectic and allegory itself into new forms of both. For, as I argue in *The Criticism of Earth* (Boer, forthcoming), such a development expresses the inner logic not only of mediaeval biblical exegesis, continually searching for the elusive, deeper meaning of Scripture, but also of Benjamin's wider work. However, there is a curious twist in all this, for in all his theological ways of thinking and writing, Benjamin was an atheist, and so the very meaning of such terms as 'God', 'redemption', 'truth' and 'messiah' must themselves begin to function allegorically for something different. And this was an elusive future, which he increasingly came to see as a communist one, for which only allegorical terms are adequate, especially theological ones.

Benjamin argues that allegory is a specifically Christian practice—the earlier Greek and Roman process of gods as various forms of human emotions, reactions, motivations and abstract concepts is a precursor—one that could arise only with the peculiarly Christian notion of guilt, tied up as it is with the Fall. For the Fall signals not merely a strong sense of evil, but also of the passing of eras, of the loss of a past that could not be retrieved. Yet the task of allegory was precisely to preserve that which was passing, finding itself at home in ruins and fragments, traces of loss that still allow contact with what has been lost. More specifically mediaeval allegory enabled the pagan gods to live on, as demons, spirits and creatures, in a complex process that both recognized their continuing power and realized that their existence was under threat in the rarified atmosphere of Christianity. But it was allegory itself that preserved them for later ages.

Benjamin's most detailed and well-known discussion of allegory comes in the final chapter of his *Trauerspielbuch* (see especially 1998: 215-35): 'For a critical understanding of the Trauerspiel, in its extreme, allegorical form, is possible only from the higher domain of theology; so long as the approach is an aesthetic one, paradox must have the last word' (1998: 216). But the moment he makes this point, history appears, for he is interested above all in a theology of history: 'Such a resolution, like the resolution of anything profane into the sacred, can only be accomplished historically, in terms of a theology of history, and only dynamically, not statically in the sense of a guaranteed economics of salvation' (1998: 216).

The origin of allegory can only be understood, argues Benjamin, in tracing its history from the Middle Ages. From this context he identifies three intimately related motifs that carry through from the Middle Ages to the Baroque (the period under analysis in the *Trauerspielbuch*): 'The struggle against the pagan gods, the triumph of allegory, the torment of the flesh' (1998: 220). Christianity's own war with the ancient gods and its rewriting of their various roles resulted in allegory. What happens is that the pagan gods were expelled from heaven and placed in hell and on earth, becoming demons instead of gods. Yet in a characteristic dialectical move, Benjamin argues that this transformation of the gods into demons, magical creatures with demonic associations, relies upon the work of Hellenistic and late Roman writers, who already produced a certain 'deadness of the figures and the abstraction of the concepts' (1998: 226). That is, the end of the living 'reality' of these gods and their interpretation as abstractions allows for a subsequent represention as demonic creatures. The third element is the body, which now becomes demonic, the location of the old gods themselves. For in certain forms of Christianity, the flesh is the locus of sin and evil, of base desires and lusts. The naked body is itself impure, just as the Greek gods and demons, and as the classical representations of gods and human beings. Allegory is then a strategy for dealing with such nakedness and the corruption of the body: '…allegorical exegesis tended above all in two directions: it was designed to establish, from a Christian point of view, the true, demonic nature of the ancient gods, and it also served the pious mortification of the flesh' (1998: 220).

Yet, in proper dialectical fashion, Benjamin does not argue that allegory was a way of reading the gods out of existence, of substituting them with abstractions and human faculties; rather, allegory enables the preservation of the gods and their world in a hostile environment: 'For an appreciation of the transcience of things, and the concern to rescue them for eternity, is one of the strongest impulses in allegory' (1998: 223). At the same time, allegory also arose as an effort to neutralize the danger of the ancient gods, a strategy to deal with them precisely because it was not possible to banish them so easily. Had it been possible to do so, then allegory would not have arisen. Instead, it is precisely because these ancient divinities had held power for so long that some method of acknowledging and transforming such a situation was required. But this allows Benjamin to make his more general argument about allegory, namely, that it is a method for preserving that which is passing away (the connections with Daniel should not be missed here). For the Middle Ages it was classical antiquity that was the prime instance of a world that had passed, that everything, all worlds and eras, were in the end impermanent and transient. As he had already intimated earlier in the chapter:

Allegory as preservator [handwritten marginal note]

> in allegory the observer is confronted with the *facies hippocratica* of history as a petrified, primordial landscape. This is the heart of the allegorical way of seeing, of the Baroque, secular explanation of history as the Passion of the world; its importance resides solely in the stations of decline (1998: 166).

By this means Benjamin arrives at a formulation of allegory that has taken on a life of its own beyond the intricacies of his argument in the *Trauerspielbuch*. Allegory takes flight out of the ruins, out of a strong sense of loss of a past that cannot be recovered:

> In the ruin history has physically merged into the setting. And in this guise history does not assume the form of the process of an eternal life so much as that of irresistible decay. Allegory thereby declares itself to be beyond beauty. Allegories are, in the realm of thoughts, what ruins are in the realm of things (1998: 177-78).

Dialectically, it is precisely in such fragmentary transience that the effort to preserve the past may be found in allegory, seeking that which is eternal in a melancholy of passing that echoes with Daniel. 'Allegory established itself most permanently where transitoriness and eternity confronted each other most closely' (1998: 224)—particularly at moments when that which was felt to be eternal most obviously underwent change, such as legal norms or religious beliefs.

But how is all of this specifically Christian, or rather, how does the Christian appropriation of the pagan past show the final dominance of Christianity? Through guilt. For guilt is the missing item among the three that Benjamin identifies as unavoidably linked—the pagan gods, the body and allegory itself—since the realm of idols and the flesh is that of guilt. And here the Fall becomes the crucial biblical and theological moment for guilt, a guilt that attaches in allegory to both the interpreter and the object interpreted, that is, to human beings and nature itself, which both suffer as a result of the Fall. Allegory is then profoundly Christian, for not only is allegory the result of the Fall, working by means of ruins in order to locate in such transient items a moment of eternity, but allegory was also, precisely because of this process, the only possible means of salvation for guilt-laden nature and antiquity. Allegory enables not merely the preservation of what was lost, but also a mode of redemption from its pagan guilt. Yet for Benjamin this has not as yet been achieved, for while the ancient gods become magical creatures—fauns, centaurs, sirens and harpies—there are transposed into the satanic. A proleptic note creeps into Benjamin's twisting argument: the redemption promised and begun by allegory awaits its completion. Benjamin's formulation of allegory, and then also history, is profoundly eschatological and even apocalyptic: allegory becomes a key not only for producing this structure, but also for realizing its hope.

If allegory is central to the analysis of the first published work by Benjamin, it becomes integral to the method of his last great unfinished Arcades Project, or *Passagenwerk* (1999). However, in the move from his study of Baroque drama to the Paris Arcades, the tension I mentioned earlier becomes stronger, for in this explicitly Marxist work he sought a way to honour the ambiguous referentiality of allegory in an explicit political programme. Modelling himself on the collector as allegorist (see Convolute H in 1999), Benjamin takes his lead from Marx's comments on the fetishism of commodities in *Capital*: here the image of the collector as one who simultaneously 'detaches the object from its functional relations' (1999: 207) and elevates 'the commodity to the status of allegory' indicates the point at which Marx and theology work together. For is not allegory a profoundly Christian practice, as he argues in the *Trauerspiel-*

buch, operating with a distinct sacred history? But if allegory also connects with the fetish character of the commodity, then this allows a Marxist analysis to appear in an integrated fashion, as the quotations from Marx that pepper the close of Convolute H indicate (1999: 209-10). Not only does allegory become part of the method of the latter work, it also operates with a double register that brings together historical materialism and theology.

Although the impetus came from Benjamin's own explicit adoption of Marxism, conjoined with the desire to maintain his earlier theological concerns, he found in Marx—especially the first part of *Capital* that was a minimal set reading for Marxist literary critics—the justification for such a dual register. The obvious symptom of this is the repetition of an oft-quoted sentence from Marx: 'A commodity appears, at first sight, to be a trivial and easily understood thing. Our analysis shows that, in reality, it is a vexed and complicated thing, abounding in metaphysical subtleties and theological niceties' (Benjamin 1999: 181; also 196-97 in a slightly different translation). Taking on a life of its own in the market, it becomes a 'material immaterial' (*sinnlich ubersinnlich*) thing, an idol full of the breath of life. Yet, apart from the juxtaposition of Marx with other quotations, what interests me here is both the historical materialist and theological dimensions of the quotation from Marx. Inseparable in Marx's work, they take on for Benjamin a less rigorous association that appears time and again throughout the *Passagenwerk*.

In both the *Trauerspielbuch* and the *Passagenwerk*, with its own Marxist integration, Benjamin has, somewhat surprisingly, produced what amounts to strong theological argument for the nature of allegory, one that relies on notions of the Fall, sin, guilt, Satan, Christ, redemption and resurrection. It is almost as though Benjamin has sought to structure his argument with a sacred history rescued from the ruins of mediaeval theology. But then, it is an ingenious move that develops the tools of analysis from the subject matter at hand, for the *Trauerspiel* is unthinkable without the fading light of a mediaeval world in which the sacred provided the primary ideological pattern for thinking, acting and living. Too often Benjamin's theory of allegory is gutted of its theological content, various critics appropriating his emphases on ramifications of the theological argument, such as transience, fragments and ruins. And yet for Benjamin the referentiality of theology operates in a curious fashion, for there are no obvious or conventional referents—divine figure, heaven, redemption from hell and so on—for Benjamin's theological arguments.

Why, then, does Benjamin develop such a complex and heavily theological theory and practice of allegory? How does one work towards the overthrow and overcoming of the present and the inauguration of a new era while avoiding the abyss of fascism as a solution to chaos? As I suggested above, there is an eschatological orientation to the future in Benjamin's theory. Too often it is assumed that the terms and conditions of the present set the conceptual and historical boundaries within which the future can be thought. So, concepts such as history, politics, economics, society, culture, along with models of the past, such as violent revolution, slower transitions, the rise to dominance of a new mode of production and social system, provide the context within which people argue for and fight for a Marxist future. But this is to admit defeat before the battle has been drawn. For the terms and conditions of the present are by definition inadequate for thinking, hoping and enacting a radically different future. Language falls short of the possibility, even while it circumscribes how one's thinking about it might move. This is why Benjamin resorts to such a curiously biblical and theological terminology and practice. Let me take a move out of Benjamin's own pages, specifically a dialectical one. It is not that various terms from the present are used in their imperfect way to give us a fleeting glimpse of that other future: rather, the socialist future provides the very terms with which we might understand our present, although these terms are but very imperfect derivatives of what that socialist future contains. In other words, rather than taking terms from our present and projecting them into the future, Benjamin works in reverse: the terms and concepts of a communist future, however degraded and partial they might be in our present perception and use of them, provide the way to think about that future itself.

The problem of course is that if the future is as radically distinct— however gradual or sudden a transition might be—as Marxists like to think, then the very ways of thinking and arguing will also be qualitatively different. It is precisely for this reason that Benjamin turns to religious, or more specifically biblical, categories in his thought. And these categories are unavoidably allegorical, for it is only by allegory that one can begin to speak of a future that connects only tangentially with our present. Allegory, particularly in Benjamin's hands, reaches across the divide between a capitalist present and a communist future to draw terms from that future itself, however imperfect they might be. This is, in the end, the dialectic that operates at the heart of Benjamin's work. For only such terms, enigmatic and religious ideas (for messianic and apocalyptic forms of religion, such as those found in Daniel, have a long history of attempting to deal with precisely this problem), give a glimpse of an alternative world.

In making this argument I have an eye on the text of Daniel, where this tension over history and the future is a crucial problem and may provide one of the reasons for the production of the language of apocalyptic itself. Ultimately, for Benjamin allegory seeks to deal with the problem of history and the future in Marxism, and yet Marxism does not appear in the *Trauerspielbuch* that was written when Benjamin was first exposed to Marxism at the hands of Asja Lacis and Ernst Bloch on the island of Capri, coming only belatedly in his later writings. The *Passagenwerk* attempts to integrate in a radical fashion the method he describes in the *Trauerspielbuch*, although now in a double register of theology and historical materialism. That is, the allegorical levels running through the various convolutes or sections of the *Passagenwerk* turn in the direction both theology and political economics. But the book of Daniel seems to do a similar thing, bringing together the specificities of historical location and an extraordinary language about the acts of God in the near future—a tension that runs close to Benjamin's efforts to integrate the possibilities of historical materialism and the esoteric language of theology.

Yet Benjamin makes use of the language without aquiescing to their truth claims. I have argued that Benjamin's use of such a schema was an attempt to overcome the blockage of conventional theories of historical change, a way of attempting to think and imagine a world that could not be thought in the terms of those theories. Yet the problem that emerges here is that a highly metaphorical and non-referential language becomes the means of understanding and enabling the movement of historical events. This is precisely the tension I explore in Daniel, between specific historical referentiality and a language used that operates at the other end of the scale. Of course, the usual understanding of apocalytpic is that it is a code. Benjamin will want to bring these together in a dialectical fashion, but his dialectic so often operates through conjunction, leaving the process to take off in its own way, rather than working through the implications.

Thus far I have traced the tension in Benjamin's thought between the need for specific political economic analysis and theology. However, despite his effort at a dialectical treatment of the problem, it seems to me that his own work raises significant questions about holding the two together. And this shows through in his theory of language. Coming from his earlier writings—the ones Adorno preferred to the later ones—it proposes a theory that leaves both history and theology in irreconcilable opposition.

Both allegory and language remained concerns of Benjamin until his last work. His work on language has an extraordinary pertinence for texts of the Bible, such as Daniel, for the question of the nature and function of language as such has rarely been broached. The key essay is 'On Language as Such and on the Language of Man' (Benjamin 1996: 62-74). Apart from the moves Benjamin makes in order to get to a linguistic theory of divine naming, what interests me here are the theories of language over against which he sets up his own position. In the text they are the ideological opponents that enable Benjamin to construct his response. They collectively appear under the empty and invalid 'bourgeois conception of language' (1996: 65), according to which language functions to communicate factual subject matter: 'It holds that the means of communication is the word, its object factual, and its addressee a human being' (1996: 65). Further, bourgeois linguistic theory holds that there is an accidental relation between word and object, agreed to by some explicit or implied convention. Language is nothing other than a system of '*mere* signs' (1996: 69). Yet Benjamin does not critique such a position with another; he prefers to account for it within the alternative theory that he proposes.

At this point he moves, significantly, into biblical interpretation, for Benjamin engages quite directly with Gen. 1–3, which itself provides the basis for his own argument. But rather than allowing the narrative sequence in these chapters of Genesis, or even the logic of Benjamin's argument that follows a similar trail, to influence my own reading, I begin with the Fall, a crucial marker in Benjamin's work at various points. Reading the story of the Tower of Babel (Gen. 11) as a consequence of the Fall—although he does note that in the biblical myth it comes somewhat later (1996: 70)—Benjamin sees its consequences as multiplicity, of human languages and thereby of translations, and of human knowledge. Further, the prelapsarian nature of language, in which the word is the name, gives way to the human word, 'in which name no longer lives intact and which has stepped out of name-language'. But what is most interesting is the nature of that new human word: 'The word must communicate *something* (other than itself). In that fact lies the true Fall of the spirit of language' (1996: 71; italics in text). This is none other than the bourgeois conception of language through which I passed a few lines ago, in which language communicates factual subject matter.

Benjamin moves on to connect this 'externally communicating word' with the knowledge of Good and Evil—a promise delivered by the serpent. Such knowledge is none other than 'prattle' (*Geschwätz*), a term Benjamin borrows from Kierkegaard, which in turn leads to the judgment of expulsion from the Garden. But 'judgment' also bears with it an eschatological note, which looms over the last paragraphs of the essay. However, I want to stay for a moment with this word 'prattle' (*Geschwätz*), for it recurs at other points. A few lines later he aligns 'the abyss of prattle' with 'the empty word', 'the word as means', 'the abyss of the mediateness of all communication'. Not only does he thereby characterize the language and function of law—as the prattle that emerged after eating from the Tree of the Knowledge and the Tree of Good and Evil, as an irony marking the mythic origins of the law—but this 'prattle' makes its way back to that same bourgeois language that has already appeared, especially the word as both empty and a means. Finally, the decline of language into prattle relates directly to confusion—a consequence of the mediateness and multiplicity of language. The steps here are subtle: it is not that language is confused, but signs are so, because of the entanglement of things. This is in direct contrast to the contemplation of things that marks the purity of the name. In other words, over against the Edenic essential connection between name and thing, the relation between sign and thing goes awry. This is, for Benjamin, a way to account for linguistic assumption that names have an entirely arbitrary relation to things—a linguistic assumption he once again describes as 'bourgeois'. While such a criticism has only hints of the Marxist analyses that would follow, in his essay on Karl Kraus (Benjamin 1986: 239-73), he explicitly argues that capitalism is the postlapsarian world in which Kraus resists the base 'prattle' (*Geschwätz*) of journalism, relevance and inauthentic language, one who holds onto to the ideal language of creation, a latter-day Adam for whom the language of naming is still an option. Kraus's practice of quotation, something Benjamin himself would develop much further, purifies and emancipates language.

By now the argument has moved through a number of twists, but there is one further step, namely a summary of the three consequences of the Fall:

> For the essential composition of language, the Fall has a threefold significance (in addition to its other meanings). In stepping outside the purer language of name, man makes language a means (that is, a knowledge inappropriate to him), and therefore also, in one part at any rate, a *mere* sign; and this later results in the plurality of languages. The second meaning is that from the Fall, in exchange for the immediacy of name that was damaged by it, a new immediacy arises: the magic of judgement, which no

longer rests blissfully in itself. The third meaning that can perhaps be tentatively ventured is that of the origin of abstraction, too, as a faculty of the spirit of language, is to be sought in the Fall. For good and evil, being unnameable and nameless, stand outside the language of names, which man leaves behind precisely in the abyss opened by this question (1996: 71-72).

In the Fall, then, the name becomes a mere sign, language a means, judgement an external magic, and abstraction itself emerges—marked by 'good' and 'evil'. Each of these features are but part of the bourgeois linguistic theory that lies behind this text. But what Benjamin attempts here is a way of dealing for the emergence of such a position in the first place and his choice, strangely enough, is the biblical myth of the Fall.

But what is this prelapsarian theory of language that is so important for Benjamin, underlying as it does the prologue to the *Trauerspiel* book, as also the translation essay? Benjamin argues that, in opposition to the bourgeois theory of language, it 'knows no means, no object, and no addressee of communication. It means: *in the name, the mental being of man communicates itself to God*' (1996: 65; italics in text). By this time, however, Benjamin has moved from the distinction between a mental entity and a linguistic entity in language, through the argument that the mental being communicates itself *in* and not *through* language (the latter being the bourgeois theory), the communication of linguistic being through language (i.e. the capacity for communication is language itself), to the conclusion that naming is the linguistic being of 'man'. The logic here is that if the communication of mental being takes place *in* language, then that communication takes place through naming. But the communication itself is directed not to other people—language thereby becomes a means of communication—but to God. Mental and linguistic being come together in the name, which is 'the innermost nature of language itself' (1996: 65). Over against the multiplicity of languages that result from the Fall, specifically through the Babel story of Genesis 11, pure language is unitary, primordial and harmonious.[2]

What interests me in the argument of the 'On Language' essay is less the philosophical lead-up, but rather the introduction of the Bible into the

---

2.   In the short essay 'Language and Logic' he writes: 'If we interpret this in the spirit of the mystics as pointing to a revealed unity of a linguistic kind, it will mean not just that this primordial language is the one originally spoken, but that the harmony originally created by those spoken languages was of incomparably greater power than any of the individual languages would possibly possess' (1996: 273).

discussion. Already appearing in parentheses,[3] the Genesis text comes into its own as a comprehensive argument for the nature of language as naming, of human beings as name-givers, which is ultimately modelled on God as name-giver. Let me summarize Benjamin's points. Both accounts of creation (Gen. 1.1–2.3; 2.3-25) emphasize a special relation between language and humans through the act of creation. In the second account it is as being created from earth and endowed with the gift of language, whereas in the first it is the creative act of God that establishes a deep relation between 'Let there be…', 'he made' and 'he named'. For Benjamin this produces the theological point that only with God are word and name one: 'God made things knowable in their names. Man, however, names them according to knowledge' (1996: 68).

However, a third feature of Genesis appears with the creation of human beings in Gen. 1.26-31. In the shift of narrative order the threefold 'he created…' in Gen. 1.27 signals for Benjamin that language itself is set free in 'man'. To be made in God's image means to know in the same language as God. After linking the earlier comments in relation to mental and linguistic being, Benjamin moves onto a fourth point, following on from this one: the connection between human language and divine is strongest with the name, firstly of animal names and then of human beings. The difference here is the proper name (Adam names her 'woman' and then 'Eve'). 'The proper name is the communion of man with the *creative* word of God. (Not the only one, however; man knows a further linguistic communion with God.)' (1996: 69). It is for this reason that there is an instrinsic relation between words and things.

I have introduced my own curious twist by ending with this text by Benjamin, for I in fact want to move from Benjamin to the biblical material and back again, and yet I will do so by means of Benjamin's reflections on the Bible. But why does he use the Bible in the first place?

> If in what follows the nature of biblical language is considered on the basis of the first chapter of Genesis, the object is neither biblical interpretation nor subjection of the Bible to objective consideration as revealed truth [*offenbarte Wahrheit*], but the discovery of what emerges of itself from the biblical text with regard to the nature of language; and the Bible is only *initially* indispensable for this purpose, because the present argument

3.   'In terming man the speaker (which, however, according to the Bible, for example, clearly means the name giver: "As man should name all kinds of living creatures, so should they be *called*"), many languages imply this metaphysical truth' (1996: 65).

broadly follows it in presupposing language as an ultimate reality, perceptible only in its manifestation, inexplicable and mystical (1996: 67).

Benjamin's reading is of course selective, the interest in language, particularly as an ultimate reality. However, there is a significant shift that takes place in this passage. Although it begins with an effort to follow the Bible on the question of language, to mine it for linguistic insights, by the end a small inversion takes place. It is not that the Bible speaks *about* language, nor that one can *follow* the Bible in order to construct a linguistic theory: the Bible itself *is* a language, the language of revelation: 'The Bible, in regarding itself as revelation (*Offenbarung*), must necessarily evolve the fundamental linguistic facts.' (Benjamin 1996: 67)

What are the implications of this for Benjamin's reflections on allegory and history? If, as I have argued, Benjamin attempts to generate an alternative system of philosophy and literary theory from theology, and that he tries to mediate between the specific concerns of historical materialism and theology by means of both allegory and his theory of history, then the reflections on language throw up a profound problem. For in the language essay he makes a distinction between various 'bourgeois' languages and a pure, prelapsarian language, between language as means, mere sign, judgment and plurality and as none of these, between language as instrumental and non-instrumental. In short, it is the difference between communication through language to pass on information to someone about an object, and communication in language, in which situation only God can be the recipient of what is now a language of naming. What Benjamin has done here is to present not only an eschatological notion of language—of that which is hoped for—but also to close down any possibility of a language that enables the kind of usage to which he puts it in his adoption of a relatively crude and idiosyncratic historical materialism. The specificity of his references to historical moments and events, to the realities of economic and political developments, fall foul of this theory of language. Yet theology also becomes an impossible option as a means to deal with the roadblocks to more conventional theories. As an allegorical effort to think through the possibilities of the future, to grasp in a distinct way what such a future might look like, it breaks down at precisely such a move.

Rather than read the earlier Benjamin and his theory of language in light of his later incorporation of Marxism, I want to read in reverse, to see the unease of this later work as the product of the earlier material. Thus, it is precisely in his effort to retool the Bible and theology for a different prupose, to break them out of their conventional and traditional referents, that such a use comes to a standstill. For by its very nature such language cannot do so: by remaining within itself, communicating in language to God through naming, biblical language is locked into its own logic and cannot provide a bridge outside itself. Even the argument that it is only by this means that language can have any effect, when there is no effort at communication through language, cannot overcome the initial problem.

I have dwelt with the problem in Benjamin's own thought, since it has direct bearing on my reading of Daniel, as I will soon show. For the Bible itself, argues Benjamin, not only provides a theory of language as the ultimate reality, as mysterious and mystical, but it is a language itself, and it is this language that I want to explore in the text of Dan. 7. I will want to put a particular spin on Benjamin's own argument, seeking to historicize in a Marxist direction his theory of language that does not try to follow his path of bringing theology and Marxism together.

The Tensions of Language in Daniel

The so-called visions of Daniel in the second half of the book (chs. 7–14) are, of course, the prime exhibit in the Hebrew Bible of apocalyptic material. Chapters 7 and 8 present two major visions, one of the lion, bear, leopard and monster, the second of the ram and the goat, each followed by a brief interpretation from a heavenly visitor, anonymous in Dan. 7.16, 10.10, 16, but Gabriel in Dan. 8.16-17, 9.21. However, after the 'prayer' of ch. 9, the rest of the collection is taken up with a lengthy interpretation/prediction of events that is a curious mix of apparent specificity and mythical motifs.

Following the cue of the text, critics have rarely been able to resist the temptation to join the dots, or rather crack the code, of the apocalyptic language. One of the standard moves is to produce a firm referent or two that can then anchor the text: the 'abomination that desolates' (שקוץ משומם) in Dan. 9.27, 11.31 and 12.11 becomes Antiochus IV Epiphanes, one of the most powerful of the Seleucid kings, who persecuted the Jews in the second century BCE (so, among a host of others, Collins 1993; Lacocque 1979; Hartmann and DiLella, 1978). Drawing on Josephus (*De Bello Judaicum* 1.37 [1984: 33]), who mentions the attack on Jerusalem as part of his conflict with Ptolemy IV over control of Palestine, the plundering of the temple and cessation of sacrifices for three and a half years (identified as 167–64 BCE), Antiochus gets locked into the book of Daniel. (No-one seems particularly interested in Pompey, who entered the Holy of Holies in 6 BCE and who may also be the 'abomination that desolates'.) Josephus includes some colourful details, such as forcing the Jews to withhold circumcision and to sacrifice pigs on the altar—hence Daniel's thrice-repeated 'abomination that desolates'. Of course the book itself, at least in its final redaction (chs. 1–6 are usually felt to come slightly earlier), must come from this time as well, when Antiochus was rampaging over Palestine and driving the Ptolemies back. Only when he dies and his son, Antiochus V, became ruler, was Judas Maccabaeus able to cleanse the temple and restore worship. For Redditt (1999), we can be a little more specific, arguing for a distinct Diaspora group responsible for Dan. 1–6, holding out for more influence in a foreign court, only to return to Jerusalem and write chs. 7–12 during the time of Atiochus IV Epiphanes. But this is merely a variation on Collins's argument that chs. 1–6 were composed in Aramaic, and that ch. 7 is a translation from Hebrew into Aramiac, with Dan. 1.1-2.4b as a Hebrew frame.

However, with the key of Antiochus in place, he can then turn up in other places, such as Dan. 5 or the king of the north in Dan. 11 over against the king of the south (Ptolemy). The description of the three kings in ch. 11 may speak of the three successors to Alexander the Great (what about the contested alliance between Caesar, Pompey and Scipio at a later date?). And the 'Kittim' of Dan. 11.30? Are they Greeks, as the word itself suggests, or in fact Romans, as seems to be the case with the Qumran material? Again the identification wavers. The problem is that even in the sections that appear to speak more directly about historical events, the language remains coded and obscure, so much so that critic after critic laments the absence of precision and clarity as a great handicap, especially without any other chronicles or annals apart from the highly unreliable Josephus.

The task of cracking the code continues, with the four beasts of ch. 7 or the ram and goat of ch. 8. The minimal interpretation of the first vision leaves critics guessing—Assyria, Babylon, Persia, Greece or Rome?—but the second vision is more helpful: the ram with the two horns are the kings of Media and Persia (Dan. 8.20), but one must take a step to identify Cyrus as the ram himself, the one who unites the Medes and the Persians. The he-goat then becomes the 'king of Greece' (Dan. 8.21), but we need to postulate Philip of Macedon to get anywhere. Or is that Alexander the Great? The four horns are the four weaker kings who follow (Dan. 8.22), but the problem here is that three of Alexander's generals divide up the empire between them, not four, unless Alexander himself is the fourth, but he is hardly a weak king. As for the one king who gets rid of the four, is that a Roman general, Pompey perhaps, but we cannot be sure. By the time the text gets to the point of superhuman intervention against this final king (Dan. 8.25), most critics feel that the text has reverted to an apocalyptic schema where myth overtakes history. If all of this was not complex enough, the convoluted material in Dan. 11 beggars identification, although many have tried to line up various Ptolemies and Seleucids.

Social scientific arguments allow one to step around the endless efforts to tie the text of Daniel down to the ebb and flow of quotidian events and the particularity of political history. Thus, drawing on the work of Ernst Troeltsch's distinction between church and sect, as well as Berger and Luckmann's notion of the social construction of reality, Hanson (1985) argues that apocalyptic material often appears in the context of oppressed groups: with no hope of any alleviation of suffering, the fevered hope of an extra-terrestial rescue becomes a way of coping. Gottwald (1985) is more specific, drawing comparison with the cargo cults of Melanesia, Polynesia and other places, where Christianity was radically redrawn in terms of the apocalyptic benefits of emergent capitalism, the material from millenarian groups in various times and places (e.g. the Hussites or Muntzer's peasants in Germany), as well as deprivation theory to make sense of the apocalyptic of Daniel. Benjamin's own apocalyptic might be understood in a similar way, given his situation in Europe, especially Germany, for assimilated Jews like Walter Benjamin at the time of the Nazis' rise to power and then the outbreak of World War II.

But the text of Daniel also spills over with references, calculations and efforts to grasp history and wrench it in a particular direction. The conventional dating formula is the most obvious, found elsewhere in the Hebrew Bible, especially Kings, and also in the first two chapters of Daniel (Dan. 1.1; 2.1). So, Dan. 7.1 has, 'In the first year of Belshazzar king of Babel'; Dan. 8.1, 'In the third year of Belshazzar the king'; Dan. 9.1, 'In the first year of Darius son of Ahasuerus'; Dan. 10.1, 'In the third year of Cyrus king of Persia'. The obvious point here is that no-one takes these dates as anything but chronological fictions, for the text of Daniel itself appears a good deal later. They are then literary devices—note the pattern of one and three that also recurs in many of the stories and visions—that attempt to place the book at a much earlier moment, turning the visions into predictions of the future. But do the specific identifications of kings and nations in the vision or dream interpretations function in a similar manner? The tendency among critics is to be not so ready to ascribe these to the whim of an anonymous author or two. Thus, the identities of Media, Persia and Greece in 8.20-21 and 10.20 seem to grant a specificity lacking elsewhere in the book. But as soon as the text allows us a whiff of history, it blows it away just as quickly, for the kings of Media and Persia are not named, nor is the king of Greece, nor are the four others of 8.22, nor the prince of Persia in 10.13 and 10.20, the prince of Greece in 10.20, the four kings of Persia in 11.2, the mighty king of Greece on 11.3, the king of the south and the king of the north in ch. 11, nor even the daughter of the king of south in 11.6, and so on. The only ones who are named apart from Daniel are characters like Gabriel (8.16; 9.21) and Michael (10.13, 21; 12.1), but only someone in an altered state of consiousness is going to suggest that these customers are verifiable historical figures.

Yet at this point, where the text takes off into the purer realms of apocalyptic speculation, it becomes very specific indeed. There seems to be a direct ratio between the communication of explicit detail and pure fantasy. I have in mind the numerological material that the heavenly visitors provide Daniel in moments of blinding insight. The key lies with the solar calculations based on the numbers seven and ten: the year itself is divided into weeks, but then the years themselves fall into lots of seven again, with key moments determined by either dividing seven (three and half is common), or multiplying sevens and tens. Thus, the jubilee itself *Emancipation* falls after 70 years, but the massive apocalyptic jubilee after 490 years.

The first of these calculations appears in Dan. 9.2: 'I, Daniel, perceived the number of years which, according to the book of Jeremiah the prophet, must pass before the end of the desolations of Jerusalem, namely, seventy years.' But the book of Daniel in fact provides the numbers, and so Gabriel the mathematician spells it out for Daniel. The end of transgression and sin, for which Daniel has just offered a prayer asking for forgiveness, will come in 'seventy weeks of years' (Dan. 9.24), that is, 490 years. This breaks into 'seven weeks' for the arrival of the anointed one (Dan. 9.25), 'sixty two weeks' to rebuild Jerusalem (9.25) until the sanctuary is destroyed (9.26). A prince—different from the anointed one or not?—will then make a covenant with 'many for one week'—the seventy are now up and we move on to the next crucial phase—and for 'half of the week' he is going to ensure that the sacrifices cease. All of these weeks seem to refer to weeks of years, so we end up with 49 years until the anointed prince, 434 years to rebuild the temple, 7 years for the covenant with the prince (a total of 490) and 3.5 years for the cessation of sacrifice. But the three weeks of Daniel's mourning and fasting last for just three normal weeks (preferable to 21 years), or 'weeks of days' as the text has it (Dan. 10.2-3) in order to distinguish from the other weeks, those of years. Other than this there is the 'appointed time' (למועד) in 11.27 and 11.29, the 'time of the end' (ובעת קץ) in 11.40 and 12.4, 9, and the curious 'a time, two times, and half a time' in 12.7 (see also Dan. 7.25) in answer to Daniel's question as to when the wonders will end. While the 1,290 days (although contrast the 2,300 evenings and mornings of Dan. 8.14) from the first desecration of the temple specifies the days of the 3.5, the 3,335 days for which those who are blessed must wait seem to fall outside any of the schemas thus far (the equivalent is a little over 9.1 years). Even though the apocalyptic speculation concerning the crucial time of the end operates with an internal logic, this has not stopped critics from trying to sort out the dates. If the 3.5 years refers to Antiochus Epiphanes's desecration of the temple, then we can start to see how the text calculates events both backwards to the exile and rebuilding of the temple and forward to the much anticpated end when Michael will roll in with the heavy artillery. But all this does is attempt to spell the esoteric logic of the system itself, often with the assistance of the book of Jubilees and the Qumran material, an internal specificity that has no hold on reality.

What the text seems to offer is a code, a hidden language that is a mix of specific dates and events—note the detail of ch. 11—and hidden references that leave one guessing. For instance, 'Then shall arise in his place one who shall send an exactor of tribute through the territory of the kingdom; but within a few days he shall be broken, neither in anger nor in battle' (Dan. 11.20). The text is tantalizingly confident about the details and yet keeps everything closed: who is the 'one', or the 'exactor of tribute' and what does the reference to his being 'broken' mean? My own suspicion is that we have the characteristic features of the coded language of political groups, insurrectionary movements that wish to keep their information hidden. The image that emerges is a small taste of the complex movement of political groups and factions, each vying for influence in reponse to the others. It is not that we need to crack the code, like some infiltrator wishing to uncover a plot, but that the language remains beyond our reach. But there is a political edge that is more than the quietism Collins finds in Daniel, in contrast to the Maccabees who appear in Josephus's account in response to the activities of Antiochus Epiphanes. In other words, it seems to me that Daniel bears an uncanny resemblance to

Benjamin's own apocalyptic language, with its evocation of creation and apocalypse as the two end points of history and the effort to bring this to bear on a Marxist politics that works towards the rupturing of capitalism. And yet the tension is not so much between his Marxist and theological agendas as between the immediate needs of Marxist politics and the esoteric and idiosyncratic language he developed. In a similar way to Daniel, critics of Benjamin struggle to determine with greater specificity what he actually means—hence the tendency for that criticism to resort to detailed exegesis of his texts. Is there a coherent system to his thought? Do some texts have priority over others? Or does his work fall to pieces in the process of interpretation?

The language of Daniel resists all of these moves to sort out the meaning, whether by critical scholars or by the text itself. What are we to make of this peculiar and for many highly uncomfortable language—violent, extra-terrestial, often misogynist, visionary? One avenue is to seek its precursors, whether in Persian dualism, Hellenistic syncretism, emergent gnostic influences, prophecy in the Hebrew Bible and its eschatological (Isa. 24–27; 40–55; 56–66; Zech. 9–14; Joel; Malachi) or visionary tendencies (Ezekiel; Zech. 1–8), cosmic wisdom, the royal cult, ancient Semitic myth, whether Babylonian or Canaanite, or a mix of some or all of these factors from both within and outside the Hebrew Bible.

Alternatively, the source of the apocalyptic language of Daniel lies with its form, although on this question critics revert to definitions of apocalyptic, such as revelation given by otherworldly beings with temporal and spatial dimensions in narrative frame (Collins 1993). The features of such language include novel phraseology, numerical systems, especially the three-plus-one pattern, quotation, allusion and paraphrase of other material in the Hebrew Bible (see Talmon 1987). The symbolic world of the text has distinct temporal and spatial coordinates that see no problem between the everyday events of politics and the extra-terrestial realm of angels, archangels, heavenly visitors and armies. In fact, these are all part of one continuum, and the distinction between worldly and other worldly is foreign to the text itself: the kings of Media and Persia, of Greece, of the north and south are as much part of this world as are Michael and Gabriel.

But I want to suggest that apart from searching for precursors and influence, or attempting to deal with the language in terms of form or symbolism when comparisons are drawn between the Greek and Aramaic version (see Meadowcroft 1995), or even as a means to furthering research into Aramaic (see Stefanovic 1992), Benjamin's own comments on language are very appropriate to Daniel. Benjamin's argument is that the notion of language as communication of a certain content, a message, by means of a lingusitic structure, is a bowdlerized and bourgeois depreciation of language itself, that the 'pure language' hinted at in the story of Gen. 2 is one in which 'mental being' communicates itself not through language—this is an instrumental view of language—but in language. And this ideal form of 'pure language' is none other that of naming, that which Adam does with the animals and with Eve. With no one to whom he can communicate, Adam communes only with God through the name, which for Benjamin is the very nature of language itself. I want to suggest that in Daniel, especially chs. 7–12, this 'pure language' of naming is also found, but in order to get there I need to make a number of moves.

To begin with, the text is full of names, whether explicit and mythical or obtuse. But what of the geographical references, such Media, Persia, Greece and Chaldea, or Edom, Moab, the Ammonites, Egypt, Libya and Ethiopia (Dan. 11.41-43), or the province of Elam in the river Ulai (Dan. 8.2, 15), or the Tigris and Uphaz, the source of gold (Dan. 10.4-5), as well as Jerusalem, Judah and Israel? It seems to me that in this case there is a mythical geography in which known and unknown place names provide the setting for an apocalyptic schema that has its own agenda. These geographical names are less concerned with the actual geography, but rather have a similar function to the personal names, such as Daniel, Belshazzar, Michael, Gabriel, Cyrus, Darius and Moses. They are names with no referent. The latter two are of course kings of the past, but for this text they belong to a mythical panoply that hardly accords with any reality. To isolate them from all the other names in the text creates a false impression of the world of the text. They need to be placed alongside the four winds of heaven, the great sea, the four beasts, the lion with eagles' wings and the mind of a man, the bear with three ribs in its mouth, the leopard with four bird's wings and four heads, the terrible beast with iron teeth, claws of bronze and ten horns, the Ancient of Days with clothes as white as snow and hair like pure wool, a son of man, the saints of the Most High, the everlasting kingdom, a ram with two horns, the one higher than the other, the floating he-goat with a single horn between his eyes subsequently replaced by four horns and a smaller horn, the Prince of the host or the Prince of princes, a holy one, another holy one, the great and terrible God, the man in linen and gold with a body of beryl, arms and legs shining like burnished bronze, and his words like the noise of a multitude, the one in the likeness of the sons of men, the book of truth, a branch of her roots, the one beloved by women, a god of the fortresses, the time of trouble, those who awake from the dust at the end time to everlasting life or to everlasting contempt, the wise who shine like the brightness of the firmament, who are like the stars, the two beings clothed in linen who stand on either side of the stream, one of whom raises both arms to heaven, and the purified ones who make themselves white.

I have run through most of the names in Dan. 7–12, for it seems to me that too often they are forgotten in the rush to speak of the names that seem to have some known referent, those that communicate information beyond the closed sytem of the apocalyptic text. Yet they cannot be isolated from the weird and wonderful names that swamp the text. This also means that the apparently historical narrative, coded to be sure, of Daniel 11 joins this fantastic realm of mythical names: the kings of the south and the north, with their battles and multitudes, a daughter, sons, a glorious land, kingdoms, an exactor of tribute, strongholds, the prince of the covenant, the table, Kittim, the temple, those who fall to refine themselves and become white, Edom, Moab, Ammon, Egypt, Libya, Ethiopia, palatial tents, the sea and the glorious holy mountain.

All of this is a rush of naming to rival that of Adam's, with which Benjamin is so enamoured. I want to take this one step further before introducing my own twist to Benjamin's argument: for Benjamin naming is the linguistic being of man, the innermost nature of language, and that language can only communicate in rather than through language. This means that the only possible communication of this pure language is with God, and in the process both mental and linguistic being come together. In Dan. 7–12 the only communication takes place between Daniel and God, especially in the prayer of 9.4-19. Otherwise communication takes place between Daniel and various heavenly visitors, names or unnamed, intermediaries for God himself. And what does Daniel do in his confession of sin for the whole people? He drags out names from the Hebrew Bible itself: the prophets, kings, princes, fathers, people of the land, Judah, Jerusalem, Israel, Moses, the laws and Egypt. Again we have a closed system, one of internal reference to the Hebrew Bible itself, which can only make sense in light of those other narratives. Apart from this, Daniel repeatedly invokes variations on God's name—Yahweh Elohim, Yahweh my Elohim, Yahweh our Elohim, Yahweh, the great and terrible Elohim, Elohim, our Elohim, my Elohim—the primary name that appears in the prayer itself.

However, Benjamin is both right and wrong with his theory. His argument, in response to theories of language that stress the communicative function of language (what he terms the bourgeois justification of prattle, the cheapening of language in capitalism), was to work towards a linguistic notion of truth. His mistake, it seems to me, is to make use of a heavily theologized form of biblical exegesis, one that based itself on the notion that the Hebrew Bible provides an antidote to the tradition of myth that derives from the Greeks. Thus, the Hebrew Bible provides an alternative model of language and history that is not mythical but rather historical. In doing so, he sought an eschatological notion of language—all language strives to return to the pure language—that he takes as the eternal nature of language itself.

What I would like to do is give Benjamin's theory on language a Marxist turn—hardly an imposition on his work—that means I will not enlist Daniel as part of his theory of language per se (although it could well enhance that argument). Rather, Benjamin's reading provides an excellent characterization of the language of Daniel in a distinctly historical sense. That is, the language of Daniel is a closed system, inaccesible to us, because it comes from vastly different cultural, ideological and political economic formation: it communicates, to use Benjamin's terminology, in language, in itself and not elsewhere. I have on previous occasions in this book used the term mode of production to characterize the way such historical difference may be understood, at times speaking of the Asiatic mode of production. For now this terminology will suffice, at least until further reflection in my conclusion. What it means is that the language of Dan. 7–12 is part of the ideological network, with a good dose of politics, of a mode of production that at times must strike us as so different, as so distant from that of capitalism, that it leaves any reader from the context of capitalism nonplussed, preferring certain options, such as those I have noted in my discussion of the critics of Daniel, over others.

To be more specific, I want to venture the hypothesis that Daniel is but one example of the cultural conjunction of what I will for now call the Asiatic and Ancient modes of production. The features of the former include the dominance of a system of empirial expansion to ensure that the small levels of tribute from vassal states reaches a sufficient volume to fund a large imperial bureaucracy, as well as an army to ensure the stability of the empire and the exaction of tribute. Trade forms a minor aspect of such an economic and political world, for the prime economic feature is the collection of tribute. However, the vassal states also operate on such a system, exacting tribute from peasants in order to pay their own tribute to the imperial centre. As I mentioned in my discussion of 1 Sam., these vassal states perpetually seek, in a centrifugal direction, to break away from the larger imperial cluster in order to set up their own empirial structures in order to exact their own tribute. In response, the larger empires, in moments of strength, enact a centripetal force that attempts to keep vassal states within their orbit. The fact that the temple was so often also the treasury indicates the cultural dominant of the sacred, as I have mentioned on a number of occasions. And it is the sacred, with its linchpin the figure of Yahweh himself, that constitutes the language in which everything was understood, what we would now term politics, economics, culture, philosophy, religion, psychology and so on.

By contrast, the ancient mode of production, the dominant form for Greece and Rome, was based on a very different economic system: work by the vast majority of slaves for the relatively few 'citizens', the proper 'human beings'. These were adult men, thereby excluding women, children, foreigners, slaves, animals and so on. A vastly more efficient system, it gradually overtook the Asiatic mode of production through superior trained armies, and the imposition of a distinct cultural form, namely 'politics', understood in terms of the notion of the *polis*, the Greek and then Roman city-state. The proper citizen was a member of the *polis*, and language shifts to deal with all aspects of life in terms of such political citizenship. But this means that human social relations were highly mediated, through the swarm of slaves and non-citizens who did all of the 'work' (citizens of the *polis* did not work). All social relations took place by means of slaves, and so the dominant ideological way of conceiving the world was in a fashion that mediated one's relationship to the *polis*. The great ideological achievement of Augustine, for instance, was to enact a fundamental shift from the notion of a people chosen by Yahweh—whether Jews or Christians—to the idea of the 'city of God'.

I have of course provided sketches of ideal systems, but modes of production are notoriously porous, full of half-measures and accommodations with other modes of production. In Daniel there seems to be an idiosyncratic fusion of both the mediated politics of the Ancient mode of production and the dominance of the sacred of the Asiatic mode of production. Thus Yahweh dominates the scene and the thought-world of the text is not conceivable without him, yet Yahweh is now a highly mediated figure, represented by Gabriel and Michael and other unnamed heavenly visitors to Daniel. And yet it remains closed to us, a world in which the king of Greece and Michael appear side by side, the terrible beast with iron teeth and claws of bronze beside Edom, the man made of beryl and bronze, dressed in linen and gold beside Moses. It is indeed a language that communicates in language, is self-contained. And the reason why the language of Daniel is so undecipherable is that the culture and ideologies of such a different mode of production are beyond our comprehension, alien, no matter how much it has contributed to our way of thinking.

CONCLUSION:
ON THE QUESTION OF MODE OF PRODUCTION

Rather than summarize the main arguments of each chapter (something I have in fact done in the introduction), I want to move the whole argument a step further in this conclusion. In some respects, the various arguments I have developed for different sections of the Hebrew Bible, ranging through from Genesis to Daniel, may stand on their own, reliant as they are on the various approaches of the Marxist critics I have engaged. However, there is a level at which the different conclusions do in fact relate to each other and that is in terms of the parts they provide of a more total picture, an overarching framework of which I have provided only fragments, even though I take them as paradigmatic of larger sections than the specific texts in question.

Thus far I have used the traditional terminology of Marxist theory, such as ideology, mode of production, cultural dominant, class and class conflict. At various moments I described the mode of production in question as the Asiatic mode of production, along with the emerging presence of the Ancient mode of production in the case of Daniel. The candidate for the cultural dominant for the Asiatic mode of production I put forward was the sacred, which, as I have indicated on a couple of occasions, may be understood as a language, a way of thinking, believing, living and articulating. The difference between such a cultural dominant and our own, under capitalism, of reification is that we are accustomed to fragment and compartmentalize into areas such as politics, religion, society, psychology and so on, whereas my suggestion was that in the Hebrew Bible such distinctions are foreign, impositions on the extraordinary dominance of the sacred, the terms in which these various concerns were articulated.

The elements of that I traced in the preceding chapters include the paradoxes of the sacred, or more specifically the figure of Yahweh in relation to social justice in my discussion of Isa. 5 through Adorno, as well as the emptiness of the language of the sacred itself in relation to liturgy, worship and devotion in the psalms and their study with the assistance of

Jameson. The effect of the sacred, where Yahweh is the central feature by which the whole system holds together, on the generic tension between historical and prophetic narratives I worked through in my study of Kings, with the assistance of Lukács. In my discussion of 1 Sam., by means of Lefebvre's spatial analysis I broached the issue of a sacred commerce, the interaction with Yahweh without which the narrative action could not proceed, in relation to Hannah's womb. In Ezekiel I argued for the presence of an implict protest against the arbitrariness and brutality of Yahweh, a protest that is more important not for its ethical value but for the way it works by bringing the logic of the system to its breaking point. But other aspects also emerged, such as the need for such a system to appropriate the maternal body in both Gen. 25 and 1 Sam. 1–2, so that the narrative itself can in fact proceed: for Genesis the issue is the promise of a people, whereas in 1 Sam. it is the need to keep the priestly system operating. In other words, one feature of the ideological patterns of the sacred is that it systematically and radically excludes women, often through their very presence in the stories. Yet it needs women in order to operate, especially since the matter of succession, of the production of sons in order to carry on the line of male succession—Esau and Jacob through Rebekah, Samuel through Hannah and Obed through Ruth—as an essential part of that system. At the same time women must be excluded, for if they appear, as Jezebel, Athaliah and Huldah in Kings indicate, they threaten to destroy the whole ideological construct with which the narratives operate. The discussion of Ruth also raised the question of class and ethnicity, where it turns out that the term 'Israel' refers to those who do not work and exploit the labour of others. In my study of Exod. 32, with Gramsci and Machiavelli as conversation partners, I also began an exploration of the whole question of political myth and its function in the Hebrew Bible, particularly for a wide range of issues, such as gender, the state, social organization, leadership, but above all the hegemonic effect—understood in terms of both force and assent—of the whole system itself. Finally, in my discussion of Exodus, as well as that of Ezekiel, I raised the question of Utopia, whether the ideological system we find in the texts of the Hebrew Bible I have examined may be characterized as utopian or dystopian, or whether the utopian possibilities are those, as in Ezekiel, that run against Yahweh and the system he holds together.

Thus far, I have assumed an overarching ideology of the sacred. Given my preference for totalizing categories, coming out of the best of Marxism, I prefer such an approach to one that sees the various ideological features of the text as splintered and unrelated. But such an approach should not be understood as uniform, unfragmented or untroubled, for it is one of the main dialectical features of a totalizing approach that it can in fact reveal all of the tensions, contradictions, paradoxes and the perpetual efforts to deal with these and threats that they perpetually pose—as the various chapters in this book illustrate only too well.

The ultimate totalizing concept within Marxism is of course mode of production, to which I want to devote the remainder of the conclusion. As a first step I want to pick up a point from my discussion of Daniel in the final chapter, namely, the sheer difference that the ideological world of Daniel exhibits, so much so that ultimately it is closed to us, remains beyond our comprehension. I initially suggested that such a closed ideological system may best be explained in terms of the historical category of mode of production, but my tentative discussion of modes of production and the sacred needs further reflection, in order to see whether it is a workable category for the analysis of ancient texts like the Hebrew Bible.

All of which means that I need to turn to economic theory, and any consideration of economic theory cannot avoid the question of Marxism. This is obvious, if occasionally debated, with the study of capitalism, for it was precisely in such study that Marxism first arose as a distinct method. It is perhaps less obvious with pre-capitalist societies, except perhaps with those social and economic forms that led into capitalism in various places. Yet a small but significant amount of work has been done in Marxist analysis of ancient economic systems, not least by Marx and Engels themselves.

In what follows I will outline the traditional notion of mode of production in Marxist thought and trace its use in biblical studies, especially in terms of the question of the Asiatic mode of production. I cannot avoid relating this to wider debates about the Asiatic mode of production, which will then lead me to raise the question about the viability of mode of production as a category of analysis, both within Marxist theory and for biblical studies.

The ultimate category for traditional Marxist criticism is mode of production. For Marx and Engels (see, for instance *The German Ideology*, 1976), the key is that human beings both produce and are produced: they are produced by the conditions under which they live but they also produce those conditions themselves, including the biological form of life known as 'human being'. Producing the means of subsistence through the organization of physical resources affects their social, cultural and biological life, but it also remakes the material life of human beings, altering the conditions under which human beings in fact live. That is, the being and nature of human beings themselves is produced by their production of subsistence in relation to nature. Thus, for Marx and Engels mode of production is the way human beings produce the possibility of their own existence in relation with both nature and the existing mode(s) of production. They identified two dimensions of mode of production: the forces or means of production, which designates human interaction with nature in terms of raw materials, technical knowledge and the uses of labour; and the relations of production, which refers to the patterns of human interaction, the organization of human resources and allocation or division of labour.

Thus far I have been considering the more precise sense of mode of production, for in this specific meaning mode of production designates the economic dimension of any socio-political formation, often described as the 'base' or 'infrastructure'. But mode of production also has a more general sense in Marxist theory, which is no less than the whole reality of a particular historical epoch, including within its orbit culture and economics, ideology and class, politics and philosophy, religion and population, nature and law, and so on. Often the term mode of production slides between these two senses—the specific and all-encompassing—although I have tended to use it in the latter sense as a total economic, social and cultural system.

In my chapter on Henri Lefebvre and 1 Samuel I gave examples of both capitalism and the Asiatic mode of production. I will add the example of tribal society, or, as it is also called, primitive communism. In this case, the means of production are primarily hunting and gathering, making use of the available natural resources and ordering life according to the cycles and patterns of seasonal availability. This is often connected with forms of animal husbandry, the keeping of herds and flocks, and the relatively limited cultivation of crops and fruit-bearing plants. The relations of production are determined mainly by age and gender, as well as the organization of groups as tribes, which is itself somewhat 'artificial' and fluid. The cultural and ideological forms of primitive communism are close to the Asiatic mode of production, except that the focus is on myth and mythic narrative, the prevalence of magical explanation and understanding of the world, especially the availability of food and life.

It becomes obvious from such descriptions that the default position is one that operates with historical periods: mode of production is then a profoundly periodizing or historicizing way of working. One of the great values of mode of production as a term of historical analysis is that it accounts for the differences betweens social, political and economic systems, as well as reminding us that each mode of production is a historical feature, with its own emergence and passing away (including that of capitalism). The obvious objection is to ask how mode of production deals with continuities, the carry-through of certain items from one mode of production to the other, such as the various forms of patriarchy, religion or money, and so on. The usual response is to stress the many overflows, anticipations, relics and leakages between the various periods defined by certain modes of production.

Mode of production, in terms of the forces and relations of production, traditionally appears with what is called the cultural dominant of a particular epoch—a particular form of culture that is specifically suited to the mode of production in question and which therefore dominates other cultural forms that are less suited. In Marxist theory the modes of production agreed upon are: hunting and gathering, agriculture and husbandry (tribal society, primitive communism or the horde) with the cultural dominant of magic and mythic narrative; neolithic agriculture (the *gens* or hierarchical kinship societies) and its cultural dominant of kinship; Asiatic mode of production ('oriental despotism') and religion or the sacred; ancient or classical mode of production (the polis or oligarchical slave-holding society) with the cultural dominant of 'politics' in terms of citizenship of the city-state; feudalism with the relations of personal domination; capitalism commodity reification; and finally the expected communism and the cultural dominant of original forms of collective and communal association. In my earlier discussion I have followed this taxonomy, refined and reworked as it has been in Marxist theory, focusing on the Asiatic and ancient modes of production as the most appropriate terms for the biblical material.

In biblical studies mode of production has been an area of continued discussion, particularly in the use of social science methods. Elsewhere (Boer 2002b) I have analyzed Norman Gottwald's influence in this regard, so I will summarize that argument here. Gottwald redescribes the Asiatic mode of production as 'tributary', arguing that emergent 'Israel' overthrew the dominant 'tributary' mode of production of the ruling Canaanites and established in the Judaean hills a 'communitarian' mode of production that he designates as more egalitarian and more cooperative than that from which it emerged. The monarchy subsequently saw a return to the 'tributary' mode under pressure of the surrounding dominance of this mode. For Gottwald, the 'communitarian' mode is the key, rising and fall-ing from the moment of emergent 'Israel' to the early Christian and Jewish practices of communal cooperation rather than domination. Thus, the message of Jesus and the reconstruction of Judaism by the Pharisees after the two revolts (67–74 CE and 132–35 CE) attempt to recover and hold onto 'communitarian' ideals whose origins lie with the first 'Israel'. This tradition is the subversive ideal of the Bible, that which holds out, with more or less success, against the 'tributary' and then later the 'slave-based' modes of production.

What Gottwald has done is shift the terminology not only from Asiatic to 'tributary', but he has also brought together both tribal society and neolithic agriculture in his 'communitarian' mode of production (the 'slave-based' or ancient mode of production remains largely the same). I have critiqued this slippage from primitive communism to 'communi-tarian' and the Asiatic mode of production to 'tributary' elsewhere (see Boer 1998: 10-11; 2002b), but I will return to a different dimension of this problem after considering some further biblical scholarship on mode of production.

David Jobling also has written on mode of production, seeking to develop and refine his debt to Gottwald. Using Fredric Jameson's method, Jobling proposed to read the contradictions of the 'golden age' of Solo-mon's reign (1 Kgs 3–10) via the three semantic fields of economics, sexuality and wisdom. The contradictions inherent in these fields turned out to be a clash between the communitarian and tributary modes of production that Gottwald had identified (Jobling 1992a). Another effort from the same period (Jobling 1992b) sought the contradictions of Ps. 72 between the 'codes' of economics and law in terms of the internal con-tradictions of the Asiatic mode of production. Already at this time, Jobling was exploring the possibility that within the law code of Deuteronomy, and thus within the Deuteronomic history as a whole, there lay a buried communitarian code of law, one that had been overlayed and broken down by the dominance of the cultural and legal dimensions of the Asiatic mode of production. In the various pieces that came together in the 1 Samuel commentary (1998), Jobling had begun to link such an explicitly economic analysis with psychoanalysis. In fact, he had suggested earlier (1987: 92; 1992b: 3) that mode of production might be understood in terms of the Freudian notions of repression and displacement, as the 'absent cause' of history that is almost impossible to conceptualize precisely because it constitutes the framework of existence. But the argument concerning the Deuteronomic law code became a much more psychoanalytic one: Jobling argued that the egalitarian ideals of this code had systematically been buried, repressed in Israel's texts, only to emerge in all sorts of unexpected ways, not least of which was setting up the possibility of *our* reading these texts in this way.

In my own work I have taken this discussion a little further, seeking to outline the major features of the Asiatic mode of production in relation to debates in sociology and economics. Apart from recalling for a moment the brief description of the Asiatic mode of production that I provided in the chapter on Lefebvre and 1 Samuel, I also take up, following a suggestion by Jobling, the inherent contradiction of this mode of production. (In fact, every mode of production is enabled and hobbled by at least one crucial contradiction). And this contradiction is that between centripetal and centrifugal forces. On the one hand, the Asiatic mode of production is a highly centralizing system, drawing in to the highly bureacratized core various forms of tribute in the forms treasure (usually from temples), produce and labour, for both building projects and armies. The standing armies undertook not only campaigns to extend the imperial holdings, but also to ensure that the all important tribute was paid—so that the army, in a vicious circle, could be maintained, among other things, to ensure the tribute came in. On the other hand, the system had strong centrifugal forces: the various subject states, such as Judah and Israel, themselves operated with a similar system, gathering tribute directly from the peasantry before passing it on to the imperial centre. But, given a chance during times of imperial weakness, these smaller states would assert their own independence and seek to expand their holdings, thereby replicating the Asiatic mode of production in their own domains. The stories of Josiah and Hezekiah in Judah, and Omri in Israel indicate such a pattern, as do the more legendary accounts of the kingdoms of David and Solomon. But centrifugal forces also operates through the money-lenders, who would acquire land from indebted peasants in the other regions of the system, through merchants trading beyond the reach of the state and gaining assets, and through tax-farmers in the collection of taxes from fringe areas. On larger (small states) and smaller (money-lenders, merchants and tax farmers), the system was inherently unstable; something reflected also in the perpetual change of the larger imperial centres, from Sumer to Asshur to Babylon and so on.

In other words, the contradictions of the Asiatic mode of production were located in size: it needs to be large to operate effectively, but this size means that there is a tendency for the distant reaches of the empire to break away and form semi-independent units. Thus, to remain effective the Asiatic mode of production must run a mobile army to keep the whole structure intact. Further, the smaller states replicate the Asiatic mode of production in their efforts to break away, but they are too small to operate effectively and tend to collapse back into the larger system.

Thus far, however, Jobling had already gone, but my interest lay in another symbolic realm that is crucial for reading the Hebrew Bible: the figure of the Oriental despot. Indeed, the Asiatic mode of production is also known as 'Oriental Despotism', since at its head was the inaccessible figure of the emperor or the despot, who invariably made some claim to divine status. So Melotti:

> The whole ideology of the system owes its shape to the prominent role played in Asiatic society by the person at the summit of the political pyramid... He tends to present himself, whether as high priest, son of heaven or son of God, as the intermediary between men and the divinity, or even as God himself... Asiatic tradition brings together the divinity or 'heaven' and the despot who rules the state: the exercise of power...is at one with the orderly functioning of the cosmos (Melotti 1975: 70-71).

The 'despot' of the Asiatic mode of production brings together political, economic and religious dimensions. As Marx writes:

> A part of their surplus labor belongs to the higher community, which exists ultimately as a *person*, and this surplus labor takes on the form of tribute etc., as well as of common labor for the exaltation of the unity, partly of the despot, partly of the imagined clan-being, the god (Marx 1973: 473).

Rather than the king or emperor himself, I argued (Boer 1996) that it is in fact Yahweh who is conceived as the 'oriental despot', that the very possibility of Yahweh was provided by the Asiatic mode of production. Perhaps a better way of putting it is that the cultural dominant of the Asiatic mode of production, the sacred or religious, provided the ground for the way people thought, believed and wrote texts, such as those in the Hebrew Bible. The problem with this, if we take Althusser's definition of ideology, is that it an unmediated relation, and imaginary representation of real conditions rather than the representation of the imaginary relations to the real conditions of social and economic life.

Others have also written of mode of production in the Hebrew Bible. Gale Yee seeks to bring together questions of class, economics and gender (Yee 1995, 1999) in terms of three modes of production, namely familial, tributary and slave. In this respect she relies heavily on Gottwald, shifting the communitarian mode of production to a familial one and reading Gen. 2–3 (Yee 1999) in terms of the transition from the former to the latter. Like Gottwald, she prefers to avoid the terminology of the Asiatic mode of production, yet her three modes of production can be read as transformations of the tribal, Asiatic and ancient modes of production in traditional Marxist theory. Ronald Simkins (1999) goes a step further, criticizing the Asiatic mode of production in light of Hindess and Hirst (1975) in order to outline a new theory of mode of production in monarchic Israel. For Hindess and Hirst, tribute is but another name for tax, and every mode of production has some form of tax: in other words, there is nothing unique about this mode of appropriating goods or surplus. Further, the absence of class, apart from the distinction between peasants and state functionaries, does not provide the mechanisms for the formation of the state that requires divisions between various groups in society, which is usually theorised in terms of class and class division. The final criticism Simkins levels at the Asiatic mode of production in relation to ancient Israel is the issue of private property, since in the traditional terms of the Asiatic mode of production all ownership was in the hands of the state. Yet the notion of private property, particularly in terms of ancestral rights, appears in the Hebrew Bible, although this should be understood in terms of proprietorship rather than the possession of things, private property in terms of rights that were divided between the state and individual peasants.

In light of these difficulties, Simkins proposes a different taxonomy for monarchic Israel, distinguishing between what has variously been termed the domestic, household or communitarian (here he follows Sahlins 1972, Meyers 1988 and Gottwald, although Jobling 1991 has also written about this), and the shift to a patron–client, or clientalistic, mode of production in monarchic Israel as the prime mode by which surplus was acquired, used and distributed, and by which social relations operated. This basic dyadic relation accounts, argues Simkins, not only for economic exchange but also the ideologies of reciprocity and societal structures (elite and peasants, king and people, Yahweh and the state) as well as unequal social relations in which the client relied on the patron for access to the means of production.

Simkins's proposal is significant, it seems to me, for reasons that will appear below. What it does is draw from a dominant social and economic pattern in ancient Rome and apply it to monarchic Israel. It does assume that we can in fact speak about monarchic Israel as some tangible reality, but his theory can operate without such a connection, and his approach tends to take mode of production as a sealed historical unit. By contrast, as I have mentioned, mode of production is an open, shifting, contradictory notion in which aspects of one—for instance, private property or money— are taken up in another and completely transformed.

Although much of this work has its own reference points, particularly the work of Gottwald in biblical studies, but also such texts as those of Sahlins and Marx, what remains absent is the consideration of other work, particularly on the Asiatic mode of production, the massive study by Ste. Croix (1981), a Marxist analysis of the slave-based or ancient mode of production in ancient Greece, and contemporary Marxist economic theory. In what follows I outline briefly some of the debates about the Asiatic mode of production, before passing on to consider the whole issue of mode of production.[1]

In the earlier work of Marx and Engels, the Asiatic mode of production was used, especially in analyzing the British colonial rule in India (see Marx 1973). Later Marx ceased to mention the Asiatic mode of production, particularly because he was less enthusiastic about the ability of British colonialism to break the stagnation they saw in Indian economies (see Ghosh 1984). Apart from the post-Marxist work of Hindess and Hirst (1975) upon which Simkins relies, there has been a long and lively debate in the former Soviet Union, much of it unavailable since it remains untranslated but also because Marxist economics from the Soviet Union were dismissed in the context of the Cold War (see especially Dunn 1981 in this regard). Even though Stalin dismissed the term from official Marxist economics, it remained a central issue in debates, returning after undergoing severe criticism. Dunn stresses, however, that official policy had little direct effect on the debates, which often turned on the interpretation of Marx and the assessment of the available information. A crucial figure, whose work has been translated (1969, 1987), was D'iakonov, who argued against the Asiatic mode of production and in favour of a single path to capitalism. The economic system of the ancient Near East thus became a form of feudalism, since it was the same mode of production found in China, leading into capitalism (whose only precursor could be feudalism) and then communism under Mao Zedong. In response, Wittfogel (see 1963) argued for the viability of the Asiatic mode of production

_____

1.   One of the urgent tasks is an assessment of the work of Ste. Croix (1981), although this is the topic for another study.

in terms of the need for and organization of irrigation, although he saw a conspiracy theory in Stalin's rejection, arguing that communism itself was the epitome of 'oriental despotism' (an argument that rendered his approach palatable in the Cold War West). Another area of debate concerned slavery in the ancient Near East, for if slavery was systemic, then it became a slave-based mode of production, such as that of ancient Greece or Rome, rather than a distinct Asiatic mode of production (see Dandamaev 1984). In the context of these Soviet debates Dunn outlines the way in which the Asiatic mode of production returned as the most useful category for speaking about ancient Mesopotamia, Egypt and Palestine.

There are other problems with the Asiatic mode of production that were raised in Soviet circles, and these include the extrapolation of a theory developed in relation to contemporary societies, especially India and China, and applied to ancient societies, such as those of the ancient Near East (see O'Leary 1989; Ghosh 1984). Further—and this is to my mind a crucial problem—there are the dangers of applying such a uniform description to a wide variety of societies that differed in terms of both place and time. The tendency with the Asiatic mode of production, and mode of production theory in general, is the application of a template of terms that were developed in the specific analysis of capitalism: social class and class conflict, the theory of value (use, exchange, surplus), commodification and reification, social revolution, ideology, superstructure, and so on.

So, the question remains as to whether there is indeed an Asiatic mode of production, or whether it is an amalgam of a number of disparate features that describe not one socio-economic form but a number. But this question is tied up with the viability of the term 'mode of production', which faces a number of problems, not only in biblical studies but also in Marxist theory itself. There is, to begin with, the proliferation of modes of production: Gottwald's communitarian and tributary, Meyers's, Jobling's, Yee's and Simkins's adoption of a 'domestic' mode of production' from feminist Marxism, often understood as a development of Gottwald's communitarian mode of production, and Simkins's clientalistic mode of production. Such a proliferation is problematic, but it also points to something within mode of production theory, namely, that such concepts as the Asiatic mode of production have had a chequered history. It also indicates that Marxist theory is an ongoing debate, constantly worked over in light of available material, that Marx's own formulations are not unalterable.

Further, the slippage between the specific and more general senses of the term that I outlined above generates its own difficulties, the one providing the ground for the other in ways that are not always clear. Thus, the restricted sense of mode of production—the means for producing and appropriating the surplus in an economic system—slips into discussions of class, ideology or culture without recognizing that the general sense of the term is now in operation. This, it seems to me, is a problem with Simkins's analysis of domestic and clientalistic modes of production. In this light, is class itself a mode of production distinct from, say, the extraction of tribute, or of trade?

What I want to do, then, is consider some of the discussions under way in contemporary Marxist economic theory before returning to the Hebrew Bible. Of the major schools of economics—neo-classical, neo-Keynesian, over-accumulation and regulation—I am interested in the last two since they are specifically Marxist. Over-accumulation theory, espoused most eloquently by such people as Mandel and Wallerstein (upon whom Jameson is dependent for his theories of late capitalism), postulates the central importance of the market in capitalism at the expense of the state. The crises in capitalism are generated through an over-accumulation of commodities that cannot not be absorbed. Over-accumulation theory has little room for the state, so state-led activities, such as minor ventures like the world wars, are aberrations. In terms of this theory, the dynamic of capitalism dominates all, and the state is part of this larger dynamic, somewhat powerless before it. Crises in capitalism are generated by periods of over-accumulation, leading to depression and economic bust, which are overcome when the accumulation drops and what is stockpiled is absorbed by consumers. In all of this, over-accumulation theory retains the notion of mode of production.

Regulation theory is more open to the vagaries of any socio-economic formation, arguing for much greater room for the state, which, although it is itself not capitalist, regulates certain areas (population in terms of the social relations of production, taxation and tax breaks, minimal welfare, workfare and medicare, etc.) so that capitalism itself may operate more smoothly. I can't help but think of Marx's observation that the state acts as the executive for capitalism. For regulation theory, the particular form of the state within capitalism is the nation-state, and that form cannot change without a significant change in socio-economic formation. Hence, under different systems the state will be different (as in the ancient Near East). Although there has been a significant discussion of regulation theory, the theorist who continues to set the agenda is Robert Boyer (1990). Regulation theory does not feel bound to the traditional idea of mode of production, preferring instead 'regimes of accumulation'. Given that the underlying drive of capitalism is the maximization of profit, the system generates various regimes by which this can happen. In a generic sense, such regimes include technology, fiscal arrangements and so on, but Boyer's main argument was that the regime of Fordism/Keynesianism dominated post war economics (note the way liberal economic schools function as the justifications for certain regimes of accumulation). The major debate is now over the regimes that succeed Fordism/Keynesianism (which is itself then a regime in itself). Boyer has distinguished between the following regimes (2000), although he favours a finance-led regime as the major successor to Fordism:

(a) Toyotism, which was dominant in Japan until the 1990s, when Japan was forced to come closer to patterns in the United States. This regime has employment stability against work malleability with a developmentalist state.

(b) A service-led regime, characteristic of the United States in the 1980s, when all the talk was of the service sector, the service industry, and how much of the economy was driven by such factors (hospitality, ranging from hotels to taxis to fast food). In this case there was strong employment inequality across industries with the state promoting flexibility.

(c) Knowledge-based, emerging in the 1990s in the United States. In this case the development and control of knowledge became a crucial factor, in regard both to the research knowledge of major corporations that they chose to make available or not and the whole explosion of the 'knowledge' available on the internet. This second factor leads into the next regime.

(d) Information and communication technology led, since the mid 1980s and driven very much from Silicon Valley. The full effect of such a transformation, from personal communication to vast commercial operations to protest movement, such as the World Trade Organization Protests in Seattle or S11 in Melbourne, has yet to be realized, but it is emerging as a major way in which profit is generated by means of an international division of labour and the role of the state in building infrastructure.

(e) Competition-led, with the espousal of neo-liberalism and the catchwords of privatization, deregulation and liberalization. Characteristic of most OECD countried since 1985 it assumes a proactive and market-enhancing state. It also operates through such organizations as the World

Trade Organization, the World Bank and the World Economic Forum—free trade, small government, a level playing field and so on—belong to this championing of neo-liberalism, a reworking of the laissez-faire of the brave new world of early capitalism.

(f) Export-led, characteristic of the East Asian new industrial countries until the financial crisis of 1997. The state is focused on a new mercantilist strategy.

(g) Finance-led, especially in the Britain and the United States in the 1990s. The particular development here is that the production of profit relies no longer upon the production of commodities and their sale: rather, speculation in money and the international exchange rates has led to a hyper-capitalism, or what is called finance capitalism. Money begets money.

These regimes of accumulation, specific to capitalism, indicate how crucial regulation theory sees the state, for Boyer's list recognizes the role of the nation-state in determining the characteristics and limits of each regime. Of course, the more powerful nation-states develop such regimes in order to dominate less economically powerful nation-states, in order to extract yet more profit from them. Further, the regimes overlap both spatially and temporally, developing in reaction to one another, and often in the same national space—thus the United States is now an amalgam of four accumulation regimes.

With its recognition of the central role of the state, regulation theory enacts a thoroughgoing revision of the traditional Marxist categories, particularly the divisions between mode of production, means and relations of production, class, ideology and culture. The regimes show how these demarcated realms are very much intertwined in ways more complex than may be described in the standard terms. At the same time, the other traditional areas of the Marxist theory, such as ideology, culture and religion, function as enabling factors for these regimes, for the focus remains on economy and the state. As for the state itself, its form under the current capitalist regimes of accumulation is the neo-liberal state, since the social-democratic one has had its day, even though there are many overlaps and remnants.

The advantages of regulation are that it is much more sensitive to the particular shape of a socio-economic formation, generating its categories from within. One cannot apply in blanket form the categories developed by Marx in the analysis of capitalism to other forms. In other words, regulation theory is much more aware of historical variabilities, although the outcome of this awareness is that a lot of work is required to determine the various regimes of accumulation in other situations as they change over time. And this applies to the Hebrew Bible and the broader context of the ancient Near East, where the resources are far more limited, with only fragmentary archaeological and dubious literary evidence.

In what can only be a preliminary discussion, notes towards further investigation (to gloss Althusser), I want to pursue the possibilities of regulation theory in relation to the Hebrew Bible and the ancient Near East. But the term 'regimes of accumulation' cannot be transposed as it is, since there is a prior question that needs to be asked. For regimes of accumulation describe the various modes by which capitalism works to generate profit, and in the ancient Near East this is not the basic economic feature. Let me put it in terms of a question: what is the fundamental dream of capitalism? The accumulation of profit so that one can have more than enough, all for oneself. This usually takes the form of a host of commodities, a standard of living—cars, houses, technological bits and pieces, valuable items and so on—that one wishes to carry through into retirement. What, then, is the fundamental dream of the Hebrew Bible? A long life with many sons. But how does one (a male) achieve this? Through the distribution or allocation of the deity, who may or may not allocate these things but whose workings are beyond one's own control or understanding. My suggestion is, therefore, that we need to speak of regimes of allocation or distribution. Under capitalism the pattern operates in the sequence of production, distribution and consumption, but this locks us into a particular economic model where the production of commodities is paramount. If, however, the question is not one of production per se, but rather the allocation of that which produces in a way that is beyond (male) knowledge—fertile land, rain and women—then the issue becomes one of attempting to ensure adequate allocation or distribution of these items that seem to produce on their own. And the way such production is accounted for is through the action of the deity. In light of what might be described as a sacred commerce, the focus of activity becomes the allocation and distribution of land, agricultural produce, plunder, people (in terms of ethnic boundaries) and so on.

The possible regimes of allocation might be sketched out as follows.

(a) A gender-determined regime of accumulation, in which the allocation of women as the producers of children, especially sons, is the major feature. Lévi-Strauss's notion of the exchange of women between men serves as the starting point for describing this process, where men attempt to allocate women but the function of women as producers of sons is ascribed to Yahweh. This regime of allocation emerges in the texts (Gen. 25; Ruth; 1 Sam. 1–2) that I have discussed, where the issue is the necessary but ideologically troubled birth of a son or sons. Each text in its own way may now be read as an effort to deal with the vexed problem of the allocation of women as producers. Under this regime of allocation must be placed the repeated ocncern with ethnic boundaries or the demarcation of distinct peoples, for women as producers of children by means of Yahweh become the focus of this concern with boundaries as well. It is not for nothing that the various food laws of Leviticus immediately precede the regulations regarding women. But the obsession with 'ethnic' boundaries overlaps with that of land.

(b) A land-based regime of allocation. The problem here is the allocation of suitably fertile land or pasture, which often appears contested between peoples. Hence the long-delayed promise of a land in the political myth of Genesis–Joshua that is finally realized through a narrative of dispossession and conquest in Joshua. As with women—women and land are closely connected in this respect—the allocation of suitable land is the focus of much narrative angst. The texts of Genesis and Exodus that I discussed earlier in this book, as well as those that deal with the return from exile, such as Ezekiel, exhibit a fair amount of narrative angst on the problem of land allocation in which Yahweh plays a key role. Given the central role of the state in regulation theory, the amount of energy expended by such imperial states as Assyria and Babylon in moving peoples to different locations in the empire must not be read merely in terms of maintaining control through keeping subject peoples in turmoil, but also as one of the major activities of the state itself in the allocation of peoples and lands. This regime also involves this the technologies of agricultural production, the types of produce, soils, and the way agricultural produce determines how people live.

(c) A tribute regime of allocation. The complex patterns of tribute, from exaction by a local state from the peasants to that by an imperial centre from subject states, comprise another form of allocation, particularly of relatively scarce financial and agricultural resources. In this respect Gottwald's notion of a tributary mode of production is on the right track. It includes the roles of tribute gatherers, the accumulation of treasure in temples and palaces and its ostentatious display, where the role of the deity or deities is once again crucial. Another aspect is the army, used for gathering tribute, which leads to the next regime.

(d) The war machine (with thanks to Deleuze and Guattari). Although the development of a large standing army was necessary to keep wayward subjects paying tribute, to expand the imperial territory so that more tribute could be gathered, and to acquire land and women, the war machine also has a distinct role, another dimension, in allocation, namely, that of plunder to the imperial state. This is one of the regimes that would mutate into other forms in different socio-economic formations for different purposes.

(e) Corvée-determined regime of allocation. This is closely related to that of tribute, for it is often seen as an imposed tribute of human labour, work for a specified period for the state in order to construct palaces, temples, roads, pyramids, etc. It is an allocation of human resources in service to the needs of the state, but it needs to be distinguished from slavery, which is characteristic of the Graeco-Roman world.

(f) Patron–client regime of allocation. Although more chacteristic of the Roman world, Simkims is correct, it seems to me, in designating the patron–client releationship as a crucial aspect of the Hebrew Bible as well. However, in light of the basic economic drive to the distribution of allocation of producing parts of the economy, the patron–client relationship takes on an important role not only in the allocation of reciprocal social relationships, but also in the allocation of land, women and produce.

These suggestions function as a preliminary effort at determining the regimes of allocation that emerge in the texts of the Hebrew Bible.[2] There are two final points that need to be made. First, the central role of the state in regulation theory accounts for the presence and function of the imperial centre in the ancient Near East, since all of its energy may be seen as a range of efforts to obtain the favour of the god(s), along with various regimes, such as the war machine, tribute, the allocation of land and women, and the patron–client relationship, in order to allocate the various producing resources of the empire in a fashion that ensured the continuation of the empire itself.

Secondly, the role of religion or the sacred in this situation should be understood as a complex metaphorization of allocation. The god or gods therefore function not only as the ones responsible for production, but also as the prime source of the allocation of those producing mechanisms. For this reason Yahweh is the one in the Hebrew Bible who chooses a people, allocates them land, controls the process of childbirth by women, blesses

---

2.   This is part of the focus of a study that follows this one, entitled 'Political Myth and the Hebrew Bible'.

the efforts of the war machine, blesses and protects the collection of tribute in the temple and functions as the prime client. The traditional Marxist term for all of this is ideology, and it seems to me that the term itself is still a very workable one. In this light my discussions of Kings, Ezekiel, Isaiah and Psalms especially may be understood as reflections on this metaphorization of allocation in the deity, riven as it is with the contradictions I identified, but it also runs through the other chapters at various levels, whether in the control of women's wombs, the dispenser of laws or land, or of the determination of the nature of a distinct state known as Israel.

The list and my brief assessments of the possibilities indicates the need to be much more sensitive to the different shape of the socio-economic formation of the ancient Near East, and I feel that many aspects of regulation theory have a contribution to make, not least of which is the need to generate categories from within the particular socio-economic formation (or 'mode of production') in question. As far as the dominant economic system itself is concerned—regulation theory assumes capitalism—that determination remains to be made.

BIBLIOGRAPHY

Adorno, Theodor W.
 1973   *The Jargon of Authenticity* (trans. Knut Tarnowski and Frederic Will;
         Evanston, IL: Northwestern University Press).
 1989   *Kierkegaard: Construction of the Aesthetic* (trans. Robert Hullot-Kentor;
         Minneapolis: University of Minnesota Press).
Alter, Robert
 1987   'Psalms', in Robert Alter and Frank Kermode (eds.), *The Literary Guide to
         the Bible* (Cambridge, MA: Belknap Press of Harvard University Press):
         244-62.
Althusser, Louis
 1971   *Lenin and Philosophy and Other Essays* (trans. Ben Brewster; London: New
         Left Books).
 1994   *The Future Lasts a Long Time* (New York: Vintage Books).
 1999   *Machiavelli and Us* (London: Verso).
Amit, Yairah
 1987   'The Dual Causality Principle and Its Effects on Biblical Literature', *VT* 37:
         385-400.
 1994   ' "Am I Not More Devoted to You Than Ten Sons?" (1 Samuel 1.8): Male
         and Female Interpretations', in Brenner (ed.) 1994: 68-76.
Anderson, A.A.
 1972   *The Book of Psalms* (New Century Bible; London: Oliphants).
Auffret, Pierre
 1982   *La sagesse a bâti sa maison: Etudes de structures littéraires dans l'Ancien
         Testament et spécialement dans les psaumes* (Fribourg: Editions Univer-
         sitaires; Göttingen: Vandenhoeck & Ruprecht).
Bailey, Anne M., and Josep R. Llobera
 1981   *The Asiatic Mode of Production: Science and Politics* (London: Routledge &
         Kegan Paul).
Baumann, Gerlinde
 2001   'Prophetic Objections to YHWH as the Violent Husband of Israel:
         Reinterpretations of the Prophetic Marriage Metaphor in Second Isaiah
         (Isaiah 40-55)', in Brenner 2001: 88-120.
Benjamin, Walter
 1986   *Reflections: Essays, Aphorisms, Autobiographical Writings* (trans. E. Jephcott;
         New York: Schoken Books).
 1996   *Selected Writings*. I. *1913–1926* (ed. Marcus Bullock and Michael W.
         Jennings; Cambridge, MA: Belknap Press).
 1998   *The Origin of German Tragic Drama* (trans. John Osborne; London: Verso).

1999   *The Arcades Project* (trans. Howard Eiland and Kevin McLaughlin; Cam-
              bridge, MA: Belknap).
Bible and Culture Collective
1995   *The Postmodern Bible* (New Haven, CT: Yale University Press).
Bledstein, Adrien J.
1993   'Female Companionships: If the Book of Ruth Were Written by a Woman…',
              in Brenner 1993: 116-33.
Bloch, Ernst
1970   *Man on his Own: Essays in the Philosophy of Religion* (trans. E.B. Ashton;
              Foreword by H. Cox; Introduction by J. Moltmann; New York: Herder and
              Herder).
1972   *Atheism in Christianity: The Religion of the Exodus and the Kingdom* (trans.
              J.T. Swann; New York: Herder & Herder).
1995   *The Principle of Hope* (trans. N. Plaice, S. Plaice and P. Knight; Cambridge,
              MA: MIT Press).
Bloch, Ernst, Georg Lukács, Bertholt Brecht, Walter Benjamin and Theodor Adorno
1990   *Aesthetics and Politics* (trans. Ronald Taylor; Afterword by Fredric Jame-
              son; London: Verso).
Blum, V., and H. Nast
1996   'Where's the Difference? The Heterosexualization of Alterity in Henri
              Lefebvre and Jacques Lacan', *Environment and Planning D: Society and
              Space* 14.4: 559-80.
Boer, Roland
1997   'National Allegory in the Hebrew Bible', *JSOT* 74: 95-116.
1997   *Novel Histories: The Fiction of Biblical Criticism* (Sheffield: Sheffield
              Academic Press).
1996   *Jameson and Jeroboam* (Semeia Studies; Atlanta: Scholars Press).
1998   'Western Marxism and the Interpretation of the Hebrew Bible', *JSOT* 78:
              3-21.
1999   *Knockin' on Heaven's Door: The Bible and Popular Culture* (London:
              Routledge).
2001   *Last Stop before Antarctica: The Bible and Postcolonialism in Australia*
              (Sheffield: Sheffield Academic Press).
2002   'Marx, Method and Gottwald', in Boer 2002a: 98-156.
Forthcoming   *The Criticism of Earth* (London: Verso).
Boer, Roland (ed.)
2002a   *Tracking 'The Tribes of Yahweh': On the Trail of a Classic* (Sheffield:
              Sheffield Academic Press).
Bowen, Nancy R.
1995   'Can God Be Trusted? Confronting the Deceptive God', in Brenner 1995:
              354-65.
Boyer, Robert
1990   *The Regulation School: A Critical Introduction* (trans. Craig Charney; New
              York: Columbia University Press).
2000   'Is a Finance-Led Growth Regime a Viable Alternative to Fordism?',
              Economy and Society 29 (February): 111-45.
Brenner, Athalya
1993   'Introduction', in Brenner 1993: 9-18.

1995   'On Prophetic Propaganda and the Politics of "Love": The Case of
           Jeremiah', in Brenner 1995: 156-74.
1999   'Ruth as a Foreign Worker and the Politics of Exogamy', in Brenner 1999:
           158-62.
Brenner, A. (ed.)
1993   *A Feminist Companion to Ruth* (Sheffield: Sheffield Academic Press).
1994   *A Feminist Companion to Samuel and Kings* (Feminist Companion to the
           Bible, 5; Sheffield: Sheffield Academic Press).
1995   *A Feminist Companion to the Latter Prophets* (Sheffield: Sheffield Aca-
           demic Press).
2001   *Prophets and Daniel: A Feminist Companion to the Bible* (Sheffield:
           Sheffield Academic Press).
Brett, Mark
1999   *Genesis: Procreation and the Politics of Identity* (London: Routledge).
Briggs, A.B., and E.G. Briggs.
1914   *A Critical and Exegetical Commentary on the Book of Psalms* (ICC; New
           York: Charles Scribner's Sons).
Broyles, Craig C.
1989   *The Conflict of Faith and Experience in the Psalms: A Form-Critical and
           Theological Study* (JSOTSup, 52; Sheffield: Sheffield Academic Press).
Buci-Glucksmann, Christine
1982   'Hegemony and Consent', in A.S. Sassoon, *Approaches to Antonio Gramsci*
           (London: Writers and Readers Publishing Cooperative): 116-26.
Butler, Judith
1993   *Bodies That Matter: On the Discursive Limits of Sex* (London: Routledge).
Callahan, Allen Dwight, Richard A. Horsley and Abraham Smith (eds.)
1998   *Slavery in Text and Interpretation* (*Semeia* 83/84; Atlanta, GA: Society of
           Biblical Literature).
Chaney, Marvin L.
1999   'Whose Sour Grapes? The Addressees of Isaiah 5.1-7 in the Light of
           Political Economy', *Semeia* 87: 105-22.
Cole, Robert L.
2000   *The Shape and Message of Book III (Psalms 73–89)* (JSOTSup, 307;
           Sheffield: Sheffield Academic Press).
Collins, John J.
1984   *Daniel, with an Introduction to Apocalyptic Literature* (Forms of Old
           Testament Literature, 20; Grand Rapids: Eerdmans).
1985   'Daniel and his Social World', *Int.* 39: 131-43.
1993   *Daniel* (Hermeneia; Philadelphia: Fortress Press).
Collins, Terence
1987   'Decoding the Psalms: A Structural Approach to the Psalter', *JSOT* 37: 41-
           60.
Creach, Jerome
1996   *Yahweh as Refuge and the Editing of the Hebrew Psalter* (JSOTSup, 217;
           Sheffield: Sheffield Academic Press).
Croatto, J. Severino
1981   *Exodus: A Hermeneutics of Freedom* (trans. Salvator Attanasio; Maryknoll,
           NY: Orbis Books).

Croft, Steven
    1987   *The Identity of the Individual in the Psalms* (JSOTSup, 44; Sheffield: Sheffield Academic Press).

Culley, Robert C.
    1967   *Oral Formulaic Language in the Biblical Psalms* (Near and Middle East Series, 5; Toronto: University of Toronto Press).
    1988   'Psalm 88 among the Complaints', in Lyle Eslinger and Glen Taylor (eds.), *Ascribe to the Lord: Biblical and Other Studies in Memory of Peter C. Craigie* (JSOTSup, 67; Sheffield: Sheffield Academic Press): 289-302.
    1993   'Psalm 103: A Complaint with a Difference', *Semeia* 62: 19-35.

Curthoys, Anne
    1998   'National Narratives, War Commemoration, and Racial Exclusion in a Settler Society: The Australian Case', in R. Nile and R. Peterson (eds.), *Becoming Australian* (Brisbane: University of Queensland Press): 173-90.

Dahood, Mitchell
    1966–70 *Psalms* (Anchor Bible, 16–17; 3 vols.; Garden City, NY: Doubleday).

Dandamaev, M.
    1984   *Slavery in Babylonia: From Nabopolassar to Alexander the Great (626–331 BC)* (DeKalb: Northern Illinois University Press).

Deleuze, Gilles and Felix Guattari
    1987   *A Thousand Plateaus: Capitalism and Schizophrenia* (trans. Brian Massumi; Minneapolis: University of Minnesota Press).

D'iakonov, I.M.
    1969   'Slave-Labor vs. Non-Slave Labor: The Problem of Definition', in M. Powell (ed.), *Labor in the Ancient Near East* (New Haven: American Oriental Society).

D'iakonov, I.M. (ed.)
    1987   *Ancient Mesopotamia: Socio-Economic History: A Collection of Studies by Soviet Scholars* (Moscow: Nauka).

Docker, John
    2001   *1492: A Poetics of Diapora* (London: Continuum).

Dunn, Stephen P.
    1981   *The Fall and Rise of the Asiatic Mode of Production* (London: Routledge & Kegan Paul).

Eagleton, Terry
    1982   *The Rape of Clarissa: Writing, Sexuality and Class Struggle in Samuel Richardson* (Minneapolis: University of Minnesota Press).
    1995   *Heathcliff and the Great Hunger: Studies in Irish Culture* (London: Verso).
    1997   *Saint Oscar and Other Plays* (Oxford: Basil Blackwell).

Eagleton, Terry (ed.)
    1989   *Raymond Williams: Critical Perspectives* (London: Polity Press).

Eaton, John H.
    1986   *Kingship in the Psalms* (Biblical Seminar, 3; Sheffield; Sheffield Academic Press).
    1995   *Psalms of the Way and the Kingdom: A Conference with the Commentators* (JSOTSup, 199; Sheffield: Sheffield Academic Press).

Fierro, Alfredo
    1983   'Exodus Event and Interpretation in Political Theologies', in Norman K.

Gottwald (ed.), *The Bible and Liberation: Political and Social Hermeneutics* (Maryknoll NY: Orbis Books): 473-81.

Flanagan, James

1996   'Construction of Ancient Space'. http:/www.cwru.edu/affil/GAIR/papers/ 96papers/constructs/flanagan/jfoutline.

1999   'Mapping the Biblical World: Perceptions of Space in Ancient Southwestern Asia'. http:/www.cwru.edu/affil/GAIR/papers/96papers/constructswindsor/ windsor.htm.

2001   'Ancient Perceptions of Space/Perceptions of Ancient Space', *Semeia* 87: 15-43.

Fokkelman, J.P.

1993   *Narrative Art and Poetry in the Books of Samuel: A Full Interpretation Based on Stylistic and Structural Analysis. IV. Vow and Desire (I Sam. 1– 12)* (Assen: Van Gorcum).

Fontana, Benedetto

1993   *Hegemony and Power: On the Relation between Gramsci and Machiavelli* (Minneapolis: University of Minnesota Press).

Freedman, David Noel

1987   'Another Look at Biblical Hebrew Poetry', in R. Follis (ed.), *Directions in Biblical Hebrew Poetry* (JSOTSup, 40; Sheffield: JSOT Press): 11-28.

Friedman, Jonathan

1998   *System, Structure, and Contradiction: The Evolution of Asiatic Social Formations* (Walnut Creek: Altamira Press, 2nd edn).

Geoghegan, Vincent

1994   *Ernst Bloch* (London: Routledge).

Gerstenberger, Erdhard S.

1988   *Psalms, Part 1; with an Introduction to Cultic Poetry* (Forms of Old Testament Literature, 14; Grand Rapids: Eerdmans).

Ghosh, Suniti Kumar

1984   'Marx on India', *Monthly Review* 35: 39-53

Girard, René

1977   *Violence and the Sacred* (trans. Patrick Gregory; Baltimore: The Johns Hopkins University Press).

Gottwald, Norman

1985   *The Hebrew Bible: A Socio-Literary Introduction.* (Philadelphia: Fortress).

1992   'Sociology of Ancient Israel', in *The Anchor Bible Dictionary*, VI: 79-89.

1993   *The Hebrew Bible in Its Social World and Ours* (Semeia Studies. Atlanta GA: Scholars Press).

1999a   *The Tribes of Yahweh: A Sociology of Liberated Israel 1050–1250* (reprint; Sheffield: Sheffield Academic Press).

1999b   'Twenty-Five Years and Counting', *Semeia* 87: 255-65.

2000   *The Politics of Ancient Israel* (Minneapolis: Fortress Press).

Goulder, Michael D.

1983   *The Psalms of the Sons of Korah* (JSOTSup, 20; Sheffield: Sheffield Academic Press).

1990   *Studies in the Psalter. II. The Prayers of David: Psalms 51–72* (JSOTSup, 102; Sheffield: Sheffield Academic Press).

1997   *Studies in the Psalter.* III. *The Psalms of Asaph and the Pentateuch* (JSOTSup, 233; Sheffield: Sheffield Academic Press).
1998   *Studies in the Psalter.* IV. *The Psalms of the Return (Book V, Psalms 107–150):* (JSOTSup, 258; Sheffield: Sheffield Academic Press).

Graffy, Adrian
1979   'The Literary Genre of Isaiah 5,1-7', *Biblica* 60: 400-409.

Gramsci, Antonio
1957   *The Modern Prince and Other Writings* (New York: International Publishers).

Grosz, Elizabeth
1995   *Space, Time and Perversion: Essays on the Politics of Bodies* (London: Routledge).

Gruber, Mayer I.
2001   'Nineveh the Adulteress', in Brenner 2001: 220-25.

Gunkel, Hermann
1967   *The Psalms: A Form Critical Introduction* (trans. Thomas M. Horner. Introduction by James Muilenburg; Facet Books, Biblical Series, 19; Philadelphia: Fortress Press).
1968   *Die Psalmen* (Göttingen: Vandenhoeck & Ruprecht, 5th edn).

Halperin, David J.
1993   *Seeking Ezekiel: Text and Psychology* (University Park, PA: Pennsylvania University Press).

Hanson, Paul D.
1985   'Apocalyptic Literature', in Douglas A. Knight and Gene M. Tucker (eds.), *The Hebrew Bible and its Modern Interpreters* (Philadelphia, PA: Fortress; Chico, CA: Scholars Press): 465-88.

Hartman, Louis F., and Alexander A. Di Lella
1978   *The Book of Daniel* (AB, 23; Garden City, NY: Doubleday).

Hauge, Martin
1995   *Between Sheol and Temple: Motif Structure and Function in the I-Psalms* (JSOTSup, 178; Sheffield: Sheffield Academic Press).

Heard, R.C.
2001   *Dynamics of Diselection: Ambiguity in Genesis 12–26 and Ethnic Boundaries in Post-Exilic Judah* (Atlanta, GA: Society of Biblical Literature).

Hindess, Barry, and Paul Q. Hirst
1975   *Precapitalist Modes of Production* (London: Routledge & Kegan Paul).

Hyppolite, Jean
1969   *Studies on Marx and Hegel* (London: Heinemann).
1971   'Hegel's Phenomenology and Psychoanalysis', in W.E. Steinkraus (ed.), *New Studies in Hegel's Philosophy* (New York: Holt, Rinehart & Winston): 57-70.
1974   *Genesis and Structure of Hegel's Phenomenology of Spirit* (Evanston, IL: Northwestern University Press.

Irigaray, Luce
1985   *This Sex Which Is Not One* (trans. Catherine Porter; Ithaca, NY: Cornell University Press).

Jameson, Fredric
1961   *Sartre: The Origins of a Style* (New Haven, CT: Yale University Press). (Reprint edn Columbia University Press, 1984.)

| 1971 | *Marxism and Form: Twentieth-Century Dialectical Theories of Literature* (Princeton, NJ: Princeton University Press). |

1971   *Marxism and Form: Twentieth-Century Dialectical Theories of Literature* (Princeton, NJ: Princeton University Press).

1972   *The Prison-House of Language: A Critical Account of Structuralism and Russian Formalism* (Princeton, NJ: Princeton University Press).

1975a   'After Armageddon: Character System in *Dr. Bloodmoney*', *Science Fiction Studies* 2.1: 31-42.

1975b   'World Reduction in Le Guin: The Emergence of Utopian Narrative', *Science Fiction Studies* 2.3: 221-30.

1976b   'The Ideology of Form: Partial Systems in *La Vielle Fille*', *Sub-stance* 15: 29-49.

1977a   'Imaginary and Symbolic in Lacan: Marxism, Psychoanalytic Criticism and the Problem of the Subject', in Shoshana Felman (ed.), *Literature and Psychoanalysis: The Question of Reading: Otherwise* (Yale French Studies, 55-56; New Haven, CN: Yale University Press): 338-95.

1977b   'Ideology, Narrative Analysis, and Popular Culture', *Theory and Society* 4: 543-59.

1979   *Fables of Aggression: Wyndham Lewis, the Modernist as Fascist* (Berkeley CA: University of California Press).

1980   'SF Novel/SF Film', *Science Fiction Studies* 7: 319-22.

1981   *The Political Unconscious: Narrative as a Socially Symbolic Act* (Ithaca, NY: Cornell University Press).

1983   'L'Éclatement du récit et la clôture californienne', *Littérature* 49: 89-101.

1984b   'Rimbaud and the Spatial Text', in Tak-wai Wong and M.A. Abbas (eds.), *Rewriting Literary History* (Hong Kong: Hong Kong University Press): 66-88.

1986   'Four Ways of Looking at a Fairy Tale', in *The Fairy Tale: Politics, Desire, and Everyday Life* (Handbook for Exhibition, Video Program, and Film Program by 'Artists Space', 30 October–26 November): 16-24.

1987   'Foreword', in A.J. Greimas, *On Meaning: Selected Writings in Semiotic Theory* (trans. Paul J. Perron; Minneapolis: University of Minnesota Press): vi-xxii.

1988   *The Ideologies of Theory: Essays 1971–1986* (2 vols., Minneapolis: University of Minnesota Press).

1990a   *Signatures of the Visible* (New York: Routledge).

1990b   *Late Marxism: Adorno, or, the Persistence of the Dialectic* (London: Verso).

1991   *Postmodernism, or, the Cultural Logic of Late Capitalism* (Durham, NC: Duke University Press).

1992   *The Geopolitical Aesthetic: Cinema and Space in the World System.* (Bloomington: Indiana University Press).

1994   *The Seeds of Time* (New York: Columbia University Press).

1998a   *Brecht and Method* (London: Verso).

1998b   *The Cultural Turn: Selected Writings on the Postmodern, 1983–1998* (London: Verso).

Jobling, David

1989   'Right-Brained Story of Left-Handed Man: An Antiphon to Yairah Amit', in J. Cheryl Exum (ed.), *Signs and Wonders: Biblical Texts in Literary Focus* (Atlanta, GA: Scholars Press): 125-31.

1987   'Sociological and Literary Approaches to the Bible: How Shall the Twain Meet?', *JSOT* 38: 85-93.

1991   'Feminism and "Mode of Production" in Israel: Search for a Method', in David Jobling, Peggy L. Day and Gerald T. Sheppard (eds.), *The Bible and the Politics of Exegesis* (Cleveland, Ohio: Pilgrim): 239-51.

1992a   '"Forced Labor": Solomon's Golden Age and the Question of Literary Representation', *Semeia* 54: 57-76.

1992b   'Deconstruction and the Political Analysis of Biblical Texts: A Jamesonian Reading of Psalm 72', *Semeia* 59: 95-127.

1998   *1 Samuel* (Collegeville, MN: The Liturgical Press).

Forthcoming 'The Salvation of Israel "The Book of the Divided Kingdom" or, was there anyn "Fall of the Northern Kingdom"?', in R. Boer and E. Conrad (eds.), *Redirected Travel: Alternative Journeys and Spaces in Biblical Studies* (London: Continuum).

Johnson, A.R.

1951   'The Psalms', in H.H. Rowley (ed.), *The Old Testament and Modern Study: A Generation of Discovery and Research: Essays by Members of the Society for Old Testament Study* (Oxford: Clarendon Press): 162-211.

Kamionkowski, S. Tamar

2001   'Gender Reversal in Ezekiel 16', in Brenner 2001: 170-85.

Kelso, Julie

2003   'Genesis 34 and the Threat of Narrative Leakage', in R. Boer and E. Conrad (eds.), *Redirected Travel: Alternative Journeys and Spaces in Biblical Studies* (London: Continuum; Sheffield: Sheffield Academic Press).

Klein, Lillian R.

1994   'Hannah: Marginalized Victim and Social Redeemer', in Brenner (ed.) 1994: 77-92.

Kojeve, Alexandre

1969   *Introduction to the Reading of Hegel: Lectures on the Phenomenology of Spirit* (ed. A. Bloom; trans. J.H. Nichols; Assembled by Raymond Queneau; New York: Basic Books).

Krader, Lawrence

1975   *The Asiatic Mode of Production: Source, Development and Critique in the Writings of Karl Marx* (Assen: van Gorcum).

Kraus, Hans-Joachim

1978   *Psalms 1–59: A Commentary* (trans. H.C. Oswald; Minneapolis: Augsburg).

Laclau, Ernesto, and Chantal Mouffe

1985   *Hegemony and Socialist Strategy: Towards a Radical Democratic Politics* (London: Verso).

Lacocque, André

1979   *The Book of Daniel* (trans. David Pellauer; English edn revised by author; Foreword by Paul Ricoeuer; Atlanta: John Knox Press).

Lefebvre, Henri

1970   *Du rural á l'urbain* (Paris: Anthropos).

1974   'La production de l'espace', *L'Homme et la société* 31.2 (January–June): 15-32.

1986   *Le retour de la dialectique. 12 mots clés* (Paris: Messidor Éditions Sociales).

1991a   *The Production of Space* (trans. Donald Nicolson-Smith; Oxford; Basil
            Blackwell [French 1974, 1984]).
1991b   *Critique of Everyday Life* (trans. John Moore; London: Verso).
1996   *Writings on Cities* (trans. and intro. by Eleonore Kofman and Elizabeth
            Lebas; Oxford: Basil Blackwell).
Lévi-Strauss, Claude.
1994   *The Raw and the Cooked: Introduction to a Science of Mythology* (New
            York: Random House).
Long, Burke O.
1984   *1 Kings with an Introduction to Historical Literature* (Forms of the Old
            Testament Literature; Grand Rapids: Eerdmans).
Lukács, Georg
1971   *Theory of the Novel: A Historico-Philosophical Essay on the Forms of Great
            Epic Literature* (trans. Anna Bostock; Cambridge, MA: MIT Press).
1983   *The Historical Novel* (trans. Hannah and Stanley Mitchell; Intro. Fredric
            Jameson; Lincoln, NA: University of Nebraska Press).
Machiavelli
1988   *The Prince* (ed. Q. Skinner and R. Price; Cambridge: Cambridge University
            Press). Originally published in Italian in 1532.
Magdalene, F. Rachel
1995   'Ancient Near Eastern Treaty-Curses and the Ultimate Texts of terror: A
            Study of the Language of Divine Sexual Abuse in the Prophetic Corpus', in
            Brenner 1995: 326-52.
Marx, Karl
1973   *Grundrisse: Foundations of the Critique of Political Economy (Rough Draft)*
            (trans. and foreword by Martin Nicolaus; Harmondsworth: Penguin Books in
            association with New Left Review).
1974   *The Eighteenth Brumaire of Louis Bonaparte* (Harmondsworth: Penguin
            Books).
Marx, Karl, and Friedrich Engels
1976   *The German Ideology* (Moscow: Progress Publishers).
Matthews, Victor H.
1999   'Treading the Winepress: Actual and Metaphorical Viticulture in the Ancient
            Near East', *Semeia* 86: 19-32.
Meadowcroft, T.J.
1995   *Aramaic Daniel and Greek Daniel: A Literary Comparison* (JSOTSup, 336;
            Sheffield: Sheffield Academic Press).
Melotti, Umberto
1975   *Marx and the Third World* (trans. Pat Ransford; London: Macmillan).
Meyers, Carol
1988   *Discovering Eve: Ancient Israelite Women in Context* (New York: Oxford
            University Press).
1994   'Hannah and her Sacrifice: Reclaiming Female Agency', in Brenner 1994:
            93-104.
Milbank, John
1992   '"I Will Gasp and Pant": Deutero-Isaiah and the Birth of the Suffering
            Subject: A Response to Norman K. Gottwald, "Social Class and Ideology in
            Isaiah 40-55"', *Semeia* 59: 59-71.

Mitchell, David C.
1997   *The Message of the Psalter: An Eschatological Programme* (JSOTSup, 252;
            Sheffield: Sheffield Academic Press).
Mowinckel, Sigmund.
1962   *The Psalms in Israel's Worship* (trans. D.R. Ap-Thomas; Oxford: Basil
            Blackwell).
Nasuti, Harry
1999   *Defining the Sacred Songs: Genre, Tradition, and the Post-Critical
            Intepretation of the Psalms* (JSOTSup, 218; Sheffield: Sheffield Academic
            Press).
Norris, Kathleen
1996   'The Story of Rebekah as a Mother', in David Rosenberg (ed.), *Genesis, as
            It Is Written: Contemporary Writers on our First Stories* (New York: Harper
            Collins): 159-68.
O'Brien, Julia M.
2001   'On Saying "No" to a Prophet', in Brenner 2001: 206-217.
O'Leary, Brendan
1989   *The Asiatic Mode of Production: Oriental Despotism, Historical
            Materialism and Indian History* (Oxford: Basil Blackwell).
Pixley, Jorge V.
1987   *On Exodus: A Liberation Perspective* (trans. Robert R. Barr; Maryknoll, NY:
            Orbis Books).
Redditt, Paul L.
1999   *Daniel* (NCB; Sheffield: Sheffield Academic Press).
Ricoeur, Paul
1970   *Freud and Philosophy* (trans. D. Savage; New Haven: Yale University
            Press).
1986   *Lectures on Ideology and Utopia* (ed. G.H. Taylor; New York: Columbia
            University Press).
Runions, Erin
2001   'Violence and the Economy of Desire in Ezekiel 16.1-45', in Brenner 2001:
            156-69.
Sahlins, Marshall
1972   *Stone Age Economics* (New York: Aldin de Gruyter).
Said, Edward
1988   'Michael Walzer's *Exodus and Revolution*: A Canaanite Reading', in E. Said
            and C. Hitchens (eds.), *Blaming the Victims: Spurious Scholarship and the
            Palestinian Question* (London: Verso): 161-78.
Ste. Croix, G.E.M. de
1981   *The Class Struggle in the Ancient Greek World: From the Archaic Age to the
            Arab Conquest* (London: Gerald Duckworth).
Sals, Ulrike
2001   'Reading Zechariah 5.5-11: Prophecy, Gender and (Ap)Perception', in
            Brenner 2001: 186-205.
Scott, Walter
1986   *Waverley; or, 'Tis Sixty Years Since* (Oxford: Oxford University Press
            [1814]).

Shields, Mary E.

2001a   'Circumcision of the Prostitute: Gender, Sexuality, and the Call to Repentance in Jeremiah 3.1–4.4', in Brenner 2001: 121-33.

2001b   'Multiple Exposure: Body Rhetoric and Gender in Ezekiel 16', in Brenner 2001: 137-53.

2001c   'An Abusive God? Identity and Power, Gender and Violence in Ezekiel 23', in A.K.M. Adam (ed.), *Postmodern Interpretations of the Bible: A Reader* (St Louis: Chalice Press): 129-51.

Shields, Rob

1999   *Lefebvre, Love and Struggle: Spatial Dialectics* (London: Routledge).

Shohat, Ella

1992   'Antinomies of Exile: Said at the Frontiers of National Narratives', in M. Sprinker (ed.), *Edward Said: A Critical Reader* (Oxford: Basil Blackwell): 121-43.

Simkins, Ronald A.

1999   'Patronage and the Political Economy of Ancient Israel', *Semeia* 87: 123-44.

Sneed, Mark (ed.)

1999   *Concepts of Class in Ancient Israel* (South Florida Studies in the History of Judaism, 201; Atlanta, GA: Scholars Press).

Soja, Edward

1996   *Thirdspace: Journeys to Los Angeles and Other Real-and-Imagined Places* (Cambridge, MA: Blackwell).

Stefanovic, Zdravko

1992   *The Aramaic of Daniel in the Light of Old Aramaic* (JSOTSup, 129; Sheffield: Sheffield Academic Press).

Talmon, Shemaryahu

1987   'Daniel', in Robert Alter and Frank Kermode (eds.), *The Literary Guide to the Bible* (Cambridge, MA: Belknap Press of Harvard University Press): 343-56.

Tournay, Raymond

1991   *Seeing and Hearing God with the Psalms: The Prophetic Liturgy of the Second Temple in Jerusalem* (JSOTSup, 118; Sheffield; Sheffield Academic Press).

Van Dijk-Hemmes, Fokkelein

1993   'Ruth: A Product of Woman's Culture?', in Brenner 1993: 134-39.

Van Iersel, B., and A. Weiler (eds.)

1987   *Exodus—A Lasting Paradigm* (Concilium, 189; Edinburgh: T. & T. Clark).

Walker, Michel Boulous

1998   *Philosophy and the Maternal Body: Reading Silence* (London: Routledge).

Walzer, Michael

1984   *Exodus and Revolution* (New York: Basic Books).

Weems, Renita J.

1995   *Battered Love: Sex, Violence and the Hebrew Prophets* (Minneapolis: Augsburg–Fortress).

Weiser, Artur

1960   'Die Legitimation des Königs David: Zur Eigenart und Entstehung der sogen. Geschichte von Davids Aufstieg', *VT* 16: 325-54.

Wesseling, Elisabeth
1991 *Writing History as a Prophet: Postmodernist Innovations of the Historical Novel* (Amsterdam: John Benjamins).
Westermann, Claus
1981 *Praise and Lament in the Psalms* (trans. K.R. Crim and R.N. Soulen; Atlanta: John Knox Press).
Williamson, G.A. (trans.)
1984 *Bellum Judaicum*. Translated as *The Jewish War* (Harmondsworth: Penguin Books, rev. edn).
Willis, John T.
1977 'The Genre of Isaiah 5.1-7', *JBL* 96: 337-62.
Wittfogel, Karl
1963 *Oriental Despotism* (New Haven: Yale University Press).
Yee, Gale
1981 'The Form-Critical Study of Isaiah 5.1-7', *CBQ* 43: 30-40.
1995 'Ideological Criticism: Judges 17-21 and the Dismembered Body', in Gale A. Yee (ed.), *Judges and Method: New Approaches in Biblical Studies* (Philadelphia: Fortress Press).
1999 'Gender, Class and the Social Scientific Study of Genesis 2–3', *Semeia* 87: 177-92.

INDEXES

INDEX OF REFERENCES

BIBLE

Genesis
1–11 36
1–3 213
1 28
1.1–2.3 216
1.26-31 216
1.27 216
2–3 5, 28, 155, 237
2 224
2.3-25 216
4 155
4.17-22 31
4.25-26 28
5.3-32 31
5.3 28
6–8 28
9 28
10 31
10.5 29, 31, 32
10.20 29, 31
10.31 29, 31
10.32 29, 32
11 213, 215
11.6 29
11.10-29 31
11.30 33, 35
12 32
12.1-3 32, 33
12.2 29
12.10-20 28
13.2 33
13.5-6 33
13.14-17 32, 33

14.1 29
14.9 29
14.16 29
15.1-18 32, 33
15.4 36
15.14 29
16.1 35
16.10 32
17.1-21 32, 33
17.4 29
17.5 29
17.6 29
17.16 29
17.20 29, 32
18.18 29
19.4 29
19.32-33 78
19.34-36 78
19.37 78
19.38 78
20 28
20.4 29
20.17-18 35
21.2 30
21.13 29, 32
21.18 29, 32
22.16-18 32, 33
22.18 29
23.7 29
23.11 29
23.12 29
23.13 29
23.19 37
24.28 37

24.67 37
25 6, 7, 14, 17, 18, 21, 25, 27-30, 32, 33, 36, 39, 40, 59, 230, 244
25.1-4 30, 31
25.3 30, 36, 37
25.6 30
25.7-11 37
25.12-18 32
25.12-16 30
25.12 31
25.13 31
25.16 30-32, 37
25.19 30, 31
25.20 35
25.21 35, 37
25.22 35, 36, 38
25.23 29, 30, 35, 36
25.24 36, 38
26 28
26.3-5 33
26.4 29
26.10 29
26.11 29
26.12-14 33
26.24 33
27.29 29, 30, 36
28.3 29
28.13-15 33
29.31 35

Genesis (cont.)
30.9	35
30.43	33
32	8, 43, 47
32.7	29
33.15	29
34.3	79
34.12	79
34.16	29
34.22	29
35.6	29
35.11-13	33
35.11	29
36	32
36.7	33
38	35, 84
41.40	29
41.55	29
42.6	29
46.3	29, 33
46.6	33
46.8-27	33
46.8	33
47.18	29
47.21	29
47.23	29
48.4	29, 33
48.16	33
48.19	29
49.10	29
49.16	29
49.29	29
50.20	29

Exodus
1.7	41
2.21	57
15	194
20.7-14	61
20.15-20	61
20.21-24	61
20.31-34	61
25–30	108
32	6, 48, 49, 51, 53-56, 58-62, 64, 230
32.1-6	56, 61
32.1	60
32.3	60
32.7	60
32.9	60
32.10	61, 62
32.11-12	60
32.11	60
32.12	60, 61
32.14	60
32.17	58
32.18	58
32.19-20	57
32.22-24	56
32.22	60
32.25-29	56
32.25	60
32.26	56
32.28	60
32.29	56
32.31	60
32.32	61, 62
32.34	60
32.35	60
32.43	61
35–40	108

Numbers
12	56
12.1	57
16	155
22–24	155

Judges
5	194
21.24-25	99

Ruth
1.2	80
1.11	80
1.12	80
1.16-17	85
1.20-21	84
1.22	78
2	78, 82, 83
2.1	80
2.2	80
2.3	79, 81, 82, 84
2.4	79
2.5	79, 84
2.6	79, 84
2.7	83
2.8	79, 80, 83
2.9	79, 83
2.13	79, 83
2.14	83
2.15-16	83
2.15	79
2.16	79
2.17	83
2.19	80
2.20	80, 81, 83
2.22-23	79
2.22	80
2.23	79, 83
3.1-4	80
3.2	81
3.3-7	79
3.3	84
3.4	84
3.7	84
3.9	84
3.10	79
3.12	81
3.13	81
3.15	84
4	81
4.1	79, 81
4.2	84
4.3	81, 82, 84
4.4	81
4.5	81, 82
4.6	81
4.7	81
4.8	81
4.9	82
4.10	81, 82
4.11	84
4.12	84, 85
4.13	84, 85
4.14	80
4.15	80, 85
4.16	80, 85
4.17	78, 80
4.18-19	85

1 Samuel
1–2   6, 9, 99,
             107-109,
             230, 244
1.1   100
1.2   100
1.3   101
1.4   104
1.6   102
1.7   104
1.8   102
1.9   101
1.11   105
1.15   103
1.16   103
1.19-20   102
1.19   101, 105
1.20   105
1.21   101
1.22   105
1.24   101, 102
2   194
2.1-10   104
2.11   101
2.19   101
7.17   101
8.4   101
9   121
15   121
15.34   101
16   121
16.13   101
16.14-23   195
18.11   195
19.18-23   101
20.1   101
25.1   101
28.3   101

2 Samuel
1.19-26   194
2.12-17   105
2.20-21   102
2.21   105
2.22-36   105
2.25   105
7.13-15   124
22.2–23.7   194

1 Kings
1–16   120, 121
1.8   121
1.10-14   121
1.22-27   121
1.32-40   121
1.44   121
2.10-12   121, 122
3–11   108
3–10   234
3.16-28   108
5   122
5.15–7.38   108
6.1   106
8   108
9.4-8   124
11.29-39   121
11.42-43   122
12   59, 127
12.15   127
12.25-33   107, 127
12.30   127
13   121
13.1-34   121
14.1-16   121
16.29-34   122
17–2 Kgs 9   120, 124
17–2 Kgs 9.10 10, 112
17.8-24   122, 126
18   122
18.38   126
18.45   126
19   122
22.1-28   128
22.1-26   122
22.37-40   122
22.39   122
22.41-46   122
22.41-44   122
22.51-53   122

2 Kings
2.6   124
2.11-12   125
2.12   125
2.17-18   122
2.19-22   126
3.1-27   122

3.1-3   122
4   122
4.1-7   126
4.11-37   126
4.38-41   126
4.42-44   126
6.1-7   126
6.15-19   125
6.17   125
8.16-29   123
8.16-19   122
8.25-27   122
8.25   122
9–10   131
9   125
9.29   122
10–25   120, 121
10   121
11.1   131
11.3   131
11.20   131
12.21   126
13.14-21   121, 125
13.14   125
13.20-21   125
13.20   125
19.1-7   121
19.19-34   121
20.1-11   121
20.14-19   121
21.10-15   121
22.14-20   121, 130
23.15-20   107
23.15-18   121
24.8-9   122
24.18-20   122
25.22-26   122

1 Chronicles
16.8-36   11, 194,
             200

2 Chronicles
1.18–4.22   108
5–7   108
10   59

Psalms		64	193		79, 229
1–41	193	65	193	5.1-7	173
3	193	68–70	193	5.1-6	173
4–6	193	72	193, 234	5.1-2	174
7	193	73–89	193	5.1	173, 174
8	193	73–83	193	5.2	173-75,
9	193	75–77	193		177
11–17	193	80	193	5.3-4	174
11–14	193	81	193	5.3	171, 173,
18–22	193	84	193		174
18	193	85	193	5.4	174, 175,
19–21	193	86	193		177
22–29	193	87	193	5.5-6	175, 176
30	193	88	193, 195	5.5	175, 177
31	193	89	193	5.6	175-77
32	193	90-106	193	5.7	169, 171,
34	193, 195	90	193		172, 174,
35–41	193	96.1-13	11, 194,		176
36	193		200	5.8-23	171-73,
39–42	193	101	193		176, 178
42–72	193	103	193	5.8-17	170
42	193	105.1-15	11, 194,	5.8-10	170
44–49	193		200	5.8	169
44–47	193	106.47-48	11, 194,	5.9	169
49	193		200	5.11-12	170
50	193	107-150	193	5.11	170
51–72	197	108-110	193	5.12	170
51–62	193	108	11, 199-	5.14	170
51	193		201	5.15	170
52	193	108.6	200	5.18-22	170
53	193	108.7	200	5.18-19	170
54	193	109	193	5.20	170
55	193	119	196	5.21	170
56	193	120-129	193	5.22	170
57	193, 195,	122	193	11	176
	200, 201	124	193	11.6-9	176
57.7-11	11, 195	127	193	24–27	223
57.8-12	199	131-134	193	40–55	147, 223
59	193	132	193	56–66	223
60	193, 200,	138–41	193		
	201	139	193	*Jeremiah*	
60.5-12	11, 195	140	193	2	147
60.6	200	142	193, 195	3	147
60.7-14	200	143-145	193	13	147
60.7	200				
61	193	*Isaiah*		*Ezekiel*	
63	193	5	6, 11, 168-	14.1-11	149
64–70	193		73, 175-	16	10, 133,

	147-49,	20.36	153	9.4-19	225
	156, 157	20.38	153	9.21	218, 221
16.1-43	148	20.39-44	153	9.24	221
16.1-13	149	20.40	153	9.25	221
20	6, 147,	20.41	153	9.26	221
	149, 150,	20.42	153	9.27	218
	152, 154-	20.43	153	10.1	220
	57	23	10, 133,	10.2-3	222
20.1-38	10, 133		147, 148,	10.4-5	224
20.5-8	150		156, 157	10.10	218
20.5	150	40–48	108	10.13	221
20.7	150			10.16	218
20.8-13	151	*Daniel*		10.20	221
20.8-9	151	1–6	219	10.21	221
20.8	150, 151	1.1–2.4	219	11	219-22
20.9	150	1.1	220	11.2	221
20.10	151, 152	2.1	220	11.3	221
20.12	151	5	219	11.6	221
20.13-21	151	7–14	218	11.20	222
20.13-14	151, 152	7–12	6, 12, 204,	11.27	222
20.13	150, 151		219, 224-	11.29	222
20.14	150		26	11.30	219
20.15	151, 152	7	218, 219	11.31	218
20.16	151	7.1	220	11.40	222
20.17	151	7.16	218	11.41-43	224
20.18	151	7.25	222	12.1	221
20.21-26	151	8	218, 219	12.4	222
20.21-22	151	8.1	220	12.7	222
20.21	150, 151	8.2	224	12.9	222
20.22	150	8.14	222	12.11	218
20.23	151, 152	8.15	224		
20.24	151	8.16-17	218	*Hosea*	
20.25-26	152, 153	8.16	221	1–3	147
20.25	10, 152-54	8.20-21	221		
20.26	152-54	8.20	219	*Zechariah*	
20.28	153	8.21	219	1–8	223
20.31	153	8.22	219, 221	5.5-11	147
20.33-39	153	8.25	220	9–14	223
20.33-38	153	9	218	14.2	147
20.34-44	153	9.1	220		
20.35	153	9.2	221		

INDEX OF AUTHORS

Adorno, T.W. 6, 10, 11, 64, 88, 135, 137, 158-68, 172-74, 178, 181, 184, 186, 190, 205, 206, 212, 229
Alter, R. 202
Althusser, L. 6-8, 14-29, 34, 35, 38-41, 50-52, 54, 59, 88, 183, 236, 243
Amit, Y. 104, 127
Anderson, A.A. 201, 202

Baumann, G. 147, 148
Benjamin, W. 6, 8, 12, 88, 135, 137, 159, 162, 164, 183, 204-18, 220, 223-26
Bible and Culture Collective 4
Bledstein, A.J. 77
Bloch, E. 2, 6, 10, 12, 88, 110, 133-47, 149, 152, 154-56, 159, 212
Blum, V. 104
Boer, R. 4, 11, 78, 106, 121, 127, 134, 135, 138, 183, 206, 233, 234, 236
Bowen, N.R. 149, 156
Boyer, R. 241, 242
Brenner, A. 76, 77, 147
Brett, M. 26
Briggs, A.B. 197, 198
Briggs, E.G. 197, 198
Broyles, C.C. 201
Buci-Glucksmann, C. 54
Butler, J. 104

Callahan, A.D. 4
Chaney, M.L. 171
Cole, R.L. 201, 202
Collins, J.J. 218, 219, 222, 223
Creach, J. 202
Croatto, J.S. 63
Croft, S. 199
Culley, R.C. 195, 201
Curthoys, A. 63

Dahood, M. 199
Dandamaev, M. 239
Deleuze, G. 88, 98, 135, 245
D'iakonov, I.M. 238
DiLella, A.A. 218
Docker, J. 63
Dunn, S.P. 238, 239

Eagleton, T. 6, 8, 14, 65-78, 83, 85, 86, 135, 180
Eaton, J.H. 199, 201
Engels, F. 19, 63, 68, 90, 231, 232, 238

Fierro, A. 63
Flanagan, J. 87
Fokkelman, J.P. 101, 107
Fontana, B. 42, 53
Frye, N. 183

Geoghegan, V. 143
Gerstenburger, E.S. 198, 199
Ghosh, S.K. 238, 239
Girard, R. 148
Gottwald, N. 3-5, 76, 100, 169, 198, 202, 220, 233, 234, 237-39
Goulder, M.D. 193, 197-99
Graffy, A. 173
Gramsci, A. 6-8, 18, 42-47, 49-55, 57-64, 135, 145, 156, 230
Grosz, E. 104
Gruber, M.I. 147
Guattari, F. 98, 245
Gunkel, H. 192, 198-201

Halperin, D.J. 149, 156
Hanson, P.D. 220
Hartmann, L.F. 218
Hauge, M. 200, 201

Heard, R.C. 32
Hindess, B. 237, 238
Hirst, P.Q. 237, 238
Horsley, R.A. 3, 4

Irigaray, L. 2, 73

Jameson, F. 6, 88, 106, 120, 135-37, 160, 180-92, 234, 240
Jobling, D. 77, 99, 100, 104, 123, 127, 234-37, 239
Johnson, A.R. 199

Kamionkowski, S.T. 149, 156
Kelso, J. 79
Klein, L.R. 104
Kraus, H.-J. 197, 199, 201, 202

Laclau, E. 67
Lacocque, A. 218
Lefebvre, H. 6, 9, 77, 87-91, 93-104, 106, 230, 232, 235
Lévi-Strauss, C. 175, 183, 190, 243
Long, B.O. 120
Lukács, G. 6, 9, 10, 42, 88, 110-20, 123, 124, 126, 130, 132, 158, 181

Machiavelli 6, 8, 42-51, 53-58, 60-64, 156, 230
Magdalene, F.R. 147, 156
Marx, K. 19, 63, 68, 78, 88, 90, 91, 100, 132, 139, 147, 160, 172, 181, 209, 210, 231, 232, 236, 238-40, 242
Matthews, V.H. 171
Meadowcroft, T.J. 223
Melotti, U. 236
Meyers, C. 102, 104, 106, 237, 239
Milbank, J. 169
Mitchell, D.C. 202
Mouffe, C. 67
Mowinckel, S. 197, 199

Nast, H. 104

Nasuti, H. 199
Norris, K. 28

O'Brien, J.M. 147
O'Leary, B. 239

Pixley, J.V. 63

Redditt, P.L. 219
Ricoeur, P. 135, 139
Runions, E. 3, 148, 149, 156

Sahlins, M. 100, 237, 238
Said, E. 63, 64
Ste. Croix, 238
Sals, U. 147
Scott, W. 116-18
Shields, R. 90, 96, 97
Shields, M.E. 147, 148, 156
Shohat, E. 63
Simkins, R.A. 5, 237-40, 245
Smith, A. 4
Sneed, M. 5, 76
Soja, E. 87
Stefanovic, Z. 223

Talmon, S. 223
Tournay, R. 197, 203

Van Dijk-Hemmes, F. 77
Van Iersel, B. 63Walker, M.B. 21

Walzer, M. 63
Weems, R.J. 148
Weiler, A. 63
Weiser, A. 199
Wesseling, E. 116
Westermann, C. 199, 202
Willis, J.T. 173
Wittfogel, K. 100, 238

Yee, G. 3, 5, 173, 236, 237, 239